Pearson New International Edition

Basics of Web Design:
HTML5 & CSS3
Terry Felke-Morris
Second Edition

PEARSON®

Pearson Education Limited
Edinburgh Gate
Harlow
Essex CM20 2JE
England and Associated Companies throughout the world

Visit us on the World Wide Web at: www.pearsoned.co.uk

© Pearson Education Limited 2014

ISBN 10: 1-292-02546-8
ISBN 13: 978-1-292-02546-9

British Library Cataloguing-in-Publication Data
A catalogue record for this book is available from the British Library

Printed in Great Britain by Ashford Colour Press Ltd

Table of Contents

HTML Basics

If you have created a web page using HTML5, you coded a web page and tested it in a browser. You used a Document Type Definition to identify the version of HTML being used along with the `<html>`, `<head>`, `<title>`, `<meta>`, and `<body>` tags. In this chapter you will study HTML and configure the structure and formatting of text on a web page using HTML elements, including the new HTML5 header, nav, and footer elements. You will also explore hyperlinks, which make the World Wide Web into a web of interconnected information. In this chapter you will configure the anchor element to connect web pages to each other with hyperlinks. As you read this chapter, be sure to work through the examples. Coding a web page is a skill, and every skill improves with practice.

You'll learn how to...

▌ Configure the body of a web page with headings, paragraphs, divs, lists, and blockquotes

▌ Configure special entity characters, line breaks, and horizontal rules

▌ Configure text with phrase elements

▌ Test a web page for valid syntax

▌ Configure a web page using new HTML5 header, nav, and footer elements

▌ Use the anchor element to link from page to page

▌ Configure absolute, relative, and e-mail hyperlinks

From Chapter 2 of *Basics of Web Design HTML5 & CSS3*, Second Edition. Terry Ann Felke-Morris. Copyright © 2014 by Pearson Education, Inc. All rights reserved.

Heading Element

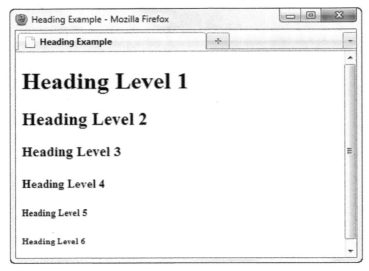

FIGURE 1 *Sample heading.html.*

Heading elements are organized into six levels: h1 through h6. The text contained within a heading element is rendered as a "block" of text by the browser (referred to as block display) and appears with empty space (sometimes called "white space" or "negative space") above and below. The size of the text is largest for **<h1>** (called the heading 1 tag) and smallest for **<h6>** (called the heading 6 tag). Depending on the font being used, the text contained within <h4>, <h5>, and <h6> tags may be displayed smaller than the default text size. All text contained within heading tags is displayed with bold font weight.

Figure 1 shows a web page document with six levels of headings.

 Hands-On Practice 1

To create the web page shown in Figure 1, launch a text editor, and open the template.html file from the chapter1 folder in the student files on the companion website at www .pearsonhighered.com/felke-morris. Modify the title element and add heading tags to the body section as indicated by the following highlighted code:

```
<!DOCTYPE html>
<html lang="en">
<head>
<title>Heading Example</title>
<meta charset="utf-8">
</head>
<body>
<h1>Heading Level 1</h1>
<h2>Heading Level 2</h2>
<h3>Heading Level 3</h3>
<h4>Heading Level 4</h4>
<h5>Heading Level 5</h5>
<h6>Heading Level 6</h6>
</body>
</html>
```

HTML Basics

2

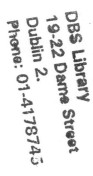

Save the document as heading2.html on your hard drive or flash drive. Launch a browser such as Internet Explorer or Firefox to test your page. It should look similar to the page shown in Figure 1. You can compare your work with the solution found in the student files (chapter2/heading.html).

FAQ Why doesn't the heading tag go in the head section?

It's common for students to try to code the heading tags in the head section of the document, but someone doing this won't be happy with the way the browser displays the web page. Even though "heading tag" and "head section" sound similar, always code heading tags in the body section of the web page document.

Accessibility and Headings

Heading tags can help to make your pages more accessible and usable. It is good coding practice to use heading tags to outline the structure of your web page content. To indicate areas within a page hierarchically, code heading tags numerically as appropriate (h1, h2, h3, and so on), and include page content in block display elements such as

paragraphs and lists. In Figure 2, the `<h1>` tag contains the name of the website in the logo header area at the top of the web page, the `<h2>` tag contains the topic or name of the page in the content area, and other heading elements are coded in the content area as needed to identify major topics and subtopics.

Visually challenged visitors who are using a screen reader can configure the software to display a list of the headings used on a page in order to focus on the topics that interest them. Your well-organized page will be more usable for every visitor to your site, including those who are visually challenged.

FIGURE 2 *Heading tags outline the page.*

More Heading Options in HTML5

You may have heard about the new HTML5 header element and hgroup element. These offer additional options for configuring headings. We'll introduce the header element later in this chapter.

Paragraph Element

Paragraph elements group sentences and sections of text together. Text that is contained by `<p>` and `</p>` tags is rendered as block display with empty space above and below.

Figure 3 shows a web page document containing a paragraph after the first heading.

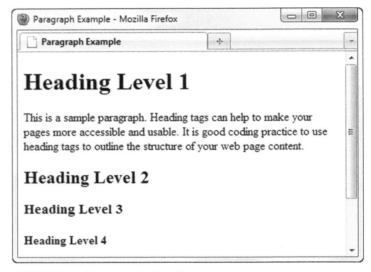

FIGURE 3 *Web page using headings and a paragraph.*

 Hands-On Practice 2 —————————————

To create the web page shown in Figure 3, launch a text editor, and open the heading.html file from the chapter2 folder in the student files. Modify the page title and add a paragraph of text to your page below the line with the `<h1>` tags and above the line with the `<h2>` tags.

```
<!DOCTYPE html>
<html lang="en">
<head>
<title>Paragraph Example</title>
<meta charset="utf-8">
</head>
<body>
<h1>Heading Level 1</h1>
<p>This is a sample paragraph. Heading tags can help to make your
pages more accessible and usable. It is good coding practice to use
heading tags to outline the structure of your web page content.
</p>
<h2>Heading Level 2</h2>
<h3>Heading Level 3</h3>
<h4>Heading Level 4</h4>
<h5>Heading Level 5</h5>
<h6>Heading Level 6</h6>
</body>
</html>
```

Save the document as paragraph2.html on your hard drive or flash drive. Launch a browser to test your page. It should look similar to the page shown in Figure 3. You can compare your work with the solution found in the student files (chapter2/paragraph.html). Notice how the text in the paragraph wraps automatically as you resize your browser window.

Alignment

As you test your web pages, you may notice that the headings and text begin near the left margin. This is called **left alignment**, and it is the default alignment for web pages. There are times when you want a paragraph or heading to be centered or right aligned (justified). In previous versions of HTML, the align attribute can be used for this. However, the align attribute is **obsolete** in HTML5, which means that the attribute has been removed from the W3C HTML5 draft specification.

Quick TIP   When writing for the Web, avoid long paragraphs. People tend to skim web pages rather than reading them word for word. Use heading tags to outline the page content along with short paragraphs (about three to five sentences each) and lists (which you'll learn about later in this chapter).

HTML Basics

Line Break and Horizontal Rule

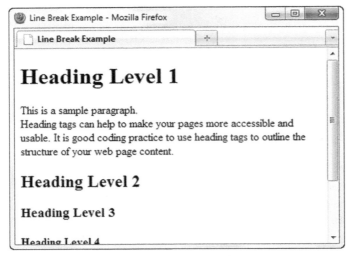

FIGURE 4 *Notice the line break after the first sentence.*

The Line Break Element

The **line break element** causes the browser to advance to the next line before displaying the next element or text on a web page. The line break tag is not coded as a pair of opening and closing tags. It is a void element and is coded as **`<br>`**. Figure 4 shows a web page document with a line break after the first sentence in the paragraph.

 Hands-On Practice 3

To create the web page shown in Figure 4, launch a text editor, and open the paragraph.html file from the chapter2 folder in the student files. Modify the text contained between the title tags to be "Line Break Example." Place your cursor after the first sentence in the paragraph (after "This is a sample paragraph."). Press the Enter key. Save your file. Test your page in a browser and notice that even though your source code displayed the "This is a sample paragraph." sentence on its own line, the browser did not render it that way. A line break tag is needed to configure the browser to display the second sentence on a new line. Edit the file in a text editor and add a `<br>` tag after the first sentence in the paragraph as shown in the following code snippet.

```
<body>
<h1>Heading Level 1</h1>
<p>This is a sample paragraph. <br> Heading tags can help to make your
pages more accessible and usable. It is good coding practice to use
heading tags to outline the structure of your web page content.
</p>
<h2>Heading Level 2</h2>
<h3>Heading Level 3</h3>
<h4>Heading Level 4</h4>
<h5>Heading Level 5</h5>
<h6>Heading Level 6</h6>
</body>
```

Save your file as linebreak2.html. Launch a browser to test your page. It should look similar to the page shown in Figure 4. You can compare your work with the solution found in the student files (chapter2/linebreak.html).

HTML Basics

6

The Horizontal Rule Element

Web designers often use visual elements such as lines and borders to separate or define areas on web pages. The **horizontal rule** element, `<hr>`, configures a horizontal line across a web page. Since the horizontal rule element does not contain any text, it is coded as a void element and not in a pair of opening and closing tags. The horizontal rule element has an additional purpose in HTML5, it can be used to indicate a thematic break or change in the content. Figure 5 shows a web page document (also found in the student files at chapter2/hr.html) with a horizontal rule after the paragraph.

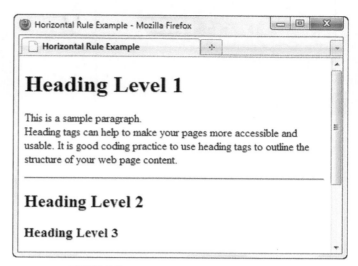

FIGURE 5 *The horizontal line is below the paragraph.*

 Hands-On Practice 4

To create the web page shown in Figure 5, launch a text editor, and open the linebreak.html file from the chapter2 folder in the student files. Modify the text contained between the title tags to be "Horizontal Rule Example". Place your cursor on a new line after the `</p>` tag. Code the `<hr>` tag on the new line as shown in the following code snippet.

```
<body>
<h1>Heading Level 1</h1>
<p>This is a sample paragraph. <br> Heading tags can help to make your
pages more accessible and usable. It is good coding practice to use
heading tags to outline the structure of your web page content.
</p>
<hr>
<h2>Heading Level 2</h2>
<h3>Heading Level 3</h3>
<h4>Heading Level 4</h4>
<h5>Heading Level 5</h5>
<h6>Heading Level 6</h6>
</body>
```

Save your file as hr2.html. Launch a browser to test your page. It should look similar to the page shown in Figure 5. You can compare your work with the solution found in the student files (chapter2/hr.html).

Quick TIP When you are tempted to use a horizontal rule on a web page, consider whether it is really needed. Usually, just leaving extra blank space (referred to as "white space" or "negative space") on the page will serve to separate the content. *Note:* The term white space is borrowed from the print industry—since paper is generally white, extra blank space is known as white space.

Blockquote Element

Besides organizing text in paragraphs and headings, sometimes you need to add a quotation to a web page. The **blockquote element** is used to display a block of quoted text in a special way—indented from both the left and right margins. A block of indented text begins with a `<blockquote>` tag and ends with a `</blockquote>` tag.

Figure 6 shows a web page document with a heading, a paragraph, and a blockquote.

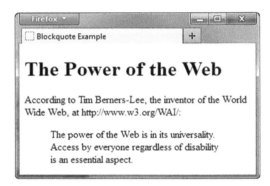

FIGURE 6 *The text within the blockquote element is indented.*

Quick TIP You've probably noticed how convenient the `<blockquote>` tag could be if you needed to indent an area of text on a web page. You may have wondered whether it would be OK to use `<blockquote>` anytime you'd like to indent text or whether the blockquote element is reserved only for long quotations. The semantically correct use of the `<blockquote>` tag is to use it only when displaying large blocks of quoted text within a web page. Why should you be concerned about semantics? Consider the future of the Semantic Web, described in *Scientific American* as "A new form of Web content that is meaningful to computers [that] will unleash a revolution of new possibilities." Using HTML in a semantic, structural manner is one step toward the Semantic Web. So, avoid using a `<blockquote>` just to indent text. Other modern techniques are available to configure margins and padding on elements.

HTML Basics

Hands-On Practice 5

To create the web page shown in Figure 6, launch a text editor, and open the template .html file from the chapter1 folder in the student files. Modify the text in the title element. Add a heading tag, a paragraph tag, and a blockquote tag to the body section as indicated by the following highlighted code.

```
<!DOCTYPE html>
<html lang="en">
<head>
<title>Blockquote Example</title>
<meta charset="utf-8">
</head>
<body>
<h1>The Power of the Web</h1>
<p>According to Tim Berners-Lee, the inventor of the World Wide Web,
at http://www.w3.org/WAI/:
</p>
<blockquote>
The power of the Web is in its universality. Access by everyone
regardless of disability is an essential aspect.
</blockquote>
</body>
</html>
```

Save the document as blockquote2.html on your hard drive or flash drive. Launch a browser such as Internet Explorer or Firefox to test your page. It should look similar to the page shown in Figure 6. You can compare your work with the solution found in the student files (chapter2/blockquote.html).

 Why does my web page still look the same?

Often, students make changes to a web page but get frustrated because their browser shows an older version of the page. The following troubleshooting tips are helpful when you know you modified your web page, but the changes do not show up in the browser:

1. Be sure that you save your web page file after you make changes.
2. Verify the location to which you save your file—the hard drive, a particular folder.
3. Verify the location from which your browser is requesting the file—the hard drive, a particular folder.
4. Be sure to click your browser's Refresh or Reload button.

HTML Basics

Phrase Elements

Phrase elements, sometimes referred to as **logical style elements**, indicate the context and meaning of the text between the container tags. It is up to each browser to interpret that style. Phrase elements are displayed right in line with the text (referred to as inline display) and can apply to either a section of text or even a single character of text. For example, the `<strong>` element indicates that the text associated with it has strong importance and should be displayed in a "strong" manner in relation to normal text on the page.

Table 1 lists common phrase elements and examples of their use. Notice that some tags, such as `<cite>` and `<dfn>`, result in the same type of display (italics) as the `<em>` tag in today's browsers. These tags semantically describe the text as a citation or definition, but the physical display is usually italics in both cases.

TABLE 1 *Phrase Elements*

Element	Example	Usage
`<abbr>`	WIPO	Identifies text as an abbreviation
`<b>`	**bold** text	Text that has no extra importance but is styled in bold font
`<cite>`	*cite* text	Identifies a citation or reference; usually displayed in italics
`<code>`	code text	Identifies program code samples; usually a fixed-space font
`<dfn>`	*dfn* text	Identifies a definition of a word or term; usually displayed in italics
`<em>`	*emphasized* text	Causes text to be emphasized; usually displayed in italics
`<i>`	*italicized* text	Text that has no extra importance but is styled in italics
`<kbd>`	kbd text	Identifies user text to be typed; usually a fixed-space font
`<mark>`	mark text	Text that is highlighted in order to be easily referenced (HTML5 only)
`<samp>`	samp text	Shows program sample output; usually a fixed-space font
`<small>`	small text	Legal disclaimers and notices ("fine print") displayed in small font size
`<strong>`	**strong** text	Strong importance; usually displayed in bold
`<sub>`	$_{sub}$text	Displays a subscript as small text below the baseline
`<sup>`	^{sup}text	Displays a superscript as small text above the baseline
`<var>`	*var* text	Identifies and displays a variable output; usually displayed in italics

HTML Basics

Note that all phrase elements are container tags—both an opening and a closing tag is used. As shown in Table 1, the `<strong>` element indicates that the text associated with it has "strong" importance. Usually the browser (or other user agent) will display `<strong>` text in bold type. A screen reader, such as JAWS or Window-Eyes, might interpret `<strong>` text to indicate that the text should be more strongly spoken. In the following line the phone number is displayed with strong importance:

Call for a free quote for your web development needs: **888.555.5555**

The code is

```
<p>Call for a free quote for your web development needs:
<strong>888.555.5555</strong></p>
```

Notice that the opening `<strong>` and closing `<strong>` tags are contained within the paragraph tags (`<p>` and `</p>`). This code is properly nested and is considered to be **well formed**. When improperly nested, the `<p>` and `<strong>` tag pairs overlap each other instead of being nested within each other. Improperly nested code will not pass validation testing (see the HTML Syntax Validation section later in this chapter) and may cause display issues.

Figure 7 shows a web page document (also found in the student files at chapter2/em.html) that uses the `<em>` tag to display the emphasized phrase, "Access by everyone," in italics.

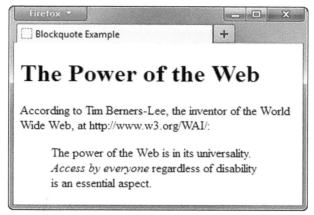

FIGURE 7 *The `<em>` tag in action.*

The code snippet is

```
<blockquote>
The power of the Web is in its universality.
<em>Access by everyone</em> regardless of disability is an essential
aspect.
</blockquote>
```

Ordered List

Lists are used on web pages to organize information. When writing for the Web, headings, short paragraphs, and lists can make your page more clear and easy to read. HTML can be used to create three types of lists—description lists, ordered lists, and unordered lists. All lists are rendered as block display with empty space above and below. This section focuses on the **ordered list**, which displays a numbering or lettering system to sequence the information contained in the list. An ordered list can be organized using numerals (the default), uppercase letters, lowercase letters, uppercase Roman numerals, and lowercase Roman numerals. See Figure 8 for a sample ordered list.

My Favorite Colors

1. Blue
2. Teal
3. Red

FIGURE 8 *Sample ordered list.*

Ordered lists begin with an `<ol>` tag and end with an `</ol>` tag. Each list item begins with an `<li>` tag and ends with an `</li>` tag. The code to configure the heading and ordered list shown in Figure 8 follows:

```
<h1>My Favorite Colors</h1>
<ol>
  <li>Blue</li>
  <li>Teal</li>
  <li>Red</li>
</ol>
```

The `type`, `start`, and `reversed` Attributes

The **`type` attribute** configures the symbol used for ordering the list. For example, to create an ordered list organized by uppercase letters, use `<ol type="A">`. Table 2 documents the type attribute and its values for ordered lists.

TABLE 2 *The* `type` *Attribute for Ordered Lists*

Value	Symbol
1	Numerals (the default)
A	Uppercase letters
a	Lowercase letters
I	Roman numerals
i	Lowercase Roman numerals

Another handy attribute that can be used with ordered lists is the **`start` attribute**, with which you can specify the start value for the list (for example, `start="10"`). In addition, you can use the new HTML5 **`reversed` attribute** (`reversed="reversed"`) to indicate that a list is in descending order.

Hands-On Practice 6 ———————————————————————————

In this Hands-On Practice you will use a heading and an ordered list on the same page. To create the web page shown in Figure 9, launch a text editor, and open the template.html file from the chapter1 folder in the student files. Modify the title element and add h1, h2, ol, and li tags to the body section, as indicated by the following highlighted code:

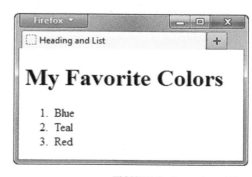

```
<!DOCTYPE html>
<html lang="en">
<head>
<title>Heading and List</title>
<meta charset="utf-8">
</head>
<body>
<h1>My Favorite Colors</h1>
<ol>
  <li>Blue</li>
  <li>Teal</li>
  <li>Red</li>
</ol>
</body>
</html>
```

FIGURE 9 *An ordered list.*

Save your file as ol2.html. Launch a browser and test your page. It should look similar to the page shown in Figure 9. You can compare your work with the solution in the student files (chapter2/ol.html).

Take a few minutes to experiment with the `type` attribute. Configure the ordered list to use uppercase letters instead of numerals. Save your file as ol3.html. Test your page in a browser. You can compare your work with the solution in the student files (chapter2/ola.html).

 FAQ Why is the web page code in the examples indented?

Actually, it doesn't matter to the browser if web page code is indented, but humans find it easier to read and maintain code when it is logically indented. This makes it easier for you or another web developer to understand the source code in the future. For example, it's common practice to indent `<li>` tags a few spaces in from the left margin because it makes it easier to "see" the list with a quick glance at the source code. There is no "rule" as to how many spaces to indent, although your instructor or the organization you work for may have a standard. Consistent indentation helps to create more easily maintainable web pages.

HTML Basics

Unordered List

Unordered lists display a bullet, or list marker, before each list entry. The default list marker is determined by the browser but is typically a disc, which is a filled-in circle. See Figure 10 for a sample unordered list.

My Favorite Colors

- Blue
- Teal
- Red

FIGURE 10 *Sample unordered list.*

Unordered lists begin with a `<ul>` tag and end with a `</ul>` tag. The ul element is a block display element and is rendered with empty space above and below. Each list item begins with an `<li>` tag and ends with an `</li>` tag. The code to configure the heading and unordered list shown in Figure 10 is

```
<h1>My Favorite Colors</h1>
<ul>
  <li>Blue</li>
  <li>Teal</li>
  <li>Red</li>
</ul>
```

? FAQ Can I change the "bullet" in an unordered list?

Back in the day before HTML5, the type attribute could be included with a `<ul>` tag to change the default list marker to a square (`type="square"`) or open circle (`type="circle"`). However, be aware that using the type attribute on an unordered list is considered obsolete in HTML5 because it is decorative and does not convey meaning. No worries, though—you'll learn techniques to configure list markers (bullets) to display images and shapes.

In this Hands-On Practice you will use a heading and an unordered list on the same page. To create the web page shown in Figure 11, launch a text editor, and open the template.html file from the chapter1 folder in the student files. Modify the title element and add h1, ul, and li tags to the body section as indicated by the following highlighted code:

FIGURE 11 *An unordered list.*

```
<!DOCTYPE html>
<html lang="en">
<head>
<title>Heading and List</title>
<meta charset="utf-8">
</head>
<body>
<h1>My Favorite Colors</h1>
<ul>
  <li>Blue</li>
  <li>Teal</li>
  <li>Red</li>
</ul>
</body>
</html>
```

Save your file as ul2.html. Launch a browser and test your page. It should look similar to the page shown in Figure 11. You can compare your work with the solution in the student files (chapter2/ul.html).

Description List

Description lists (formerly called definition lists in XHTML and HTML4) help to organize terms and their descriptions. The terms stand out, and their descriptions can be as long as needed to convey your message. Each term begins on its own line at the margin. Each description begins on its own line and is indented. Description lists are also handy for organizing Frequently Asked Questions (FAQs) and their answers. The questions and answers are offset with indentation. Any type of information that consists of a number of corresponding terms and associated descriptions is well suited to being organized in a description list. See Figure 12 for an example of a web page that uses a description list.

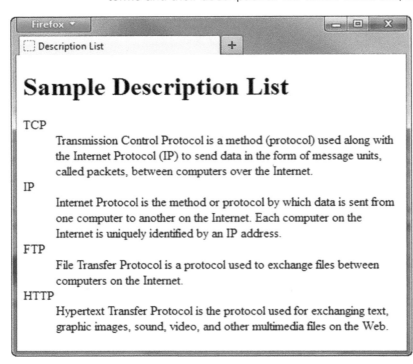

Sample Description List

TCP
> Transmission Control Protocol is a method (protocol) used along with the Internet Protocol (IP) to send data in the form of message units, called packets, between computers over the Internet.

IP
> Internet Protocol is the method or protocol by which data is sent from one computer to another on the Internet. Each computer on the Internet is uniquely identified by an IP address.

FTP
> File Transfer Protocol is a protocol used to exchange files between computers on the Internet.

HTTP
> Hypertext Transfer Protocol is the protocol used for exchanging text, graphic images, sound, video, and other multimedia files on the Web.

FIGURE 12 *A description list.*

Description lists begin with the `<dl>` tag and end with the `</dl>` tag. Each term or name in the list begins with the `<dt>` tag and ends with the `</dt>` tag. Each term description begins with the `<dd>` tag and ends with the `</dd>` tag.

 Hands-On Practice 8

In this Hands-On Practice you will use a heading and a description list on the same page. To create the web page shown in Figure 12, launch a text editor, and open the template.html file from the chapter1 folder in the student files. Modify the title element and add h1, dl, dd, and dt tags to the body section as indicated by the following highlighted code:

HTML Basics

```
<!DOCTYPE html>
<html lang="en">
<head>
<title>Description List</title>
<meta charset="utf-8">
</head>
<body>
<h1>Sample Description List</h1>
<dl>
  <dt>TCP</dt>
    <dd>Transmission Control Protocol is a method (protocol) used along
with the Internet Protocol (IP) to send data in the form of message
units, called packets, between computers over the Internet.</dd>
  <dt>IP</dt>
    <dd>Internet Protocol is the method or protocol by which data is
sent from one computer to another on the Internet. Each computer on
the Internet is uniquely identified by an IP address.</dd>
  <dt>FTP</dt>
    <dd>File Transfer Protocol is a protocol used to exchange files
between computers on the Internet.</dd>
  <dt>HTTP</dt>
    <dd>Hypertext Transfer Protocol is the protocol used for exchanging
text, graphic images, sound, video, and other multimedia files on the
Web.</dd>
</dl>
</body>
</html>
```

Save your file as description2.html. Launch a browser and test your page. It should look similar to the page shown in Figure 12. Don't worry if the word wrap is a little different—the important formatting is that each <dt> term should be on its own line and the corresponding <dd> description should be indented under it. Try resizing your browser window and notice how the word wrap on the description text changes. You can compare your work with the solution in the student files (chapter2/description.html).

? FAQ **Why does the text in my web page wrap differently than the examples?**

The text may wrap a little differently because your screen resolution or browser viewport size may not be the same as those on the computer used for the screen captures. That's part of the nature of working with the Web—expect your web pages to look slightly different in the multitude of screen resolutions, browser viewport sizes, and devices that people will use to view your designs.

Special Entity Characters

In order to use special characters such as quotation marks, the greater-than sign (>), the less-than sign (<), and the copyright symbol (©) in your web page document, you need to use special characters, sometimes called entity characters. For example, if you want to include a copyright line on your page as follows:

© Copyright 2014 My Company. All rights reserved.

you need to use the special character **©** to display the copyright symbol, as shown in here:

```
&copy; Copyright 2014 My Company. All rights reserved.
```

Another useful special character is ** **, which stands for nonbreaking space. You may have noticed that web browsers treat multiple spaces as a single space. If you want multiple spaces to display in your text, you can use   multiple times to indicate multiple blank spaces. This is acceptable if you simply need to tweak the position of an element a little. If you find that your web pages contain many   special characters in a row, you should use a different method to align elements, such as configuring the margin or padding with Cascading Style Sheets.

See Table 3 and the companion website at http://webdevbasics.net/2e/chapter2.html for a description of more special characters and their codes.

TABLE 3 *Common Special Characters*

Character	Entity Name	Code
"	Quotation mark	"
©	Copyright symbol	©
&	Ampersand	&
Empty space	Nonbreaking space	
'	Right single quote	’
—	Long dash	—
|	Vertical Bar	|

HTML Basics

Figure 13 shows the web page you will create in this Hands-On Practice. Launch a text editor, and open the template.html file from the chapter1 folder in the student files.

Change the title of the web page to "Web Design Steps" by modifying the text between the `<title>` and `</title>` tags.

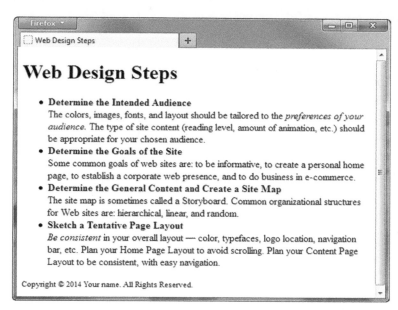

The sample page shown in Figure 13 contains a heading, an unordered list, and copyright information. You will add these elements to your file next.

Configure the phrase, "Web Design Steps", as a level 1 heading (`<h1>`) as follows:

```
<h1>Web Design Steps</h1>
```

Now create the unordered list. The first line of each bulleted item is the title of the web design step. In the sample, each step title should be strong or stand out from the rest of the text. The code for the beginning of the unordered list is

FIGURE 13 *Sample design.html.*

```
<ul>
  <li><strong>Determine the Intended Audience</strong>
  <br> The colors, images, fonts, and layout should be tailored to
  the <em>preferences of your audience.</em> The type of site content
  (reading level, amount of animation, etc.) should be appropriate for
  your chosen audience.</li>
```

Edit your design.html file and code the entire ordered list shown in Figure 13. Remember to code the closing `</ul>` tag at the end of the list. Finally, configure the copyright information in a paragraph and apply the small element. Use the special character `&copy;` for the copyright symbol. The code for the copyright line is

```
<p><small>Copyright &copy; 2014 Your name. All Rights
Reserved.</small></p>
```

Save your file as design2.html. Launch a browser and test your page. How did you do? Compare your work to the sample in the student files (chapter2/design.html).

HTML Syntax Validation

VideoNote
*HTML
Validation*

The W3C has a free Markup Validation Service available at http://validator.w3.org that will check your code for syntax errors and validate your web pages. **HTML validation** provides you with quick self-assessment—you can prove that your code uses correct syntax. In the working world, HTML validation serves as a quality assurance tool. Invalid code may cause browsers to render the pages slower than otherwise.

 Hands-On Practice 10

In this Hands-On Practice you will use the W3C Markup Validation Service to validate a web page file. Launch a text editor, and open the design.html file from the chapter2 folder in the student files.

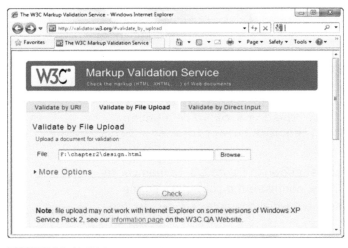

FIGURE 14 *Validate your page.*

1. We will add an error to the design.html page. Delete the first closing `</strong>` tag. This modification should generate several error messages.

2. Next, attempt to validate the design.html file. Launch a browser and visit the W3C Markup Validation Service file upload page at http://validator.w3.org and select the "Validate by File Upload" tab. Click the Browse button and select the chapter2/design.html file from your computer. Click the Check button to upload the file to the W3C site (Figure 14).

3. An error page will display. Notice the "Errors found while checking this document" message. You can view the errors by scrolling down the page, as shown in Figure 15.

4. Notice that the message indicates line 12, which is the first line after the missing closing `</strong>` tag. HTML error messages often point to a line that follows the error. The text of the message "End tag for li seen, but there were unclosed elements" lets you know that something is wrong. It's up to you to figure out what it is. A good place to start is to check your container tags and make sure they are in pairs. In this case, that is the problem. You can scroll down to view the other errors. However, since multiple error messages are often displayed after a single error occurs, it's a good idea to fix one item at a time and then revalidate.

HTML Basics

5. Edit the design.html file in a text editor and add the missing `</strong>` tag. Save the file. Launch a browser and visit http://validator.w3.org and select the "Validate by File Upload" tab. Select your file, select More Options, and verify the Show Source and Verbose Output check boxes are checked. Click the Revalidate button to begin the validation.

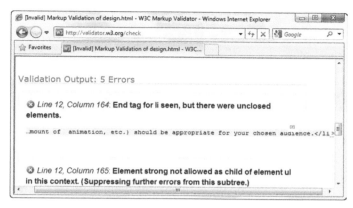

FIGURE 15 *The error indicates line 12.*

6. Your display should be similar to that shown in Figure 16. Notice the "This document was successfully checked as HTML5" message. This means that your page passed the validation test. Congratulations, your design.html page is valid! You may also notice a warning message that indicates the HTML5 conformance checker is in experimental status.

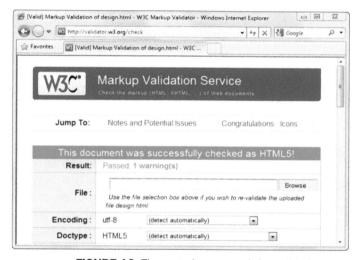

FIGURE 16 *The page has passed the validation test.*

 It's a good practice to validate your web pages. However, when validating code, use common sense. Since web browsers still do not completely follow W3C recommendations, there will be situations, such as when adding multimedia to a web page, when HTML code configured to work reliably across a variety of browsers and platforms will not pass validation.

In addition to the W3C validation service, there are other tools that you can use to check the syntax of your code. Explore the HTML5 validator at http://html5.validator.nu and the HTML5 "lint" tool at http://lint.brihten.com/html.

HTML Basics

Structural Elements

The Div Element

The **div element** has been used for many years to configure a generic structural area or "division" on a web page as a block display with empty space above and below. A div element begins with a `<div>` tag and ends with a `</div>` tag. Use a div element when you need to format an area of a web page that may contain other block display elements such as headings, paragraphs, unordered lists, and even other div elements. You'll use Cascading Style Sheets (CSS) to style and configure the color, font, and layout of HTML elements.

HTML5 Structural Elements

In addition to the generic div element, HTML5 introduces a number of semantic structural elements that can be used to configure specific areas on a web page. These new HTML5 elements are intended to be used in conjunction with div and other elements to structure web page documents in a more meaningful manner that indicates the purpose of each structural area. You'll explore three of these new elements in this section: the header element, the nav element, and the footer element. Figure 17 shows a diagram of a page (called a wireframe) that indicates how the structure of a web page could be configured with the header, nav, div, and footer elements.

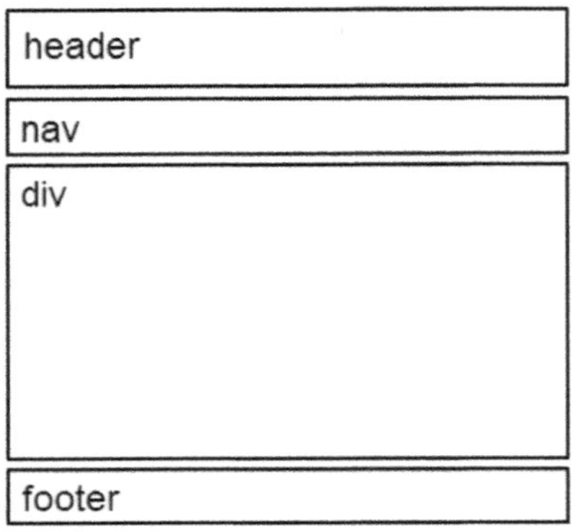

FIGURE 17 *Structural elements.*

The Header Element

The purpose of the new HTML5 **header element** is to contain the headings of either a web page document or an area within the document such as a section or article. The header element begins with the `<header>` tag and ends with the `</header>` tag. The header element is block display and typically contains one or more heading level elements (h1 through h6).

The Nav Element

The purpose of the new HTML5 **nav element** is to contain a section of navigation links. The block display nav element begins with the `<nav>` tag and ends with the `</nav>` tag.

The Footer Element

The purpose of the new HTML5 **footer element** is to contain the footer content of a web page or section of a web page. The block display footer element begins with the `<footer>` tag and ends with the `</footer>` tag.

HTML Basics

Hands-On Practice 11

In this Hands-On Practice you will practice using structural elements as you create the Trillium Media Design home page, shown in Figure 18. Launch a text editor, and open the template.html file from the chapter1 folder in the student files. Edit the code as follows:

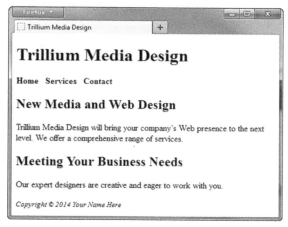

1. Modify the title of the web page by changing the text between the `<title>` and `</title>` tags to Trillium Media Design.

2. Position your cursor in the body section and code the header element with the text, "Trillium Media Design" contained in an h1 element:

```
<header>
  <h1>Trillium Media Design</h1>
</header>
```

FIGURE 18 *Trillium home page.*

3. Code a nav element to contain text that will indicate the main navigation for the website. Configure bold text (use the b element) and use the ` ` special character to add extra blank space:

```
<nav>
  <b>Home   Services   Contact</b>
</nav>
```

4. Code the content within a div element that contains the h2 and paragraph elements:

```
<div>
  <h2>New Media and Web Design</h2>
  <p>Trillium Media Design will bring your company&rsquo;s Web
presence to the next level. We offer a comprehensive range of
services.</p>
  <h2>Meeting Your Business Needs</h2>
  <p>Our expert designers are creative and eager to work with you.</p>
</div>
```

5. Configure the footer element to contain a copyright notice displayed in small font size (use the small element) and italic font (use the i element). Be careful to properly nest the elements as shown here:

```
<footer>
  <small><i>Copyright &copy; 2014 Your Name Here</i></small>
</footer>
```

Save your page as structure2.html. Test your page in a browser. It should look similar to Figure 18. You can compare your work to the sample in the student files (chapter2/structure.html).

 Older browsers (such as Internet Explorer 8 and earlier) do not support the new HTML5 elements. For now, be sure to use a current version of any popular browser to test your pages.

Anchor Element

Use the **anchor element** to specify a **hyperlink**, often referred to as a *link*, to another web page or file that you want to display. Each anchor element begins with an `<a>` tag and ends with an `</a>` tag. The opening and closing anchor tags surround the text that the user can click to perform the hyperlink. Use the `href` **attribute** to configure the hyperlink reference, which identifies the name and location of the file to access.

Figure 19 shows a web page document with an anchor tag that configures a hyperlink to this text's website, http://webdevbasics.net.

The code for the anchor tag in Figure 19 is

```
<a href="http://webdevbasics.net">Basics of Web Design Textbook
Companion</a>
```

Notice that the href value is the URL for the website and will display the home page. The text that is typed between the two anchor tags displays on the web page as a hyperlink and is underlined by most browsers. When you move the mouse over a hyperlink, the cursor changes to a pointing hand, as shown in Figure 19.

 Hands-On Practice 12 ────────────────────────────

To create the web page shown in Figure 19, launch a text editor, and open the template.html file from the chapter1 folder in the student files. Modify the title element and add an anchor tag to the body section as indicated by the following highlighted code:

FIGURE 19 *Sample hyperlink.*

```
<!DOCTYPE html>
<html lang="en">
<head>
<title>Anchor Example</title>
<meta charset="utf-8">
</head>
<body>
<a href="http://webdevbasics.net">Basics of Web
Design Textbook Companion</a>
</body>
</html>
```

Save the document as anchor2.html on your hard drive or flash drive. Launch a browser and test your page. It should look similar to the page shown in Figure 19. You can compare your work with the solution found in the student files (chapter2/anchor.html).

──

 Can images be hyperlinks?

Yes. Although we'll concentrate on text hyperlinks in this chapter, it is also possible to configure an image as a hyperlink.

Targeting Hyperlinks

You may have noticed in Hands-On Practice 12 that when a visitor clicks a hyperlink, the new web page automatically opens in the same browser window. You can configure the **target attribute** on an anchor tag with `target="_blank"` to open a hyperlink in a *new* browser window or browser tab. Note that you cannot control whether the web page opens in a new window or opens in a new tab—that is dependent on your visitor's browser configuration. To see the target attribute in action, try the example in the student files at chapter2/target.html.

Absolute Hyperlinks

An **absolute hyperlink** indicates the absolute location of a resource on the Web. The hyperlink in Hands-On Practice 12 is an absolute hyperlink. Use absolute hyperlinks when you need to link to resources on other websites. The href value for an absolute hyperlink to the home page of a website includes the http:// protocol and the domain name. The following hyperlink is an absolute hyperlink to the home page of this text's website:

```
<a href="http://webdevbasics.net">Basics of Web Design</a>
```

Note that if we want to access a web page other than the home page on the text's website, we can also include a specific folder name and file name. For example, the following anchor tag configures an absolute hyperlink for a file named chapter1.html located in a folder named 2e on this text's website:

```
<a href="http://webdevbasics.net/2e/chapter1.html">Chapter 1</a>
```

Relative Hyperlink

When you need to link to web pages within your site, use a **relative hyperlink**. The href value for a relative hyperlink does not begin with http:// and does not include a domain name. For a relative hyperlink, the href value will contain only the file name (or folder and file name) of the web page you want to display. The hyperlink location is relative to the page currently being displayed. For example, if you are coding a home page (index.html) for a website and want to link to a page named contact.html located in the same folder as index.html, you can configure a relative hyperlink as shown in the following code sample:

```
<a href="contact.html">Contact Us</a>
```

Block Anchor

It's typical to use anchor tags to configure phrases or even just a single word as a hyperlink. HTML5 provides a new function for the anchor tag—the block anchor. A block anchor can configure one or more entire elements (even those that display as a block, such as a div, h1, or paragraph) as a hyperlink. See an example in the student files (chapter2/block.html).

Accessibility and Hyperlinks

Visually challenged visitors who are using a screen reader can configure the software to display a list of the hyperlinks in the document. However, a list of hyperlinks is only useful if the text describing each hyperlink is actually helpful and descriptive. For example, on your college website, a "Search the course schedule" link would be more useful than a hyperlink that simply says "More information" or "click here." Keep this in mind as you are coding hyperlinks in your web pages.

HTML Basics

Practice with Hyperlinks

The best way to learn how to code web pages is by actually doing it! In this section you'll create three pages in a small website so that you can practice using the anchor tag to configure hyperlinks.

Site Map

Figure 20 displays the site map for your new website—a Home page with two content pages: a Services page and a Contact page.

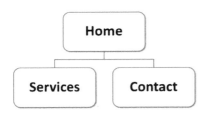

FIGURE 20 *Site map.*

A **site map** represents the structure, or organization, of pages in a website in a visual manner. Each page in the website is represented by a box on the site map. Review Figure 20 and notice that the Home page is at the top of the site map. The second level in a site map shows the other main pages of the website. In this very small three-page website, the other two pages (Services and Contact) are included on the second level. The main navigation of a website usually includes hyperlinks to the pages shown on the first two levels of the site map.

Hands-On Practice 13

Figure 20 displays the site map for your new website—a home page (index.html) with two content pages services page (services.html) and contact page (contact.html).

1. **Create a Folder.** If you had printed papers to organize you would probably store them in a paper folder. Web designers store and organize their computer files by

How do I create a new folder?

FAQ

Before you begin to learn how to code web pages, it's a good idea to be comfortable using your computer for basic tasks such as creating a new folder. If you don't remember how to create a folder, review your computer's handbook for instructions. You may also benefit from a brush-up course on either the Windows or Mac operating systems before you continue. For a quick review on how to use your operating system to create a folder, check out the following resources:

▶ *Mac:* http://support.apple.com/kb/HT2476
▶ *Windows:* http://windows.microsoft.com/en-us/windows7/Create-a-new-folder

HTML Basics

creating a folder on a hard drive (or portable storage such as an SD card or Flash drive) for each website. This helps them to be efficient as they work with many different websites. You will organize your own web design work by creating a new folder for each website and storing your files for that website in the new folder. Use your operating system to create a new folder named mypractice for your new website.

2. **Create the Home Page.**   Use the Trillium Media Design web page (Figure 18) from Hands-On Practice 11 as a starting point for your new home page (shown in Figure 21). Copy the sample file for Hands-On Practice 11 (chapter2/structure.html) into your mypractice folder. Change the file name of structure.html to index.html. It's common practice to use the file name index.html for the home page of a website.

FIGURE 21 *New index.html web page.*

Launch a text editor, and open the index.html file.

a. The navigation hyperlinks will be located within the nav element. You will edit the code within the nav element to configure three hyperlinks:

▶ The text "Home" will hyperlink to index.html

▶ The text "Services" will hyperlink to services.html

▶ The text "Contact" will hyperlink to contact.html

Modify the code within the nav element as follows:

```
<nav>
  <b><a href="index.html">Home</a>  
    <a href="services.html">Services</a>  
    <a href="contact.html">Contact</a>
  </b>
</nav>
```

b. Save the index.html file in your mypractice folder. Test your page in a browser. It should look similar to Figure 21. You can compare your work to the sample in the student files (chapter2/practice/index.html).

HTML Basics

3. **Create the Services Page.** It is common practice to create a new web page based on an existing page. You will use the index.html file as a starting point for the new services page, shown in Figure 22.

FIGURE 22 *The services.html web page.*

Open your index.html file in a text editor and save the file as services.html. Edit the code as follows:

a. Modify the title of the web page by changing the text between the `<title>` and `</title>` tags to "Trillium Media Design - Services". In order to create a consistent header, navigation, and footer for the web pages in this website, do not change the code within the header, nav, or footer elements.

b. Position your cursor in the body section and delete the code and text between the opening and closing div tags. Code the main page content (heading 2 and description list) for the services page between the div tags as follows:

```
<h2>Our Services Meet Your Business Needs</h2>
  <dl>
    <dt><strong>Website Design</strong></dt>
      <dd>Whether your needs are large or small, Trillium can get
      you on the Web!</dd>
    <dt><strong>E-Commerce Solutions</strong></dt>
      <dd>Trillium offers quick entry into the e-commerce
      marketplace.</dd>
    <dt><strong>Search Engine Optimization</strong></dt>
      <dd>Most people find new sites using search engines.
      Trillium can get your website noticed.</dd>
  </dl>
```

c. Save the services.html file in your mypractice folder. Test your page in a browser. It should look similar to Figure 22. You can compare your work to the sample in the student files (chapter2/practice/services.html).

HTML Basics

28

4. **Create the Contact Page.** Use the index.html file as a starting point for the new Contact page, shown in Figure 23. Open your index.html file in a text editor and save the file as contact.html. Edit the code as follows:

a. Modify the title of the web page by changing the text between the `<title>` and `</title>` tags to "Trillium Media Design - Contact". In order to create a consistent header, navigation, and footer for the web pages in this website, do not change the code within the header, nav, or footer elements.

b. Position your cursor in the body section and delete the code and text contained between the opening div tag and the closing div tag. Code the main page content for the contact page between the div tags:

```
<h2>Contact Trillium Media Design Today</h2>
   <ul>
     <li>E-mail: contact@trilliummediadesign.com</li>
     <li>Phone: 555-555-5555</li>
   </ul>
```

c. Save the contact.html file in your mypractice folder. Test your page in a browser. It should look similar to Figure 23. Test your page by clicking each link. When you click the "Home" hyperlink, the index.html page should display. When you click the "Services" hyperlink, the services.html page should display. When you click the "Contact" hyperlink, the contact.html page will display. You can compare your work to the sample in the student files (chapter2/practice/contact.html).

 What if my relative hyperlink doesn't work?

Check the following:

▶ Did you save files in the specified folder?

▶ Did you save the files with the names as requested? Use Windows Explorer, My Computer, or Finder (Mac users) to verify the actual names of the files you saved.

▶ Did you type the file names correctly in the anchor tag's href property? Check for typographical errors.

▶ When you place your mouse over a link, the file name of a relative link will display in the status bar in the lower edge of the browser window. Verify that this is the correct file name. On many operating systems, such as UNIX or Linux, the use of uppercase and lowercase letters in file names matters—make sure that the file name and the reference to it are in the same case. It's a good practice to always use lowercase for file names used on the Web.

E-Mail Hyperlinks

The anchor tag can also be used to create e-mail hyperlinks. An e-mail hyperlink will automatically launch the default mail program configured for the browser. It is similar to an external hyperlink with the following two exceptions:

- It uses `mailto:` instead of `http://`.
- It launches the default e-mail application for the visitor's browser with your e-mail address as the recipient.

For example, to create an e-mail hyperlink to the e-mail address help@webdevbasics.net, code the following:

```
<a href="mailto:help@webdevbasics.net">help@webdevbasics.net</a>
```

It is good practice to place the e-mail address both on the web page and within the anchor tag. Not everyone has an e-mail program configured with his or her browser. By placing the e-mail address in both places, you increase usability for all of your visitors.

 Hands-On Practice 14 ——————————————————

In this Hands-On Practice you will modify the contact page (contact.html) of the website you created in Hands-On Practice 13 and configure an e-mail link in the page content area. Launch a text editor, and open the contact.html file from your mypractice folder. This example uses the contact.html file found in the student files in the chapter2/practice folder.

FIGURE 24 *An e-mail hyperlink has been configured on the contact page.*

Configure the e-mail address in the content area as an e-mail hyperlink as follows:

```
<li>E-mail:
<a href="mailto:contact@trilliummediadesign.com">contact@trilliummediadesign.com</a>
</li>
```

Save and test the page in a browser. The browser display should look similar to the page shown in Figure 24. Compare your work with the sample in the student files (chapter2/practice2/contact.html).

Quick TIP

Free web-based e-mail is offered by many providers, such as Yahoo!, Google, Hotmail, and so on. You can create one or more free e-mail accounts to use when communicating with new websites or signing up for free services, such as newsletters. This will help to organize your e-mail into those you need to access and respond to right away (such as school, work, or personal messages) and those you can get to at your convenience.

FAQ

Won't displaying my actual e-mail address on a web page increase spam?

Yes and no. While it's possible that some unethical spammers may harvest web pages for e-mail addresses, the chances are that your e-mail application's built-in spam filter will prevent your inbox from being flooded with messages. When you configure an easily readable e-mail hyperlink you increase the usability of your website for your visitors in the following situations:

▶ The visitor may be at a public computer with no e-mail application configured. In this case, when the e-mail hyperlink is clicked, an error message may display, and the visitor will have difficulty contacting you using the e-mail link.

▶ The visitor may be at a private computer but may prefer not to use the e-mail application (and address) that is configured by default to work with the browser. Perhaps he or she shares the computer with others, or perhaps he or she wishes to preserve the privacy of the default e-mail address

If you prominently displayed your actual e-mail address, in both of these situations the visitor can still access your e-mail address and use it to contact you (in either their e-mail application or via a web-based e-mail system such as Google's Gmail). The result is a more usable website for your visitors.

HTML Basics

Review and Apply

Review Questions

1. Which tag is used to hyperlink web pages to each other?
   - a. `<hyperlink>` tag
   - b. `<a>` tag
   - c. `<link>` tag
   - d. `<body>` tag

2. Which tag pair configures the largest heading?
   - a. `<h1> </h1>`
   - b. `<h9> </h9>`
   - c. `<h type="largest"> </h>`
   - d. `<h6> </h6>`

3. Which tag configures the following text or element to display on a new line?
   - a. `<new line>`
   - b. `<nl>`
   - c. `<br>`
   - d. `<line>`

4. Which tag pair configures a paragraph?
   - a. `<para> </para>`
   - b. `<paragraph> </paragraph>`
   - c. `<p> </p>`
   - d. `<body> </body>`

5. Which of the following is an HTML5 element used to indicate navigational content?
   - a. nav
   - b. header
   - c. footer
   - d. p

6. When should you code an absolute hyperlink?
   - a. when linking to a web page that is internal to your website
   - b. when linking to a web page that is external to your website
   - c. always; the W3C prefers absolute hyperlinks
   - d. never; absolute hyperlinks are obsolete

7. Which tag pair is the best choice to emphasize text with italic font on a web page?
   - a. `<b> </b>`
   - b. `<strong> </strong>`
   - c. `<em> </em>`
   - d. `<bold> </bold>`

8. Which tag configures a horizontal line on a web page?
   - a. `<br>`
   - b. `<h1>`
   - c. `<hr>`
   - d. `<line>`

9. Which type of HTML list will automatically number the items for you?
   - a. numbered list
   - b. ordered list
   - c. unordered list
   - d. description list

10. Which statement is true?
    - a. The W3C Markup Validation Service describes how to fix the errors in your web page.
    - b. The W3C Markup Validation Service lists syntax errors in a web page.
    - c. The W3C Markup Validation Service is only available to W3C members.
    - d. None of the above statements are true

Hands-On Exercises

1. Write the markup language code to display your name in the largest-size heading element.

2. Write the markup language code for an unordered list to display the days of the week.

HTML Basics

3. Write the markup language code for an ordered list that uses uppercase letters to order the items. This ordered list will display the following: Spring, Summer, Fall, and Winter.

4. Think of a favorite quote by someone you admire. Write the HTML code to display the person's name in a heading and the quote in a blockquote.

5. Modify the following code snippet to indicate that the bolded text has strong importance.

```
<p>A diagram of the organization of a website is called a <b>site
map</b> or <b>storyboard</b>. Creating the <b>site map</b> is one
of the initial steps in developing a website.</p>
```

6. Write the code to create an absolute hyperlink to a website whose domain name is google.com.

7. Write the code to create a relative hyperlink to a web page named clients.html.

8. Create a web page about your favorite musical group. Include the name of the group, the members of the group, a hyperlink to the group's website, your favorite three (or fewer if the group is new) CD releases, and a brief review of each CD. Be sure to use the following elements: html, head, title, meta, body, header, footer, div, h1, h2, p, ul, li, and a. Configure your name in an e-mail link in the page footer area. Save the page as band.html. Open your file in a text editor and print the source code for the page. Display your page in a browser and print the page. Hand in both printouts to your instructor.

Focus on Web Design

Markup language code alone does not make a web page—design is very important. Access the Web and find two web pages—one that is appealing to you and one that is unappealing to you. Print each page. Create a web page that answers the following questions for each of your examples.

a. What is the URL of the website?

b. Is the page appealing or unappealing? List three reasons for your answer.

c. If the page is unappealing, what would you do to improve it?

d. Would you encourage others to visit this site? Why or why not?

Answers to Review Questions

1. b   2. a   3. c
4. c   5. a   6. b
7. c   8. c   9. b
10. b

Credits

Figures 14–16 © Microsoft Corporation

Figures 1–7, 9, 11–13, 18, 19, 21–24, 27, 28, 31, 32 © Terry Ann Morris, Ed.D. | Mozilla Foundation

Web Design Basics

As a website visitor, you have probably found that certain websites are appealing and easy to use, while others seem awkward or just plain annoying. What separates the good from the bad? This chapter discusses recommended website design practices. The topics include site organization, site navigation, page design, text design, graphic design, and accessibility considerations.

You'll learn how to...

- Describe the most common types of website organization
- Describe principles of visual design
- Design for your target audience
- Create clear, easy-to-use navigation
- Improve the readability of the text on your web pages
- Use graphics appropriately on web pages
- Apply the concept of universal design to web pages
- Describe web page layout design techniques
- Describe the concept of responsive web design
- Apply best practices of web design

From Chapter 3 of *Basics of Web Design HTML5 & CSS3*, Second Edition. Terry Ann Felke-Morris. Copyright © 2014 by Pearson Education, Inc. All rights reserved.

Design for Your Target Audience

Whatever your personal preferences, your website should appeal to your **target audience**—the people who will use your site. Your intended target audience may be specific, such as kids, college students, young couples, or seniors, or you may intend your site to appeal to everyone. The purpose and goals of your visitors will vary—they may be casually seeking information, performing research for school or work, comparison shopping, job hunting, and so on. The design of a website should appeal to and meet the needs of the target audience.

For example, NASA's website, www.nasa.gov, as shown in Figure 1, features compelling graphics and has a different look and feel from the text-based, link-intensive website of the Bureau of Labor Statistics, www.bls.gov (Figure 2).

The first site engages you, draws you in, and invites exploration. The second site provides you with a wide range of choices so that you can quickly get down to work. Keep your target audience in mind as you explore the web design practices in this chapter.

FIGURE 1 *The compelling graphic draws you in.*

FIGURE 2 *This text-intensive website immediately offers numerous choices.*

Web Design Basics

Browsers

Just because your web page looks great in your favorite browser doesn't automatically mean that all browsers will render it well. Recent surveys by Net Market Share (http://marketshare.hitslink.com) indicate that while Microsoft Internet Explorer is still the most popular desktop web browser, the Mozilla Firefox and Google Chrome browsers have been gaining ground. Net Market Share reported the market share of the top four desktop browsers in a recent month as: Internet Explorer (54%), Firefox (20%), Chrome (19%), and Safari (2%). The market share of the top four mobile/tablet browsers was reported by Net Market Share: Safari (64%), Android Browser (19%), Opera Mini (12%), and Symbian Browser (1%).

Apply the principle of progressive enhancement: Design a website so that it looks good in commonly used browsers and then add enhancements with CSS3 and/or HTML5 for display in the most recent versions of browsers.

Always try to test your pages with the most popular versions of browsers on both PC and Mac operating systems. Many web page components, including default text size and default margin size, are different among browsers, browser versions, and operating systems. Also try to test your website on other types of devices such as tablets and smartphones. Opera offers free simulators for the Opera Mini mobile browser at www.opera.com/mobile/demo.

Screen Resolution

Your website visitors will use a variety of screen resolutions. A recent survey by Net Market Share (http://marketshare.hitslink.com/report.aspx?qprid=17) reported the use of more than 90 different screen resolutions, with the top four being 1024×768 (with 16%), 1366×768 (14%), 1280×800 (12%), and 1280×1024 (8%). Mobile use will vary with the purpose of the website, but it is expected to grow as the use of smartphones and tablets increases. Be aware that some smartphones have low screen resolution, such as 240×320, 320×480, or 480×800. Popular tablet devices offer a higher screen resolution: Apple iPad (1024×768), Motorola Xoom (1280×800), Samsung Galaxy Tab (1200×800), and Kindle Fire (1024×600). CSS media queries is a technique for configuring a web page to display well on various screen resolutions.

?FAQ **How can I create web pages that look exactly the same on all browsers?**

You can't. Design with the most popular browsers and screen resolutions in mind, but expect your web pages to look slightly different when displayed by different browsers and on monitors with different screen resolutions. Expect web pages to look even more different when displayed on mobile devices. You'll learn about responsive web design techniques later in this chapter.

Website
Organization

How will visitors move around your site? How will they find what they need? This is largely determined by the website's organization or architecture. There are three common types of website organization:

- ▶ Hierarchical
- ▶ Linear
- ▶ Random (sometimes called web organization)

A diagram of the organization of a website is called a **site map**. Creating the site map is one of the initial steps in developing a website.

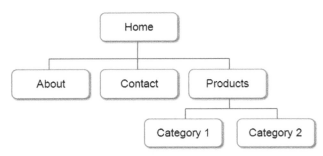

FIGURE 3 *Hierarchical site organization.*

Hierarchical Organization

Most websites use **hierarchical organization**. A site map for hierarchical organization, such as the one shown in Figure 3, is characterized by a clearly defined home page with links to major site sections. Web pages within sections are placed as needed. The home page plus the first level of pages in a hierarchical site map typically indicates the hyperlinks that will be displayed on the main navigation bar of each web page within the website.

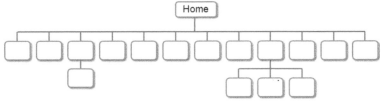

FIGURE 4 *This site design uses a shallow hierarchy.*

It is important to be aware of pitfalls of hierarchical organization. Figure 4 shows a site design that is too shallow—there could be too many major site sections. This site design needs to be organized into fewer, easily managed topics or units of information, a process called **chunking**. In the case of web page design, each unit of information is a page. Nelson Cowan, a research psychologist at the University of Missouri, found that adults are typically able to keep about four items or chunks of items (such as the three parts of a phone number 888-555-5555) in their short-term memory (http://web.missouri.edu/~cowann/research.html). Following this principle, be aware of the number of major navigation links and try to group them into visually separate sections on the page, with each group having no more than about four links.

Web Design Basics

Another potential design pitfall of hierarchical website design is creating a site whose structure is too deep. Figure 5 shows an example of this. The interface design "three-click rule" says that a web page visitor should be able to get to any page on your site with a maximum of three hyperlinks. In other words, a visitor who cannot get what he or she wants in three mouse clicks will begin to feel frustrated and may leave your site. This rule may be very difficult to satisfy on a large site, but in general, the goal is to organize your site so that your visitors can easily navigate from page to page within the site structure.

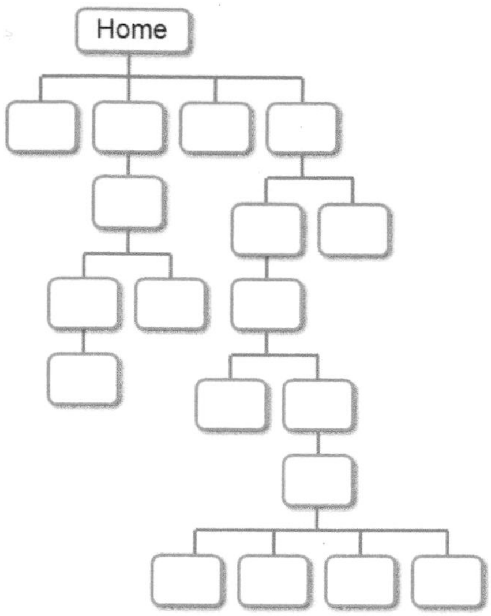

Linear Organization

Linear organization, shown in Figure 6, is useful when the purpose of a website or series of pages within a site is to provide a tutorial, tour, or presentation that needs to be viewed sequentially.

FIGURE 6 *Linear site organization.*

FIGURE 5 *This site design uses a deep hierarchy.*

In linear organization, the pages are viewed one after another. Some websites use hierarchical organization in general but with linear organization in a few small areas.

Random Organization

Random organization (sometimes called web organization) offers no clear path through the site, as shown in Figure 7. There is often no clear home page and no discernible structure. Random organization is not as common as hierarchical or linear organization and is usually found only on artistic sites or sites that strive to be especially different and original. This type of organization is typically not used for commercial websites.

FIGURE 7 *Random site organization.*

FAQ

What's a good way to organize my site map?

Sometimes it is difficult to begin creating a site map for a website. Some design teams meet in a room with a blank wall and a package of large Post-it Notes. They write the titles of topics and subtopics needed on the site on the Post-it Notes. They arrange the notes on the wall and discuss until a site structure evolves and there is consensus within the group. If you are not working in a group, you can try this on your own and then discuss the way you have chosen to organize the website with a friend or fellow student.

Web Design Basics

Principles of Visual Design

VideoNote
Principles of Visual Design

There are four visual design principles that you can apply to the design of just about anything: repetition, contrast, proximity, and alignment. Whether you are designing a web page, a button, a logo, a DVD cover, a brochure, or a software interface, the design principles of repetition, contrast, proximity, and alignment will help to create the "look" (visual aesthetic), of your project and will determine whether your message is effectively communicated.

Repetition: Repeat Visual Components Throughout the Design

When applying the principle of **repetition**, the web designer repeats one or more components throughout the page. The repeating aspect ties the work together. Figure 8 displays the home page for a bed and breakfast business. The page design demonstrates the use of repetition in a variety of design components, including color, shape, font, and images.

- ▶ The photographs displayed on the web page use similar colors (brown, tan, dark green, and off-white) which are repeated in other areas on the web page. Browns are used for background color of the navigation area, call-to-action "Search" and "Subscribe" buttons, and the color of text in the center and right columns. An off-white color is used for the logo text, navigation text, and center column background. The dark green is used as the background color of the navigation area and also as the topic headings in the center column.

- ▶ The call-to-action "Reservations" and "Newsletter" areas have a similar shape and format with heading, content, and button.

- ▶ The use of only two font typefaces on the page also demonstrates repetition and helps to create a cohesive look. The website name and page topic headings are configured with Trebuchet font. Other page content uses Arial font.

Whether it is color, shape, font, or image, repetition helps to unify a design.

Contrast: Add Visual Excitement and Draw Attention

To apply the principle of **contrast**, emphasize the differences between page elements in order to make the design interesting and direct attention. There should be good contrast between the background color and the text color on a web page. If there is too little contrast, the text will be difficult to read. Notice how the upper right navigation area in Figure 8 uses a text color that has good contrast with the dark background color. The left column features a medium dark background that has good contrast with the light off-white text. The middle column features dark text on a medium-light background to provide good visual contrast and easy reading. The dark text in the footer area contrasts well with the medium-light background color.

FIGURE 8 *The design principles of repetition, contrast, proximity, and alignment are well used on this web page.*

Proximity: Group Related Items

When designers apply the principle of **proximity**, related items are placed physically close together. Unrelated items should have space separating them. The placing of "Reservations" form controls close together gives visual clues to the logical organization of the information or functionality. In Figure 8, the horizontal navigation links are all placed in close proximity to each other. This creates a visual group on the page and makes the navigation easier to use. Proximity is used well on this page to group related elements.

Alignment: Align Elements to Create Visual Unity

Another principle that helps to create a cohesive web page is **alignment**. When applying this principle, the designer organizes the page so that each element placed has some alignment (vertical or horizontal) with another element on the page. The page shown in Figure 8 also applies this principle. Notice how the page components are vertically aligned in columns of equal height.

Repetition, contrast, proximity, and alignment are four visual design principles that can greatly improve your web page designs. If you apply these principles effectively, your web pages will look more professional and you will communicate your message more clearly. Keep these principles in mind as you design and build web pages.

Web Design Basics

Design to Provide for Accessibility

Let's consider the concept of **universal design**. The Center for Universal Design defines universal design as "the design of products and environments to be usable by all people, to the greatest extent possible, without the need for adaptation or specialized design."

Who Benefits from Universal Design and Increased Accessibility?

Consider the following scenarios:

▶ Maria is a young woman in her twenties with physical challenges who cannot manipulate a mouse and who uses a keyboard with much effort. Accessible web pages designed to function without a mouse will help Maria access content.

▶ Leotis is a college student who is deaf and wants to be a web developer. Captions for audio/video content and transcripts will provide Leotis access to content.

▶ Jim is a middle-aged man who has a dial-up Internet connection and is using the Web for personal enjoyment. Alternate text for images and transcripts for multimedia will provide Jim improved access to content.

▶ Nadine is a mature woman with age-related macular degeneration who has difficulty reading small print. Web pages designed so that text can be enlarged in the browser will make it easier for Nadine to read.

▶ Karen is a college student using a smart phone to access the Web. Accessible content organized with headings and lists will make it easier for Karen to surf the Web on a mobile device.

▶ Prakesh is a man in his thirties who is legally blind and needs access to the Web to do his job. Web pages designed to be accessible (which are organized with headings and lists, display descriptive text for hyperlinks, provide alternate text descriptions for images, and are usable without a mouse) will help Prakesh access content when using a screen reader application such as JAWS or Window-Eyes.

All of these individuals benefit from web pages designed with accessibility in mind. A web page that is designed to be accessible is typically more usable for all—even a person who has no physical challenges and is using a broadband connection benefits from the improved presentation and organization of a well-designed web page (Figure 9).

Accessible Design Can Benefit Search Engine Listing

Search engine programs (commonly referred to as bots or spiders) walk the Web and follow hyperlinks on websites. An accessible website with descriptive page titles that is well organized with headings, lists, descriptive text for hyperlinks, and alternate text for images is more visible to search engine robots and may result in better ranking.

Legal Requirements

The Internet and World Wide Web are such a pervasive part of our culture that accessibility is mandated by laws in the United States. Section 508 of the Rehabilitation Act requires electronic and information technology, including web pages, used by federal agencies to be accessible to people with disabilities. The accessibility recommendations presented in this text are intended to satisfy the Section 508 standards and the W3C Web Accessibility Initiative guidelines. At the time this was written the Section 508 standards were undergoing revision; see www.access-board.gov for current information.

FIGURE 9 *Everyone benefits from an accessible web page.*

Accessibility Is the Right Thing to Do

The federal government is promoting accessibility by law, and the private sector is following its lead. The W3C is also active in this cause and has created the Web Accessibility Initiative (WAI) to create guidelines and standards applicable to web content developers, authoring-tool developers, and browser developers. You can access WAI's Web Content Accessibility Guidelines 2.0 (WCAG 2.0) at www.w3.org/TR/WCAG20/Overview. The following four content accessibility principles are essential to conformance with WCAG 2.0—**P**erceivable, **O**perable, **U**nderstandable, and **R**obust—referred to by the acronym **POUR**.

1. Content must be **Perceivable**. Perceivable content is easy to see or hear. Any graphic or multimedia content should be available in a text format, such as text descriptions for images, closed captions for videos, and transcripts for audio.

2. Interface components in the content must be **Operable**. Operable content has interactive features, such as navigation forms, that can be used or operated with either a mouse or keyboard. Multimedia content should be designed to avoid flashing, which may cause a seizure.

3. Content and controls must be **Understandable**. Understandable content is easy to read, organized in a consistent manner, and provides helpful error messages when appropriate.

4. Content should be **Robust** enough to work with current and future user agents, including assistive technologies. Robust content is written to follow W3C Recommendations and should be compatible with multiple operating systems, browsers, and assistive technologies such as screen reader applications.

You'll learn to include accessibility features as you create practice pages, including the importance of the title tag, heading tags, and descriptive text for hyperlinks.

Web Design Basics

Use of Text

Writing for the Web

Long-winded sentences and explanations are often found in academic textbooks and romance novels, but they really are not appropriate on a web page. Long blocks of text and long paragraphs are difficult to read on the Web. The following suggestions will help to increase the readability of your web pages.

- Be concise. Use the text equivalent of sound bytes—short sentences and phrases.
- Organize the page content with headings and subheadings.
- Use lists to help text stand out and make content easier to read.

The web page shown in Figure 10 provides an example of using headings and brief paragraphs to organize web page content so that it is easy to read and visitors can quickly find what they need.

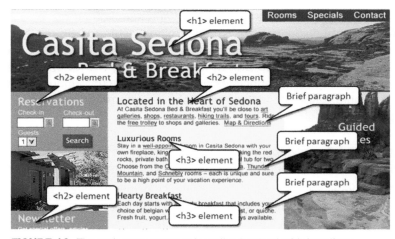

FIGURE 10 *The web page content is well organized with headings.*

Text Design Considerations

You may be wondering how to know whether a web page is easy to read. Readable text is crucial to providing content of value for your web page visitors. Carefully consider the typeface, size, weight, and color when you select fonts for your web pages. The following are some suggestions that will help increase the readability of your pages:

- **Use Common Fonts**

  Use common fonts such as Arial, Verdana, or Times New Roman. Remember that the web page visitor must have the font installed on his or her computer in order for

Web Design Basics

that particular font to appear. Your page may look great with Gill Sans Ultra Bold Condensed, but if your visitor doesn't have this typeface, the browser's default font will be displayed. Explore the list of "web-safe" fonts at www.ampsoft.net/webdesign-l/WindowsMacFonts.html.

Carefully Choose Fonts

Serif fonts, such as Times New Roman, were originally developed for printing text on paper, not for displaying text on a computer monitor. Research shows that sans serif fonts, such as Arial and Verdana, are easier to read than serif fonts when displayed on a computer screen (see www.alexpoole.info/academic/literaturereview.html or www.wilsonweb.com/wmt6/html-email-fonts.htm for details).

Check Font Size

Be aware that fonts display smaller on a Mac than on a PC. Even within the PC platform, the default font size displayed by browsers may not be the same. Consider creating prototype pages of your font size settings to test on a variety of browsers and screen resolution settings.

Check Font Weight

Bold or *emphasize* important text (use the `<strong>` element for bold and the `<em>` element to configure italics). However, be careful not to bold everything—that has the same effect as bolding nothing.

Check Font Color for Contrast

Use appropriate color combinations. Newbie web designers sometimes choose color combinations for web pages that they would never dream of using in their wardrobe. An easy way to choose colors that contrast well and look good together is to select colors from an image or logo that you will use for your site. Make sure that your page background color properly contrasts with your text and hyperlink colors.

Check Line Length

Be aware of line length—use white space and multiple columns if possible. Christian Holst at the Baymard Institute (http://baymard.com/blog/line-length-readability) recommends using between 50–75 characters per line for readability. Look ahead to Figure 30 for examples of text placement on a web page.

Check Alignment

A paragraph of centered text is more difficult to read than left-aligned text.

Carefully Choose Text in Hyperlinks

Use hyperlinks for keywords and descriptive phrases. Do not hyperlink entire sentences. Also avoid the use of the words "click here" in hyperlinks—users know what to do by now.

Check Spelling and Grammar

Unfortunately, many websites contain misspelled words. Most web-authoring tools have built-in spell checkers; consider using this feature.

Finally, be sure that you proofread and test your site thoroughly. It's very helpful if you can find web developer buddies—you check their sites, and they check yours. It's always easier to see someone else's mistake than your own.

Web Design Basics

Web Color Palette

Red: #FF0000

Green: #00FF00

Blue: #0000FF

Black: #000000

White: #FFFFFF

Grey: #CCCCCC

FIGURE 11
Sample colors.

Computer monitors display color as a combination of different intensities of red, green, and blue, also known as **RGB color**. RGB intensity values are numeric from 0 to 255.

Each RGB color has three values, one each for red, green, and blue. These are always listed in the same order (red, green, blue) and specify the numerical value of each color (see examples in Figure 11). You will usually use hexadecimal color values to specify RGB color on web pages.

Hexadecimal Color Values

Hexadecimal is the name for the base 16 numbering system, which uses the characters 0, 1, 2, 3, 4, 5, 6, 7, 8, 9, A, B, C, D, E, and F to specify numeric values.

Hexadecimal color values specify RGB color with numeric value pairs ranging from 00 to FF (0 to 255 in base 10). Each pair is associated with the amount of red, green, and blue displayed. Using this notation, one would specify the color red as #FF0000 and the color blue as #0000FF. The # symbol signifies that the value is hexadecimal. You can use either uppercase or lowercase letters in hexadecimal color values; #FF0000 and #ff0000 both configure the color red.

Don't worry—you won't need to do calculations to work with web colors. Just become familiar with the numbering scheme. See Figure 12 for an excerpt from the companion website at http://webdevbasics.net/color.

#FFFFFF	#FFFFCC	#FFFF99	#FFFF66	#FFFF33	#FFFF00
#FFCCFF	#FFCCCC	#FFCC99	#FFCC66	#FFCC33	#FFCC00
#FF99FF	#FF99CC	#FF9999	#FF9966	#FF9933	#FF9900
#FF66FF	#FF66CC	#FF6699	#FF6666	#FF6633	#FF6600
#FF33FF	#FF33CC	#FF3399	#FF3366	#FF3333	#FF3300
#FF00FF	#FF00CC	#FF0099	#FF0066	#FF0033	#FF0000

FIGURE 12 *Partial color chart.*

Web-Safe Colors

It is easy to tell whether a color is a web-safe color—check the hexadecimal color values.

Web-Safe Hexadecimal Values

00, 33, 66, 99, CC, FF

Look at the color chart at the end of the chapter (also shown at http://webdevbasics.net/color). Note that all the colors listed follow this numbering scheme—they comprise the Web Safe Color Palette.

Web Design Basics

Must I use only web-safe colors?

No, you are free to choose any color, as long as you check that there is adequate contrast between your text and background colors—you want your visitors to be able to read the content on your site! Back in the day of eight-bit color it was very important to use web-safe colors. Today, it is less important since most video drivers support millions of colors.

Accessibility and Color

Everyone who visits your website may not be able to see or distinguish between colors. Keep in mind that you'll need to convey information even if color cannot be viewed. According to VisCheck (http://vischeck.com/vischeck), one out of twenty people experiences some type of color perception deficiency.

Color choices can be crucial. For example, red text on a blue background, as shown in Figure 13, is usually difficult for everyone to read. Also avoid using red, green, brown, gray, or purple next to each other. White, black, and shades of blue and yellow are easier for most people to differentiate.

Choose text and background colors with enough contrast so the text can be easily read. Use the tool at http://juicystudio.com/services/luminositycontrastratio.php to verify the amount of contrast.

Can you read this easily?

FIGURE 13 *Some color combinations are difficult to read.*

Check out the following websites for some color ideas. Then continue with the next section for more tips on choosing colors for your web pages.

▶ www.colorschemedesigner.com
▶ http://0to255.com
▶ www.colorsontheweb.com/colorwizard.asp

Web Design Basics

Use of Color

The first section in this chapter focused on the importance of designing for your target audience. In this section, we consider how to use color to appeal to a target audience.

FIGURE 14 *A web page intended to appeal to children.*

Appealing to Children and Preteens

Younger audiences, such as children and preteens, prefer bright, lively colors. The web page shown in Figure 14, features bright graphics, lots of color, and interactivity. Examples of websites designed to appeal to children:

- www.sesamestreet.org/games
- www.nick.com
- www.usmint.gov/kids

Appealing to Young Adults

Individuals in their late teens and early twenties generally prefer dark background colors with occasional use of bright contrast, music, and dynamic navigation. Figure 15 shows a web page designed for this age group. Note how it has a completely different look and feel from the site designed for young children. Examples of websites designed to appeal to young adults:

- http://us.battle.net/wow
- www.nin.com
- www.thresholdrpg.com

FIGURE 15 *Many teens and young adults find dark sites appealing.*

Web Design Basics

Appealing to Everybody

If your goal is to appeal to everyone, follow the example of the popular Amazon.com and eBay.com websites in their use of color. These sites display a neutral white background with splashes of color to add interest and highlight page areas. Use of white as a background color was found to be quite popular by Jakob Nielsen and Marie Tahir in *Homepage Usability: 50 Websites Deconstructed*, a book that analyzed 50 top websites. According to this study, 84 percent of the sites used white as the background color, and 72 percent used black as the text color. This maximized the contrast between text and background— providing maximum ease of reading.

FIGURE 16 *A compelling graphic along with white background for the content area.*

You'll also notice that websites targeting "everyone" often include compelling visual graphics. The National Park Service home page (www.nps.gov), shown in Figure 16, engages the visitor with color and graphics while providing the main content on a white background for maximum contrast.

Appealing to Older Adults

For an older target audience, light backgrounds, well-defined images, and large text are appropriate. The screenshot of the National Institutes of Health Senior Health site (http://nihseniorhealth.gov) shown in Figure 17 is an example of a web page intended for the 55-and-older age group. Examples of websites designed to appeal to older adults:

- www.aarp.org
- www.theseniornews.com
- http://senior.org

FIGURE 17 *A site designed specifically for the 55-and-older age group.*

Use of Graphics and Multimedia

As shown in Figure 16, a compelling graphic can be an engaging element on a web page. However, be aware that you should avoid relying on images to convey meaning. Some individuals may not be able to see your images and multimedia—they may be accessing your site with a mobile device or using an assistive technology such as a screen reader to visit your page. You may need to include text descriptions of important concepts or key points that a graphic image or multimedia file conveys. In this section, you'll explore recommended techniques for use of graphics and multimedia on web pages.

File Size and Dimensions Matter

Image optimization is the process of creating an image with the lowest file size that still renders a good-quality image—balancing image quality and file size. The dimensions of the image should be as close to possible as the actual display size to enable speedy browser rendering of the image. Other approaches to image optimization are to crop an image or create a thumbnail image that links to a larger version of the image. Adobe Photoshop and Adobe Fireworks are often used by web professionals to optimize images for the Web. A free online tool for image editing and optimization is Pixlr Editor at www.pixlr.com/editor.

Antialiased

FIGURE 18 *Antialiased text.*

FIGURE 19 *This graphic has a jagged look and was not saved using antialiasing.*

Antialiased/Aliased Text Considerations

Refer back to Figure 14 and notice how easy it is to read the text in the navigation buttons—the text in each button is **antialiased text**. Antialiasing introduces intermediate colors to smooth jagged edges in digital images. Graphic applications such as Adobe Photoshop and Adobe Fireworks can be used to create antialiased text images. The graphic shown in Figure 18 was created using antialiasing. Figure 19 displays an image created without antialiasing; note the jagged edges.

Use Only Necessary Multimedia

Use animation and multimedia only if it will add value to your site. Limit the use of animated items. Only use animation if it makes the page more effective. Consider limiting how long an animation plays. Don't include an animated GIF or a Flash animation just because you happen to have one.

Web Design Basics

In general, younger audiences find animation more appealing than older audiences. The web page shown in Figure 14 is geared to children and uses lots of animation. This would be too much animation for a website targeted to adult shoppers. However, a well-done navigation animation or an animation that describes a product or service could be appealing to almost any target group. Adobe Flash is often used on the Web to add visual interest and interactivity to web pages, as shown in Figure 20.

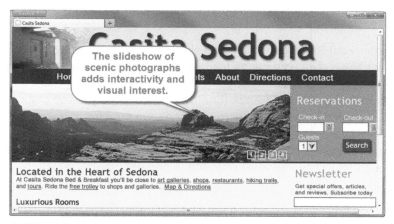

FIGURE 20 *The slideshow adds visual interest and interactivity.*

Provide Alternate Text

Each image on your web page should be configured with alternate text. Alternate text may be displayed instead of the image when the page is displayed by mobile devices, while the image is loading (when the image is slow to load), and when a browser is configured to not show images. Alternate text is also read aloud when a person with a disability uses a screen reader to access your website. In Figure 21, the Firefox Web Developer extension was used to display the alt text for an image on the National Park Service website (http://nps.gov).

FIGURE 21 *The alt text is displayed above the image by the Web Developer Extension for Firefox.*

Web Design Basics

More Design Considerations

Load Time

The last thing you want to happen is for your visitors to leave your page before it has even finished loading! Make sure your pages load as quickly as possible. Web usability expert Jakob Nielsen reports that visitors will often leave a page after waiting more than 10 seconds. It takes less than 9 seconds at 56Kbps for a browser to display a web page and associated files of 60KB. It's a good practice to try to limit the total file size of a website's home page and all of its associated images and media files to less than 60KB. However, it's common to go over this recommended limit for content pages when you're sure your visitors will be interested enough to wait to see what your site is presenting.

According to a recent study by the PEW Internet and American Life Project, the percentage of U.S. Internet users with a broadband connection (cable, DSL, and so on) at home or at work is rising. Sixty-six percent of adult Americans have access to broadband at home. Even with the trend of increasing bandwidth available to your visitors, keep in mind that 34 percent of households do not have broadband Internet access. Visit www.pewinternet.org for the most up-to-date statistics. The chart shown in Figure 22 compares file sizes and connection speed download times, and was created using the calculator at www.t1shopper.com/tools/calculate/downloadcalculator.php.

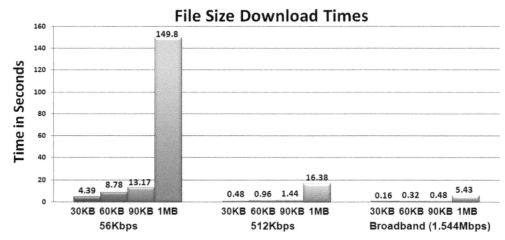

FIGURE 22 *File size download times and internet connection speeds.*

Web Design Basics

One method to help determine whether the load time of your page is acceptable is to view the size of your website files in Windows Explorer or MacOS Finder. Calculate the total file size of your web page plus all of its associated images and media. If the total file size for a single page and of its associated files is greater than 60KB and it is likely that your target audience may not be using broadband access, take a closer look at your design. Consider whether you really need to use all the images to convey your message. Perhaps the images can be better optimized for the Web or the content of the page should be divided into multiple pages. This is a time for some decision-making! Popular web-authoring tools such as Microsoft Expression Web and Adobe Dreamweaver will calculate load time at various transmission speeds.

Perceived Load Time

Perceived load time is the amount of time a web page visitor is aware of waiting while your page is loading. Since visitors often leave a website if a page takes too long to load, it is important to shorten their perception of waiting. In addition to optimizing all images, another common technique for shortening perceived load time is to utilize image sprites, which combine multiple small images into a single file.

Above the Fold

Placing important information **above the fold** is a technique borrowed from the newspaper industry. When newspapers are sitting on a counter or in a vending machine waiting to be sold, you can see the portion of the page that is "above the fold." Publishers noticed that more papers were sold when the most important, attention-getting information was placed in this location. You may use this technique to attract visitors and to keep visitors on your web pages. Arrange interesting content above the fold. On web pages, this is the area the visitor sees without scrolling down the page. At one of the most popular screen resolutions of 1024×768, the amount of screen viewable above the fold (after accounting for browser menus and controls) is about 600 pixels. Avoid placing important information and navigation on the far right side because this area may not be initially displayed by browsers at some screen resolutions.

Adequate White Space

The term **white space** is also borrowed from the publishing industry. Placing blank or white space (because paper is usually white) in areas around blocks of text increases the readability of the page. Placing white space around graphics helps them to stand out. Allow for some blank space between blocks of text and images. How much is adequate? It depends—experiment until the page is likely to look appealing to your target audience.

Horizontal Scrolling

In order to make it easy for visitors to view and use your web pages, avoid creating pages that are too wide to be displayed in the browser window. These pages require the user to scroll horizontally. Cameron Moll (www.cameronmoll.com/archives/001220.html) suggests that the optimal web page width for display at 1024×768 screen resolution is 960 pixels. Be mindful that many of your web page visitors will not maximize their browser viewport.

Web Design Basics

Navigation Design

Ease of Navigation

Sometimes web developers are so close to their sites that they can't see the forest for the trees. A new visitor will wander onto the site and not know what to click or how to find the information he or she seeks. Clearly labeled navigation on each page is helpful and should be in the same location on each page for maximum usability.

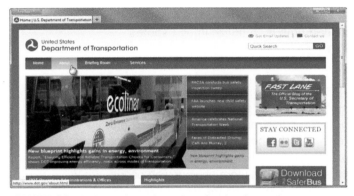

FIGURE 23 *Horizontal text-based navigation is used at www.dot.gov.*

Navigation Bars

Clear **navigation bars**, either graphic or text based, make it obvious to website users where they are and where they can go next. It's quite common for site-wide navigation to be located in either a horizontal navigation bar placed under the logo (see Figure 23) or in a vertical navigation bar on the left side of the page (see Figure 24). Less common is a vertical navigation bar on the right side of the page—this area can be cut off at lower screen resolutions.

Breadcrumb Navigation

Jakob Nielsen, a well-known usability and web design professional, favors what he calls a **breadcrumb trail** for larger sites, which indicates the path of web pages a visitor has viewed during the current session. Figure 24 shows a page with a well-organized main navigation area below the logo area in addition to the breadcrumb trail navigation above the main content area that indicates the pages the visitor has viewed during this visit: Home > News and Features > News Topics > Solar System. Visitors can easily retrace their steps or jump back to a previously viewed page. The left side of this page also contains a vertical navigation bar with links for the "News Topics" section. This NASA page illustrates that it's common for a website to use more than one type of navigation.

FIGURE 24 *Visitors can follow the "breadcrumbs" to retrace their steps through www.nasa.gov.*

Using Graphics for Navigation

Sometimes graphics are used to provide navigation, as in the pink navigation buttons on the web page shown in Figure 14. The "text" for the navigation is actually stored in image files. Be aware that using graphics for navigation is an outdated design technique. A website with text navigation is more accessible and more easily indexed by search engines.

Even when image hyperlinks instead of text hyperlinks provide the main navigation of the site, you can use two techniques that provide for accessibility:

▶ Configure each image with an alternate text description.

▶ Configure text hyperlinks in the footer area.

Dynamic Navigation

In your experiences visiting websites you've probably encountered navigation menus that display additional options when your mouse cursor moves over an item. This is dynamic navigation, which provides a way to offer many choices to visitors while at the same time avoid overwhelming them. Instead of showing all the navigation links all the time, menu items are dynamically displayed (typically using a combination of HTML and CSS) as appropriate. The additional items are made available when a related top-level menu item is selected by the cursor. The U.S. Bureau of Labor Statistics website (www.bls.gov) has a dynamic navigation menu. In Figure 25, "Publications" has been selected, causing the vertical menu to appear.

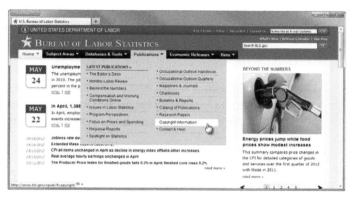

FIGURE 25 *Dynamic navigation with HTML, CSS, and JavaScript.*

Site Map

Even with clear and consistent navigation, visitors sometimes may lose their way on large websites. A site map, also referred to as a site index, provides an outline of the organization of the website with hyperlinks to each major page. This can help visitors find another route to get to the information they seek, as shown in the National Park Service website in Figure 26.

Site Search Feature

Note the search feature on the left side of the web page in Figure 26. The site search feature helps visitors find information that is not apparent from the navigation or the site map.

FIGURE 26 *This large site offers a site search and a site map to visitors.*

Wireframes and Page Layout

A **wireframe** is a sketch or diagram of a web page that shows the structure (but not the detailed design) of basic page elements such as the header, navigation, content area, and footer. Wireframes are used as part of the design process to experiment with various page layouts, develop the structure and navigation of the site, and provide a basis for communication among project members. Note that the exact content (text, images, logo, and navigation) does not need to be placed in the wireframe diagram—the wireframe depicts the overall structure of the page.

Figures 27, 28, and 29 show wireframe diagrams of three possible page designs with horizontal navigation. The wireframe in Figure 27 is adequate and may be appropriate for when the emphasis is on text information content, but it's not very engaging.

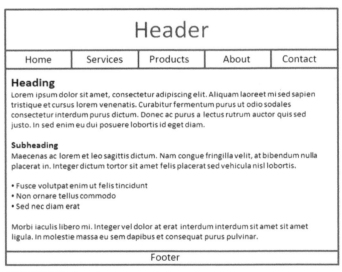

FIGURE 27 *An adequate page layout.*

Figure 28 shows a diagram of a web page containing similar content formatted in three columns along with an image. This is an improvement, but something is still missing.

Figure 29 shows a diagram of the same content but formatted in three columns of varying width with a header area, navigation area, content area (with headings, subheadings, paragraphs, and unordered lists), and a footer area. This is the most appealing layout of the three. Notice how the use of columns and images in Figures 28 and 29 increase the appeal of the page.

Web Design Basics

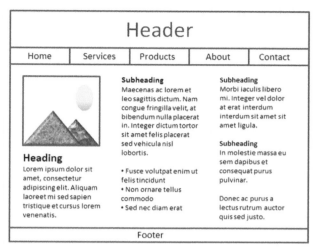

FIGURE 28 *The image and columns make this page layout more interesting.*

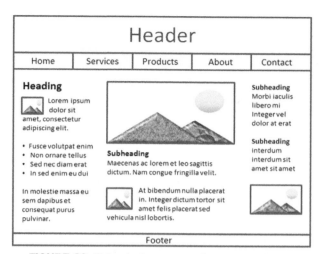

FIGURE 29 *This wireframe page layout uses images and columns of various widths.*

The wirefame in Figure 30 displays a webpage with a header, vertical navigation area, content area (with headings, subheadings, images, paragraphs, and unordered lists), and a footer area.

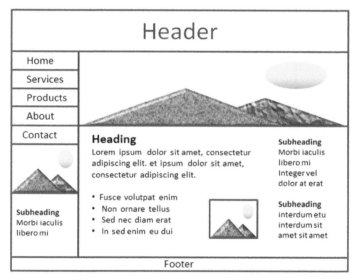

FIGURE 30 *Wireframe with vertical navigation.*

Often the page layout for the home page is different from the page layout used for the content pages. Even in this situation, a consistent logo header, navigation, and color scheme will produce a more cohesive website. Cascading Style Sheets (CSS) can be used along with HTML to configure color, text, and layout. In the next section you will explore two commonly used layout design techniques: fixed layout and fluid layout.

Web Design Basics

Fixed and Fluid Layouts

Now that you have been introduced to wireframes as a way to sketch page layout, let's explore two commonly used design techniques to implement those wireframes: fixed layout and fluid layout.

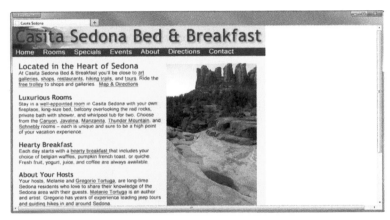

FIGURE 31 *This page is configured with a fixed layout design.*

FIGURE 32 *This fixed width centered content is balanced on the page by left and right margins.*

Fixed Layout

The **fixed layout** technique is sometimes referred to as a solid or "ice" design. The web page content has a fixed width and may hug the left margin as shown in Figure 31.

Notice the empty space in the right side of the browser viewport in Figure 31. To avoid this unbalanced look, a popular method to create a fixed layout design is to configure the content with a specific width in pixels (such as 960px) and center it in the browser viewport as shown in Figure 32 (www.nps.gov). As the browser is resized, it will expand or contract the left and right margin areas to center the content in the viewport.

Web Design Basics

Fluid Layout

The **fluid layout** technique, sometimes referred to as a "liquid" layout, results in a fluid web page with content typically configured with percentage values for widths—often taking up 100% of the browser viewport. The content will flow to fill whatever size browser window is used to display it, as shown in Figure 33. Other examples of liquid layout can be found at http://amazon.com and http://sears.com. One disadvantage of liquid layout is that when displayed in maximized browser viewports using high screen resolutions the lines of text may be quite wide and become difficult to scan and read.

Figure 34 shows an adaptation of liquid layout that utilizes a 100 percent width for the header and navigation area along with an 80 percent width for the centered page content. Compare this to Figure 33. The centered content area grows and shrinks as the browser viewport is resized. Readability can be ensured by using CSS to configure a maximum width value for this area.

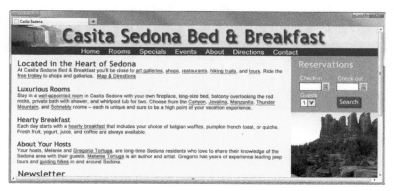

FIGURE 33 *This fluid layout expands to fill 100% of the browser viewport.*

FIGURE 34 *This fluid layout also has a maximum width value configured for the centered content area.*

Websites designed using fixed and fluid layout techniques can be found throughout the Web. Fixed-width layouts provide the web developer with the most control over the page configuration but can result in pages with large empty areas when viewed at higher screen resolutions. Fluid designs may become less readable when viewed at high screen resolutions due to the page stretching to fill a wider area than originally intended by the developer. Configuring a maximum width on text content areas can alleviate the text readability issues. Even when using an overall fluid layout, portions of the design can be configured with a fixed width (such as the "Reservations" column on the right side of the web page in Figures 33 and 34). Whether employing a fixed or fluid layout, web pages with centered content are typically pleasing to view on a variety of desktop screen resolutions.

Design for the Mobile Web

The desktop browser is not the only way that people access websites. Access to the Web from cell phones, smartphones, and tablets makes it possible to always be online. Internet analyst Mary Meeker of Morgan Stanley predicts that more users will access websites using mobile devices than desktop computers by 2015 (www.scribd.com/doc/69353603/Mary-Meekers-annual-Internet-Trends-report). Visit http://mashable.com/2012/08/22/mobile-trends-ecommerce for an infographic about trends in mobile device usage. With this growth in mind, it's becoming more important to design web pages that are appealing and usable for your mobile visitors.

Three Approaches

There are three different approaches to providing a satisfactory mobile experience for your website visitor:

1. Develop a separate mobile site with a .mobi TLD. Visit JCPenney at http://jcp.com and http://jcp.mobi to see this in practice.
2. Create a separate website hosted within your current domain that is targeted for mobile users.
3. Apply techniques of responsive web design (see the next section) by using CSS to configure your current website for display on mobile devices.

Mobile Device Design Considerations

No matter which approach you choose to use, here are some considerations to keep in mind when designing a mobile website.

- **Small screen size.** Common mobile phone screen sizes include 320×240, 320×480, 480×800, 640×960 (Apple iPhone 4), and 1136×640 (Apple iPhone 5). Even on one of the large phones, that's not a lot of pixels to work with!

- **Low bandwidth (slow connection speed).** Although the use of faster 3G and 4G networks is becoming more widespread, many mobile users experience slow connection speeds. Images usually take up quite a bit of bandwidth on a typical website. Depending on the service plan, some mobile web visitors may be paying per kilobyte. Be aware of this and eliminate unnecessary images.

- **Font, color, and media issues.** Mobile devices may have very limited font support. Configure font size using ems or percentages and configure generic font family names. Mobile devices may have very limited color support. Choose colors carefully to maximize contrast. Many mobile devices do not support Adobe Flash media.

Web Design Basics

- **Awkward controls; limited processor and memory.** While smartphones with touch controls are becoming more popular, many mobile users will not have access to mouselike controls. Provide keyboard access to assist these users. Although mobile device processing speed and available memory are improving, they still cannot compare to the resources of a desktop computer. While this won't be an issue for the websites you create for the exercises in this text, be mindful of this issue in the future as you continue to develop your skills and create web applications.
- **Functionality.** Provide easy access to your website's features with prominent hyperlinks or a prominent search button.

Example Desktop Website and Mobile Website

The website for the White House utilizes the second approach—separate websites within the same domain for desktop display and mobile display.

The desktop site for the White House (www.whitehouse.gov) shown in Figure 35 features a large graphic and interactive slideshow.

The White House's mobile site (http://m.whitehouse.gov) shown in Figure 36 is quite text-intensive with links to featured content, a search feature, and a prominent link to the regular (desktop) website.

FIGURE 35 *http://whitehouse.gov in a desktop browser.*

Mobile Design Quick Checklist

- Be aware of the small screen size and bandwidth issues.
- Configure nonessential content, such as sidebar content, to not display.
- Consider replacing desktop background images with graphics optimized for small screen display.
- Provide descriptive alternate text for images.
- Use a single-column layout for mobile display.
- Choose colors to maximize contrast.

FIGURE 36 *A text-intensive mobile site features hyperlinks to frequently accessed information.*

Web Design Basics

Responsive
Web Design

As mentioned earlier in this chapter, a recent survey by Net Market Share reported the use of more than 90 different screen resolutions and that websites are expected to display and function well on desktop browsers, tablets, and smartphones. While you can develop separate desktop and mobile websites, a more streamlined approach is to utilize the same website for all devices. The W3C's **One Web** initiative refers to the concept of providing a single resource that is configured for optimal display on multiple types of devices.

Responsive web design is a term coined by noted web developer Ethan Marcotte (www .alistapart.com/articles/responsive-web-design) to describe progressively enhancing a web page for different viewing contexts (such as smartphones and tablets) through the use of coding techniques, including fluid layouts, flexible images, and media queries. CSS **media queries** is a technique for configuring a web page to display well at various screen resolutions.

Visit the Media Queries website (http://mediaqueri.es) to view a gallery of sites that demonstrate this method for responsive web design. The screen captures in the Media Queries gallery show web pages at the following screen widths: 320px (smartphone display), 768px (tablet portrait display), 1024px (netbook display and landscape tablet display), and 1600px (large desktop display).

You might be surprised to discover that Figures 37, 38, 39, and 40 are actually the same web page .html file that is configured with CSS to display differently, depending

FIGURE 37 *Desktop display of the web page.*

Web Design Basics

on the viewport size detected by media queries. Figure 38 shows the standard desktop browser display.

Display for netbooks and tablets using landscape orientation is depicted in Figure 38. Figure 39 demonstrates how the page would render on a tablet using portrait orientation. Figure 40 shows the web page displayed on a mobile device such as a smartphone—note the reduction of the logo area, removal of images, and prominent phone number.

FIGURE 38 *Netbook display of the web page.*

FIGURE 39 *Portrait orientation tablet display of the web page.*

FIGURE 40 *Smartphone display of the web page.*

Web Design Basics

Web Design Best Practices Checklist

Use Table 1 as a guide to help you create easy-to-read, usable, and accessible web pages.

TABLE 1 *Web Design Best Practices Checklist*

Page Layout Criteria

- ☐ 1. Consistent site header/logo
- ☐ 2. Consistent navigation area
- ☐ 3. Informative page title that includes the company/organization/site name
- ☐ 4. Page footer area—copyright, last update, contact e-mail address
- ☐ 5. Good use of basic design principles: repetition, contrast, proximity, and alignment
- ☐ 6. Displays without horizontal scrolling at 1024×768 and higher resolutions
- ☐ 7. Balance of text/graphics/white space on page
- ☐ 8. Repetitive information (header/logo and navigation) takes up no more than one fourth to one third of the browser window at 1024×768 resolution
- ☐ 9. Home page has compelling information before scrolling at 1024×768 resolution
- ☐ 10. Home page downloads within 10 seconds on dial-up connection

Navigation Criteria

- ☐ 1. Main navigation links are clearly and consistently labeled
- ☐ 2. Navigation is easy for the target audience to use
- ☐ 3. When the main navigation consists of images and/or multimedia, the page footer area contains plain text hyperlinks (accessibility)
- ☐ 4. Navigational aids, such as site map, skip to content link, or breadcrumbs, are used

Color and Graphics Criteria

- ☐ 1. Use of different colors is limited to a maximum of three or four plus neutrals
- ☐ 2. Color is used consistently
- ☐ 3. Background and text colors have good contrast
- ☐ 4. Color is not used alone to convey meaning (accessibility)
- ☐ 5. Use of color and graphics enhances rather than distracts from the site
- ☐ 6. Graphics are optimized and do not slow download significantly
- ☐ 7. Each graphic used serves a clear purpose
- ☐ 8. Image tags use the alt attribute to configure alternate text (accessibility)
- ☐ 9. Animated images do not distract from the site and do not loop endlessly

Web Design Basics

Multimedia Criteria

- ☐ 1. Each audio/video/Flash file used serves a clear purpose
- ☐ 2. The audio/video/Flash files used enhance rather than distract from the site
- ☐ 3. Captions or transcripts are provided for each audio or video file used (accessibility)
- ☐ 4. Download times for audio or video files are indicated
- ☐ 5. Hyperlinks are provided to downloads for media plug-ins

Content Presentation Criteria

- ☐ 1. Common fonts such as Arial or Times New Roman are used
- ☐ 2. Techniques of writing for the Web are applied: headings, subheadings, bulleted lists, short sentences in brief paragraphs, use of white space
- ☐ 3. Fonts, font sizes, and font colors are consistently used
- ☐ 4. Content provides meaningful, useful information
- ☐ 5. Content is organized in a consistent manner
- ☐ 6. Information is easy to find (minimal clicks)
- ☐ 7. Timeliness: The date of the last revision and/or copyright date is accurate
- ☐ 8. Content is free of typographical and grammatical errors
- ☐ 9. Avoids the use of "Click here" when writing text for hyperlinks
- ☐ 10. Hyperlinks use a consistent set of colors to indicate visited/nonvisited status
- ☐ 11. Alternate text equivalent of content is provided for graphics and media (accessibility)

Functionality Criteria

- ☐ 1. All internal hyperlinks work
- ☐ 2. All external hyperlinks work
- ☐ 3. All forms function as expected
- ☐ 4. No error messages are generated by the pages

Additional Accessibility Criteria

- ☐ 1. Use attributes designed to improve accessibility such as alt and title where appropriate
- ☐ 2. The html element's lang attribute indicates the spoken language of the page

Browser Compatibility Criteria

- ☐ 1. Displays on current versions of Internet Explorer (9+)
- ☐ 2. Displays on current versions of Firefox
- ☐ 3. Displays on current versions of Safari (both Mac and Windows)
- ☐ 4. Displays on current versions of Google Chrome
- ☐ 5. Displays on current versions of Opera
- ☐ 6. Displays on popular mobile devices (including tablets and smartphones)

Web Design Basics

Review and Apply

Review Questions

1. Which of the following would a consistent website design *not* have?
   a. a similar navigation area on each content page
   b. the same fonts on each content page
   c. a different background color on each page
   d. the same logo in the same location on each content page

2. Which of the following are the three most common methods of organizing websites?
   a. horizontal, vertical, and diagonal
   b. hierarchical, linear, and random
   c. accessible, readable, maintainable
   d. none of the above

3. Which of the following is not a web design recommended practice?
   a. design your site to be easy to navigate
   b. colorful pages appeal to everyone
   c. design your pages to load quickly
   d. limit the use of animated items

4. Which are the four principles of the Web Content Accessibility Guidelines?
   a. contrast, repetition, alignment, proximity
   b. perceivable, operable, understandable, robust
   c. accessible, readable, maintainable, reliable
   d. hierarchical, linear, random, sequential

5. Which of the following is a sketch or diagram of a web page that shows the structure (but not the detailed design) of basic page elements?
   a. drawing
   b. HTML code
   c. site map
   d. wireframe

6. Which of the following is influenced by the intended or target audience of a site?
   a. the amount of color used on the site
   b. the font size and styles used on the site
   c. the overall look and feel for the site
   d. all of the above

7. Which of the following recommended design practices applies to a website that uses images for its main site navigation?
   a. provide alternative text for the images
   b. place text links at the bottom of the page
   c. both a and b
   d. no special considerations are needed

8. Which of the following is a mobile web design best practice?
   a. Configure a single column page layout
   b. Configure a multiple column page layout
   c. Avoid using lists to organize information
   d. Embed text in images wherever possible

9. Which of the following should you do when creating text hyperlinks?
   a. create the entire sentence as a hyperlink
   b. include the words "click here" in your text
   c. use a key phrase as a hyperlink
   d. none of the above

10. Which of the following is the design technique used to create pages that stretch to fill the browser window?
    a. fixed
    b. fluid
    c. wireframe
    d. sprites

Web Design Basics

Hands-On Exercise

1. **Website Design Evaluation.** In this chapter you've explored web page design, including navigation design techniques and the design principles of contrast, repetition, alignment, and proximity. In this Hands-On Exercise, you'll review and evaluate the design of a website. Your instructor may provide you with the URL of a website to evaluate. If not, choose a website to evaluate from the following list of URLs:

   www.arm.gov
   www.telework.gov
   www.dcmm.org
   www.sedonalibrary.org
   http://bostonglobe.com
   www.alistapart.com

   Visit the website you are evaluating. Write a paper that includes the following information:
   a. URL of the website
   b. Name of the website
   c. Target audience
   d. Screen shot of the home page
   e. Indicate the type(s) of navigation evident.
   f. Describe how the design principles of contrast, repetition, alignment, and contrast are applied. Be specific.
   g. Complete the Web Design Best Practices Checklist (see Table 1).
   h. Recommend three improvements for the website.

2. **Responsive Web Design.** Visit the Media Queries website at http://mediaqueri.es to view a gallery of sites that demonstrate responsive web design. Choose one of the example responsive websites to explore. Write a paper that includes the following:
   a. URL of the website
   b. Name of the website
   c. Target audience
   d. Three screen shots of the website (desktop display, tablet display, and smartphone display).
   e. Describe the similarities and differences between the three screen shots.
   f. Describe two ways in which the display has been modified for smartphones.
   g. Does the website meet the needs of its target audience in all three display modes? Why or why not? Justify your answer.

Focus on Web Design

Choose two sites that are similar in nature or have a similar target audience, such as the following:

- http://amazon.com and http://bn.com
- http://chicagobears.com and http://greenbaypackers.com
- http://cnn.com and http://msnbc.com

Web Design Basics

1. Describe how the two sites that you chose to review exhibit the design principles of repetition, contrast, alignment, and proximity.

2. Describe how the two sites that you chose to review exhibit web design best practices. How would you improve these sites? Recommend three improvements for each site.

Answers to Review Questions

1. c	**2.** b	**3.** b
4. b	**5.** d	**6.** d
7. c	**8.** a	**9.** c
10. b		

Credits

Web Design Basics

68

Cascading Style Sheets Basics

In this chapter, we'll explore **Cascading Style Sheets (CSS)**. Web designers use CSS to separate the presentation style of a web page from the information on the web page. CSS is used to configure text, color, and page layout.

CSS first became a W3C Recommendation in 1996. Additional properties for positioning web page elements were introduced to the language with CSS level 2 (CSS2) in 1998. CSS continues to evolve, with proposals for CSS level 3 (CSS3) properties to support features such as embedding fonts, rounded corners, and transparency. This chapter introduces you to the use of CSS on the Web as you explore configuring color on web pages.

You'll learn how to...

- Describe the purpose of Cascading Style Sheets
- List advantages of using Cascading Style Sheets
- Configure color on web pages with Cascading Style Sheets
- Configure inline styles
- Configure embedded style sheets
- Configure external style sheets
- Configure web page areas with element name, class, id, and descendant selectors
- Test your Cascading Style Sheets for valid syntax

From Chapter 4 of *Basics of Web Design HTML5 & CSS3*, Second Edition. Terry Ann Felke-Morris. Copyright © 2014 by Pearson Education, Inc. All rights reserved.

Cascading Style Sheets Overview

For years, style sheets have been used in desktop publishing to apply typographical styles and spacing instructions to printed media. CSS provides this functionality (and much more) for web designers. CSS allows web designers to apply typographical styles (typeface, font size, and so on), color, and page layout instructions to a web page.

The CSS Zen Garden (www.csszengarden.com) exemplifies the power and flexibility of CSS. Visit this site for an example of CSS in action. Notice how the content looks dramatically different depending on the design (configured with CSS style rules) that you select. Although the designs on CSS Zen Garden are created by CSS masters, at some point these designers were just like you—starting out with CSS basics.

CSS is a flexible, cross-platform, standards-based language developed by the W3C (see www.w3.org/Style). Be aware that even though CSS has been in use for many years, it is still considered an emerging technology, and different browsers do not support it in exactly the same way. We concentrate on aspects of CSS that are well supported by popular browsers.

Advantages of Cascading Style Sheets

There are several advantages to using CSS (see Figure 1):

- **Typography and page layout can be better controlled.** These features include font size, line spacing, letter spacing, indents, margins, and element positioning.
- **Style is separate from structure.** The format of the text and colors used on the page can be configured and stored separately from the body section of the web page document.
- **Styles can be stored.** You can store styles in a separate document and associate them with the web page. When the styles are modified, the web page code remains intact. This means that if your client decides to change the background color from red to white, you only need to change one file that contains the styles, instead of each web page document.
- **Documents are potentially smaller.** The formatting is separate from the document; therefore, the actual documents should be smaller.
- **Site maintenance is easier.** Again, if the styles need to be changed, it's possible to complete the modifications by changing only the style sheet file.

An issue to be aware of when using CSS is that CSS technology is still not uniformly supported by browsers. We focus on features of CSS that are well-supported by modern browsers in this book.

Cascading Style Sheets Basics

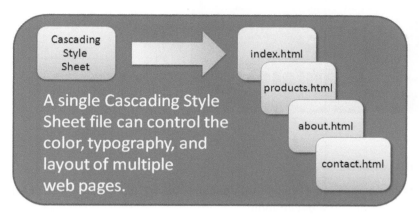

FIGURE 1 *The power of a single CSS file.*

Methods of Configuring Cascading Style Sheets

Web designers use four methods to incorporate CSS technology in a website: inline, embedded, external, and imported.

> **Inline styles** are coded in the body of the web page as an attribute of an HTML tag. The style only applies to the specific element that contains it as an attribute.

> **Embedded styles** are defined in the head section of a web page. These style instructions apply to the entire web page document.

> **External styles** are coded in a separate text file, called an external style sheet. This text file is associated with a web page by coding a link element in the head section.

> **Imported styles** are similar to external styles in that they can connect styles coded in a separate text file with a web page document. An external style sheet can be imported into embedded styles or into another external style sheet by using the `@import` directive.

The "Cascade" in Cascading Style Sheets

Figure 2 shows the "cascade" (**rules of precedence**) that applies the styles in order from outermost (external styles) to innermost (HTML attributes coded on the page). This allows the site-wide styles to be configured with an external style sheet file but overridden when needed by more granular, page-specific styles (such as embedded or inline styles).

You'll learn to configure inline styles, embedded styles, and external styles in this chapter.

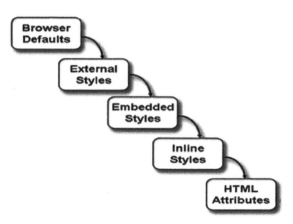

FIGURE 2 *The "cascade" of Cascading Style Sheets.*

Cascading Style Sheets Basics

CSS Selectors and Declarations

Style Rule Basics

Style sheets are composed of **rules** that describe the styling to be applied. Each **rule** has two parts: a **selector** and a **declaration**.

> ### CSS Style Rule Selector
>
> There are several different types of selectors. The selector can be an HTML element name, a class name, or an id name. In this section we'll focus on applying styles to element name selectors. You'll work with class selectors and id selectors later in this chapter.

> ### CSS Style Rule Declaration
>
> The declaration indicates the CSS property you are setting (such as color) and the value you are assigning to the property.

FIGURE 3 *Using CSS to set the text color to blue.*

For example, the CSS rule shown in Figure 3 would set the color of the text used on a web page to blue. The selector represents the body element, and the declaration sets the color property to the value of blue.

The `background-color` Property

The CSS property to configure the background color of an element is `background-color`. The following style rule will configure the background color of a web page to be yellow:

```
body { background-color: yellow }
```

Notice how the declaration is enclosed within braces and how the colon symbol (:) separates the declaration property and the declaration value.

Cascading Style Sheets Basics

The `color` Property

The CSS property to configure the text color of an element is `color`. The following CSS style rule will configure the text color of a web page to be blue:

```
body { color: blue }
```

Configure Background and Text Color

To configure more than one property for a selector, use a semicolon (`;`) to separate the declarations as follows (see Figure 4):

```
body { color: blue; background-color: yellow; }
```

FIGURE 4 *A web page with yellow background color and blue text color.*

You might be asking how you would know what properties and values are allowed to be used. See the CSS Cheat Sheet at the end of the chapter for a detailed list of CSS properties. This chapter introduces you to the CSS properties commonly used to configure color, shown in Table 1.

TABLE 1 *CSS Properties Used in This Chapter*

Property	Description	Value
background-color	Background color of an element	Any valid color value
color	Foreground (text) color of an element	Any valid color value

Cascading Style Sheets Basics

CSS Syntax for Color Values

The previous section used color names to configure color with CSS. You can find a list of color names and numerical color values on the textbook's companion website at http://webdevbasics.net/color. However, there are a limited number of color names, and all the names may not be supported by all browsers.

For more flexibility and control, use a numerical color value, such as the hexadecimal color values. The Web Safe Color Palette, located on the companion website (at http://webdevbasics.net/color) provides examples of colors created with hexadecimal values.

A style rule to configure the web page displayed in Figure 5 with medium blue text (#3399CC) on a soft yellow back-ground (#FFFFCC) is

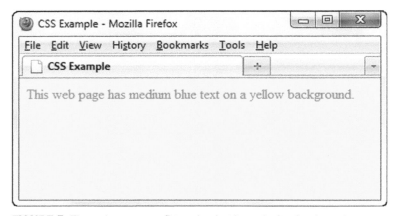

FIGURE 5 *The color was configured using hexadecimal color values.*

```
body { color: #3399CC; background-color: #FFFFCC; }
```

The spaces in these declarations are optional. The ending semicolon (;) is also optional but useful in case you need to add additional style rules at a later time. The following alternative versions of the code above are also valid:

EXAMPLE 1:
```
body {color:#3399CC;background-color:#FFFFCC}
```

EXAMPLE 2:
```
body { background-color:#FFFFCC; color:#3399CC; }
```

EXAMPLE 3:
```
body {
color: #3399CC;
background-color: #FFFFCC;
}
```

EXAMPLE 4:
```
body { color: #3399CC;
       background-color: #FFFFCC;
}
```

Cascading Style Sheets Basics

CSS syntax allows you to configure colors in a variety of ways:

- color name
- hexadecimal color value
- hexadecimal shorthand color value
- decimal color value (RGB triplet)
- HSL (Hue, Saturation, and Lightness) color value notation new to CSS3; see www.w3.org/TR/css3-color/#hsl-color

Visit http://meyerweb.com/eric/css/colors/ to view a chart with examples of configuring color values using different notations. We'll typically use hexadecimal color values in this book. Table 2 shows a variety of CSS syntax examples that configure a paragraph with red text.

TABLE 2 *Syntax to Configure a Paragraph with Red Text*

CSS Syntax	Color Type
`p { color: red }`	Color name
`p { color: #FF0000 }`	Hexadecimal color value
`p { color: #F00 }`	Shorthand hexadecimal (one character for each hexadecimal pair—only used with web-safe colors)
`p { color: rgb(255,0,0) }`	Decimal color value (RGB triplet)
`p { color: hsl(0, 100%, 50%) }`	Color Type: HSL color values

Although hexadecimal color notation is commonly used on most web pages, the W3C developed a new color notation called HSL (Hue, Saturation, and Lightness) as part of CSS3 to provide a more intuitive way to describe color on web pages. The hue is the actual color which is represented by numeric values ranging from 0 to 360 (like the 360 degrees in a circle). For example, red is represented by both the values 0 and 360, green is represented by 120, and blue is represented by 240. Saturation is indicated by a percentage value (full color saturation= 100%, gray=0%). A percentage value is also used to configure lightness (normal color=50%, white=100%, black=0%). Table 2 includes the HSL representation for the color red. A dark blue color could be represented by hsl(240, 100%, 25%). Explore the color tools at www.colorhexa.com and www.workwithcolor.com/color-converter-01.htm. Visit www.w3.org/TR/css3-color/#hsl-color for more information about HSL color.

Are there other methods to configure color with CSS?
Yes, the CSS3 Color Module provides a way for web designers to configure not only color, but also the transparency of the color with RGBA (Red, Green, Blue, Alpha) color and HSLA (Hue, Saturation, Lightness, Alpha) color. Also new to CSS3 is the opacity property, and CSS gradient backgrounds.

Configure Inline CSS

There are four methods for configuring CSS: inline, embedded, external, and imported. In this section we focus on inline CSS.

The `style` Attribute

Inline styles are coded as an attribute on an HTML tag using the **`style` attribute**. The value of the `style` attribute is set to the style rule declaration that you need to configure. Recall that a declaration consists of a property and a value. Each property is separated from its value with a colon (:). The following code will set the text color of an `<h1>` tag to a shade of red:

```
<h1 style="color:#cc0000">This is displayed as a red heading</h1>
```

If there is more than one property, each is separated by a semicolon (;). The following code configures the heading with a red text color and a gray background color:

```
<h1 style="color:#cc0000;background-color:#cccccc;">
This is displayed as a red heading on a gray background</h1>
```

 Hands-On Practice 1

In this Hands-On Practice you will configure a web page with inline styles. The inline styles will specify the following:

▌ Global body tag styles for an off-white background with teal text. These styles will be inherited by other elements within the body of the web page by default.

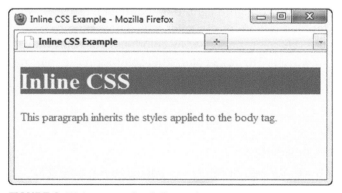

▌ Styles for an h1 element with a teal background with off-white text. This will override the global styles configured on the body element.

A sample is shown in Figure 6. Launch a text editor, and open the template.html file from the chapter1 folder in the student files on the companion website at www.pearsonhighered .com/felke-morris.

FIGURE 6 *Web page using inline styles.*

Cascading Style Sheets Basics

Modify the title element and add heading tag, paragraph tags, style attributes, and text to the body section as indicated by the following highlighted code:

```
<!DOCTYPE html>
<html lang="en">
<head>
<title>Inline CSS Example</title>
<meta charset="utf-8">
</head>
<body style="background-color:#F5F5F5;color:#008080;">
  <h1 style="background-color:#008080;color:#F5F5F5;">Inline CSS</h1>
  <p>This paragraph inherits the styles applied to the body tag.</p>
</body>
</html>
```

Save the document as inline2.html on your hard drive or flash drive. Launch a browser to test your page. It should look similar to the page shown in Figure 6. Note that the inline styles applied to the body tag are inherited by other elements on the page (such as the paragraph) unless more-specific styles are specified (such as those coded on the `<h1>` tag. You can compare your work with the solution found in the student files (chapter4/inlinep.html).

Let's continue and add another paragraph with the text color configured to be dark gray.

```
<p style="color:#333333"> This paragraph overrides the text color style applied to the body tag.</p>
```

Save the document as inline3.html. It should look similar to the page shown in Figure 7. You can compare your work with the solution at chapter4/inlinep.html in the student files.

Note that the inline styles applied to the second paragraph override the global styles applied to the body of the web page. What if you had ten paragraphs that needed to be configured in this manner? You'd have to code an inline style on *each* of the ten paragraph tags. This would add quite a bit of redundant code to the page. For this reason, inline styles are not the most efficient way to use CSS. In the next section you'll learn how to configure embedded styles, which can apply to the entire web page document.

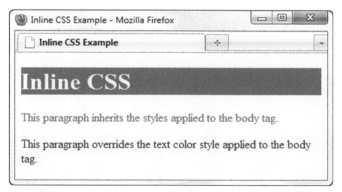

FIGURE 7 *The second paragraph's inline styles override the global styles configured on the body tag.*

> **Quick TIP**
> While inline styles can sometimes be useful, you'll find that you won't use this technique much in practice—it's inefficient, adds extra code to the web page document, and is inconvenient to maintain. However, inline styles can be quite handy in some circumstances, such as when you post an article to a content management system or blog and need to tweak the site-wide styles a bit to help get your point across.

Configure Embedded CSS

The Style Element

Embedded styles apply to the entire document and are placed within a **style element** located in the head section of a web page. The opening `<style>` tag begins the area with

embedded style rules, and the closing `</style>` tag ends the area containing embedded style rules. When using XHTML syntax, the `<style>` tag requires a `type` attribute that should have the value of `"text/css"` to indicate the CSS MIME type. HTML5 syntax does not require the type attribute.

FIGURE 8 *Web page using embedded styles.*

The web page in Figure 8 uses embedded styles to set the text color and background color of the web page document with the body element selector. See the example in the student files at chapter4/embed.html.

```
<!DOCTYPE html>
<html lang="en">
<head>
<title>Embedded CSS Example</title>
<meta charset="utf-8">
<style>
body { background-color: #E6E6FA;
       color: #191970;
}
</style>
</head>
<body>
  <h1>Embedded CSS</h1>
  <p>This page uses embedded styles.</p>
</body>
</html>
```

Notice the way the style rules were coded with each rule on its own line. This makes the styles more readable and easier to maintain than one long row of text. The styles are in effect for the entire web page document because they were applied to the `<body>` tag using the body element selector.

 Hands-On Practice 2

Launch a text editor and open the starter.html file from the chapter4 folder in the student files. Save your page as embedded2.html and test it in a browser. Your page should look similar to the one shown in Figure 9.

Cascading Style Sheets Basics

Open the file in a text editor and view the source code. Notice that the web page code uses the `<h1>`, `<h2>`, `<div>`, `<p>`, `<ul>`, and `<li>` elements. In this Hands-On Practice you'll code embedded styles to configure selected background and text colors. You'll use the body element selector to configure the default background color (#E6E6FA) and default text color (#191970) for the entire page. You'll also use the h1 and h2 element selectors to configure different background and text colors for the heading areas.

Edit the embedded2.html file in a text editor and add the following code in the head section above the closing `</head>` tag:

```
<style>
body { background-color: #E6E6FA;
       color: #191970; }
h1 { background-color: #191970;
     color: #E6E6FA; }
h2 { background-color: #AEAED4;
     color: #191970; }
</style>
```

Save and test your file in a browser. Figure 10 displays the web page along with color swatches. A monochromatic color scheme was chosen. Notice how the repetition of a limited number of colors adds interest and unifies the design of the web page.

View the source code for your page and review the CSS and HTML code. An example of this web page is in the student files at chapter4/embedded.html. Note that all the styles are in a single location on the web page. Since embedded styles are coded in a specific location, they are easier to maintain over time than inline styles. Also notice that you only needed to code the styles for the h2 element selector once (in the head section)

FIGURE 9 *The web page without any styles.*

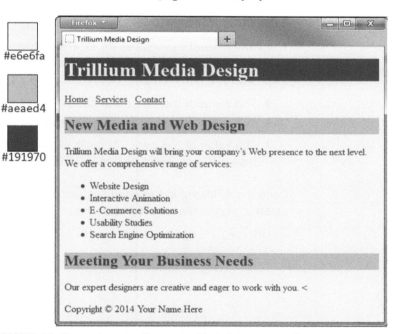

#e6e6fa

#aeaed4

#191970

FIGURE 10 *The web page after embedded styles are configured.*

and *both* of the `<h2>` tags applied the h2 style. This is more efficient than coding the same inline style on each `<h2>` tag.

However, it's uncommon for a website to have only one page. Repeating the CSS in the head section of each web page file is inefficient and difficult to maintain. In the next section, you'll use a more efficient approach—configuring an external style sheet.

Cascading Style Sheets Basics

Configure
External CSS

VideoNote
External Style Sheets

The flexibility and power of CSS are best utilized when the CSS is external to the web page document. An external style sheet is a text file with a .css file extension that contains CSS style rules. The external style sheet file is associated with a web page using the link element. This provides a way for multiple web pages to be associated with the same external style sheet file. The external style sheet file does not contain any HTML tags—it only contains CSS style rules.

The advantage of external CSS is that styles are configured in a single file. This means that when styles need to be modified, only one file needs to be changed, instead of multiple web pages. On large sites this can save a web developer much time and increase productivity. Let's get some practice with this useful technique.

The Link Element

The **link element** associates an external style sheet with a web page. It is placed in the head section of the page. The link element is a stand-alone, void tag. Three attributes are used with the link element: `rel`, `href`, and `type`.

- The value of the `rel` attribute is `"stylesheet"`.
- The value of the `href` attribute is the name of the style sheet file.
- The value of the `type` attribute is `"text/css"`, which is the MIME type for CSS. The type attribute is optional in HTML5 and required in XHTML.

Code the following in the head section of a web page to associate the document with the external style sheet named color.css:

```
<link rel="stylesheet" href="color.css">
```

Let's practice using external styles. First, you'll create an external style sheet. Then you'll configure a web page to be associated with the external style sheet.

Create an External Style Sheet. Launch a text editor and type style rules to set the background color of a page to blue and the text color to white. Save the file as color.css. The code is as follows:

```
body { background-color: #0000FF;
       color: #FFFFFF; }
```

Figure 11 shows the external color.css style sheet displayed in Notepad. Notice that there is no HTML in this file. HTML tags are not coded within an external style sheet. Only CSS rules (selectors, properties, and values) are coded in an external style sheet.

FIGURE 11 *The external style sheet color.css.*

Configure the Web Page. To create the web page shown in Figure 12, launch a text editor and open the template.html file from the chapter1 folder in the student files. Modify the title element, add a link tag to the head section, and add a paragraph to the body section as indicated by the following highlighted code:

```
<!DOCTYPE html>
<html lang="en">
<head>
<title>External Styles</title>
<meta charset="utf-8">
<link rel="stylesheet" href="color.css">
</head>
<body>
<p>This web page uses an external style sheet.</p>
</body>
</html>
```

Save your file as external2.html in the same folder as your color.css file. Launch a browser and test your page. It should look similar to the page shown in Figure 12. You can compare your work with the solution in the student files (chapter4/external.html).

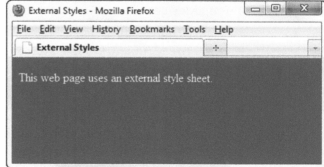

FIGURE 12 *This page is associated with an external style sheet.*

The color.css style sheet can be associated with any number of web pages. If you ever need to change the style of formatting, you only need to change a single file (color.css) instead of multiple files (all of the web pages). As mentioned earlier, this technique can boost productivity on a large site. This is a simple example, but the advantage of having only a single file to update is significant for both small and large websites.

CSS Selectors: Class, Id, and Descendant

The Class Selector

Use a CSS **class selector** to apply a CSS declaration to one or more areas on a web page. When setting a style for a class, configure the class name as the selector. Place a dot or period (.) in front of the class name in the style sheet. A class name must begin with a letter and may contain numbers, hyphens, and underscores. Class names may not contain spaces. The following code configures a class called `feature` in a style sheet with a foreground (text) color set to red: `.feature { color: #FF0000; }`

The styles set in the new class can be applied to any element you wish. You do this by using the class attribute, such as `class="feature"`. The following code will apply the feature class styles to a `<li>` element: `<li class="feature">Usability Studies</li>`

The Id Selector

Use an **id selector** to identify and apply a CSS rule uniquely to a *single area* on a web page. Unlike a class selector which can be applied multiple times on a web page, an id may only be applied once per web page. When setting a style for an id, place a hash mark (#) in front of the id name in the style sheet. An id name may contain letters, numbers, hyphens, and underscores. Id names may not contain spaces. The following code will configure an id called `content` in a style sheet:

`#content { color: #333333; }`

The styles set in the `content` id can be applied to the element you wish by using the id attribute, `id="content"`. The following code will apply the content id styles to a div tag:

`<div id="content">This sentence will be displayed using styles configured in the content id.</div>`

The Descendant Selector

Use a **descendant selector** to specify an element within the context of its container (parent) elements. Using descendant selectors can help you to reduce the number of different classes and ids but still allow you to configure CSS for specific areas on the web page. To configure a descendant selector, list the container selector (which can be an element selector, class, or id) followed by the specific selector you are styling. For example, to specify a green text color for paragraphs located *within* the `content` id, code the following style rule:

`#content p { color: #00ff00; }`

Hands-On Practice 4

In this Hands-On Practice you will modify the Trillium Media Design page while you practice configuring a class and an id. Launch a text editor and open the embedded.html file from the chapter4 folder in the student files. Save the file as classid.html.

Configure the CSS. Code CSS to configure a class named `feature` and an id named `content`.

1. Create a class named `feature` that configures red (#FF0000) text. Add the following code to the embedded styles in the head section of the web page:

   ```
   .feature { color: #FF0000; }
   ```

2. Create an id named `content` that configures an off-white background color. Add the following code to the embedded styles in the head section of the web page:

   ```
   #content {
       background-color: #F6F6FD; }
   ```

Configure the HTML. Associate HTML elements with the class and id you just created.

FIGURE 13 *CSS class and id selectors are used on this page.*

1. Modify the last two `<li>` tags in the unordered list. Add a class attribute that associates the `<li>` with the `feature` class as follows:

   ```
   <li class="feature">Usability Studies</li>
   <li class="feature">Search Engine Optimization</li>
   ```

2. Modify the opening div tag (located below the closing nav tag). Add an id attribute that associates the div with the id named `content`:

   ```
   <div id="content">
   ```

Save your classid.html file, and test it in a browser. Your page should look similar to the image shown in Figure 13. Notice how the class and id styles are applied. The student files contain a sample solution at chapter4/classy.html.

 For maximum compatibility choose your class and id names carefully. Always begin with a letter. Do not use any blank spaces. Feel free to use numerals, the dash character, and the underscore character in addition to letters. See the following URLs for lists of commonly used class and id names:

▶ http://code.google.com/webstats/2005-12/classes.html

▶ http://dev.opera.com/articles/view/mama-common-attributes

Span Element

The Span Element

The inline **span element** defines a section on a web page that is displayed inline without empty space above and below. A span element begins with a `<span>` tag and ends with a `</span>` tag. Use the span element when you need to format an area that is contained within another, such as within a `<p>`, `<blockquote>`, or `<div>` element.

 Hands-On Practice 5

In this Hands-On Practice you will experiment with div and span elements in the Trillium Media Design home page. Launch a text editor and open the starter.html file from the chapter4 folder in the student files. Save your page as span2.html and test it in a browser. Your page should look similar to the one shown in Figure 9.

Open span2.html in a text editor and view the source code. In this Hands-On Practice you'll code embedded styles to configure selected background and text colors. You'll also add `<span>` tags to the web page. When you are finished with the first part of this Hands-On Practice, your web page will be similar to Figure 14.

FIGURE 14 *This page uses the span element.*

Part 1

Configure the Embedded Styles. Edit span2.html in a text editor and add embedded styles in the head section above the closing `</head>` tag. You will configure styles for a class named `companyname` and for the body, h1, h2, nav, and footer element selectors. The code is

```
<style>
body { background-color:#FFFFFF;
      color: #191970; }
h1 { background-color:#191970;
     color: #E6E6FA; }
h2 { color: #6A6AA7; }
nav { background-color: #E2E2EF;  }
footer { color: #666666; }
.companyname { color: #6A6AA7; }
</style>
```

Cascading Style Sheets Basics

Configure the Company Name. View Figure 14 and notice that the company name, Trillium Media Design, is displayed in a different color than the other text within the first paragraph. You've already created a class named `companyname` in the CSS. You'll use a span to apply this formatting. Find the text "Trillium Medium Design" in the first paragraph. Configure a span element to contain this text. Assign the span to the class named `companyname`. A sample code excerpt is

```
<p><span class="companyname">Trillium Media Design</span> will bring
```

Save your file and test in a browser. Your page should look similar to the one shown in Figure 14. The student files contain a sample solution at chapter4/span.html.

Part 2

As you review your web page and Figure 14, notice the empty space between the h1 element and the navigation area—the empty space is the default bottom margin of the h1 element. The margin is one of the components of the CSS box model with which you'll work. One technique that will cause the browser to collapse this empty space is to configure the margin between the elements. Add the following style to the h1 element selector in the embedded CSS: `margin-bottom: 0;`

Save the file and launch in a browser. Your web page should now be similar to Figure 15. Notice how the display of the h1 and navigation area has changed. The student files contain a sample solution at chapter4/rework.html.

FIGURE 15 *The new header area.*

? FAQ How do I know when to use an id, a class, or a descendent selector?

The most efficient way to configure CSS is to use HTML elements as selectors. However, sometimes you need to be more specific—that's when other types of selectors are useful. Create a class when you need to configure one or more specific objects on a web page in the same way. A class can be applied more than once per web page. An id is similar to a class, but be mindful that it is not valid to apply an id more than once on a web page. To repeat: an id can be used once and only once on each web page. Use an id for a unique item, such as the navigation hyperlink that indicates the current page. As you become more comfortable with CSS, you'll begin to see the power and efficiency of descendent selectors, which allow you to target elements within a specific context (such as all paragraphs in the footer area) without the need to code additional classes or ids within the HTML code.

Cascading Style Sheets Basics

Practice with CSS

 Hands-On Practice 6 ————————————————————————

In this Hands-On Practice you'll continue to gain experience using external style sheets as you modify the Trillium Media Design website to use an external style sheet. You'll create the external style sheet file named trillium.css, modify the home page (index.html) to use external styles instead of embedded styles, and associate a second web page with the trillium.css style sheet.

Launch a browser and open the span.html file from the chapter4 folder in the student files. This file is a version of the Trillium home page. The display should be the same as the web page shown in Figure 14 from Hands-On Practice 5.

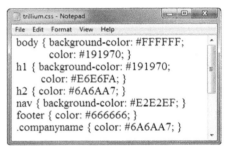

FIGURE 16 *The external style sheet named trillium.css.*

Now that you've seen what you're working with, let's begin. Launch a text editor and open the span.html file from the chapter4 folder in the student files. Save the file as index.html in a folder named trillium.

Convert the Embedded CSS to External CSS Edit the index.html file and select the CSS rules (all the lines of code between, but not including, the `<style>` and `</style>` tags). Select Edit > Copy to copy the CSS code to the clipboard. You will place the CSS in a new file. Launch a text editor, select File > New to create a new file, paste the CSS style rules by selecting Edit > Paste, and save the file as trillium.css in the trillium folder. See Figure 16 for a screenshot of the new trillium.css file in the Notepad text editor. Notice that there are no HTML elements in trillium.css—not even the `<style>` element. The file contains CSS rules only.

Associate the Web Page with the External CSS File Next, edit the index.html file in a text editor. Delete the CSS code you just copied. Delete the closing `</style>` tag. Replace the opening `<style>` tag with a `<link>` element to associate the style sheet named trillium.css. The `<link>` element code follows:

```
<link href="trillium.css"
rel="stylesheet">
```

Save the file, and test it in a browser. Your web page should look just like the one shown in Figure 14. Although it looks the same, the difference is in the code—the page now uses external instead of embedded CSS.

Now, for the fun part—you'll associate a second page with the style sheet. The student files contain a services.html page for Trillium at chapter4/services.html. When you display this

FIGURE 17 *The services.html page is not yet associated with a style sheet.*

Cascading Style Sheets Basics

page in a browser it should look similar to the one shown in Figure 17. Notice that although the structure of the page is similar to the home page, the styling of the text and colors is absent.

Launch a text editor to edit the services.html file. Code a `<link>` element to associate the services.html web page with the trillium.css external style sheet. Place the following code in the head section above the closing `</head>` tag:

```
<link href="trillium.css"
rel="stylesheet">
```

Save your file in the trillium folder and test in a browser. Your page should look similar to Figure 18—the CSS rules have been applied!

If you click the "Home" and "Services" hyper-links, you can move back and forth between the index.html and services.html pages in the browser. The student files contain a sample solution in the chapter4/trillium folder.

FIGURE 18 *The services.html page has been associated with trillium.css.*

Notice that when using an external style sheet, if the style rule declarations need to be changed in the future, you'll typically only have to modify *one* file—the external style sheet. Think about how this can improve productivity on a site with many pages. Instead of modifying potentially hundreds of pages to make a color or font change, only a single file— the CSS external style sheet—needs to be updated. Becoming comfortable with CSS will be important as you develop your skills and increase your technical expertise.

 FAQ

My CSS doesn't work; what can I do?

Coding CSS is a detail-oriented process. There are several common errors that can cause the browser not to apply CSS correctly to a web page. With a careful review of your code and the following tips, you should get your CSS working:

▶ Verify that you are using the colon ":" and semicolon ";" symbols in the right spots—they are easy to confuse. The : symbol should separate the properties from their values. The ; symbol should be placed between each property:value configuration.

▶ Check that you are not using = signs instead of : between each property and its value.

▶ Verify that the { and } symbols are properly placed around the style rules for each selector.

▶ Check the syntax of your selectors, their properties, and property values for correct usage.

▶ If part of your CSS works and part doesn't, read through the CSS and check to determine the first rule that is not applied. Often the error is in the rule *above* the rule that is not applied.

▶ Use the W3C's CSS validator at http://jigsaw.w3.org/css-validator to help you find syntax errors. See the next section for an overview of how to use this tool to validate your CSS.

Cascading Style Sheets Basics

CSS Syntax Validation

VideoNote

CSS Validation

The W3C has a free Markup Validation Service (http://jigsaw.w3.org/css-validator) that will validate your CSS code and check it for syntax errors. CSS validation provides students with quick self-assessment—you can prove that your code uses correct syntax. In the working world, CSS validation serves as a quality assurance tool. Invalid code may cause browsers to render the pages slower than otherwise.

 Hands-On Practice 7

In this Hands-On Practice you will use the W3C CSS Validation Service to validate an external CSS style sheet. This example uses the color.css file completed in Hands-On Practice 3 (student files chapter4/color.css). Locate color.css and open it in a text editor. We will add an error to the color.css file. Find the body element selector style rule and delete the first "r" in the `background-color` property. Remove the # from the `color` property value. Save the file.

Next, attempt to validate the color.css file. Visit the W3C CSS Validation Service page at http://jigsaw.w3.org/css-validator, and select the "By file upload" tab. Click the "Browse" button, and select the color.css file from your computer. Click the "Check" button. Your display should be similar to that shown in Figure 19. Notice that two errors were found. The selector is listed, followed by the reason an error was noted.

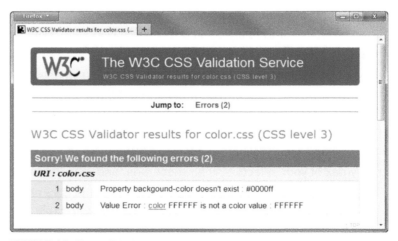

FIGURE 19 *The validation results indicate errors.*

Cascading Style Sheets Basics

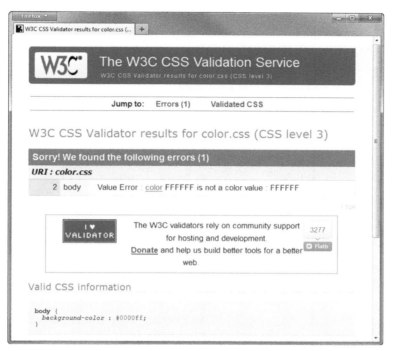

FIGURE 20 *The valid CSS is displayed below the errors (and warnings, if any).*

Notice that the first message in Figure 19 indicates that the "backgound-color" property does not exist. This is a clue to check the syntax of the property name. Edit color.css and correct the error. Test and revalidate your page. Your browser should now look similar to the one shown in Figure 20 and report only one error.

The error reminds you that FFFFFF is not a color value—the validator expects you to already know that you need to add a "#" character to code a valid color value, #FFFFFF. Notice how any valid CSS rules are displayed below the error messages. Correct the color value, save the file, and test again.

Your results should look similar to those shown in Figure 21. There are no errors listed. The Valid CSS Information contains all the CSS style rules in color.css. This means that your file passed the CSS validation test. Congratulations, your color.css file contains valid CSS syntax! It's a good practice to validate your CSS style rules. The CSS validator can help you to identify code that needs to be corrected quickly and indicate which style rules a browser is likely to consider valid. Validating CSS is one of the many productivity techniques that web developers commonly use.

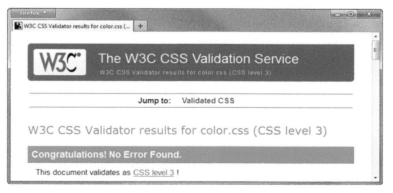

FIGURE 21 *The CSS is valid!*

Review and Apply

Review Questions

1. Which of the following can be a CSS selector?
   a. an HTML element name
   b. a class name
   c. an id name
   d. all of the above

2. Which of the following is the CSS property used to set the background color?
   a. `bgcolor`
   b. `background-color`
   c. `color`
   d. none of the above

3. Which type of CSS is coded in the body of the web page as an attribute of an HTML tag?
   a. embedded
   b. inline
   c. external
   d. imported

4. Which of the following describe two components of CSS rules?
   a. selectors and declarations
   b. properties and declarations
   c. selectors and attributes
   d. none of the above

5. Which of the following associates a web page with an external style sheet?
   a. `<style rel="external" href="style.css">`
   b. `<style src="style.css">`
   c. `<link rel="stylesheet" href="style.css">`
   d. `<link rel="stylesheet" src="style.css">`

6. Which of the following configures a CSS class called news with red text (#FF0000) and light gray background (#EAEAEA)?

   a. `news { color: #FF0000; background-color: #EAEAEA; }`
   b. `.news {color: #FF0000; background-color: #EAEAEA; }`
   c. `.news {text: #FF0000; background-color: #EAEAEA; }`
   d. `#news { color: #FF0000; background-color: #EAEAEA; }`

7. An External Style Sheet uses the _____ file extension.
   a. ess
   b. css
   c. htm
   d. No file extension is necessary

8. Where do you place the code to associate a web page with an external style sheet?
   a. in the external style sheet
   b. in the DOCTYPE of the web page document
   c. in the body section of the web page document
   d. in the head section of the web page document

9. Which of the following configures a background color of #FFF8DC for a web page using CSS?
   a. `body { background-color: #FFF8DC; }`
   b. `document { background: #FFF8DC; }`
   c. `body {bgcolor: #FFF8DC;}`
   d. none of the above

10. Which of the following do you configure to apply a style to more than one area on a web page?
   a. id
   b. class
   c. group
   d. link

Cascading Style Sheets Basics

Hands-On Exercise

Practice with External Style Sheets. In this exercise you will create two external style sheet files and a web page. You will experiment with linking the web page to the external style sheets and note how the display of the page is changed.

a. Create an external style sheet (call it format1.css) to format as follows: document background color of white, document text color of #000099.

b. Create an external style sheet (call it format2.css) to format as follows: document background color of yellow, document text color of green.

c. Create a web page about your favorite movie that displays the movie name in an `<h1>` tag, a description of the movie in a paragraph, and an unordered (bulleted) list of the main actors and actresses in the movie. The page should also include a hyperlink to a website about the movie and an e-mail link to yourself. This page should be associated with the format1.css file. Save the page as moviecss1.html. Be sure to test your page in more than one browser.

d. Modify the moviecss1.html page to be associated with the format2.css external style sheet instead of the format1.css file. Save the page as moviecss2.html and test it in a browser. Notice how different the page looks!

Focus on Web Design

In this chapter you learned how to configure color with CSS. In this activity you will design a color scheme, code an external CSS file for the color scheme, and code an example web page that applies the styles you configured. Use any of the following sites to help you get started with color and web design ideas:

Psychology of Color

- www.infoplease.com/spot/colors1.html
- www.sensationalcolor.com/meanings.html
- http://designfestival.com/the-psychology-of-color
- www.designzzz.com/infographic-psychology-color-web-designers

Color Theory

- www.colormatters.com/colortheory.html
- http://colortheory.liquisoft.com
- www.digital-web.com/articles/color_theory_for_the_colorblind

Color Scheme Generators

- http://meyerweb.com/eric/tools/color-blend
- http://colorschemer.com/schemes
- www.colr.org
- http://colorsontheweb.com/colorwizard.asp
- http://kuler.adobe.com
- http://colorschemedesigner.com

You have the following tasks:

    a. Design a color scheme. List three hexadecimal color values in addition to white (#FFFFFF) or black (#000000) in your design.

    b. Describe the process you went through as you selected the colors. Describe why you chose these colors. What type of website would they be appropriate for? List the URLs of any resources you used.

    c. Create an external CSS file name color1.css that configures text color and background color selections for the document, h1 element selector, p element selector, and footer element selector using the colors you have chosen.

    d. Create a web page named color1.html that shows examples of the CSS style rules.

Answers to Review Questions

1. d	2. b	3. b
4. a	5. c	6. b
7. b	8. d	9. a
10. b		

Credits

Figures 11, 16 © Terry Ann Morris, Ed.D. | Microsoft Corporation

Figures 4–10, 12–15, 17–22, 24, 26, 28, 29© Terry Ann Morris, Ed.D. | Mozilla Foundation

Web Graphics
Styling Basics

A key component of a compelling website is the use of interesting and appropriate graphics. This chapter introduces you to working with visual elements on web pages. When you include images on your website, it is important to remember that not all web users are able to view them. Some users may have vision problems and need assistive technology such as a screen reader application that reads the web page to them. In addition, search engines send out spiders and robots to walk the web and catalog pages for their indexes and databases; such programs do not access your images. Some of your visitors may be using a mobile device that may not display your images. As a web designer, strive to create pages that are enhanced by graphical elements but that are usable without them.

You'll learn how to...

- Describe types of graphics used on the Web
- Apply the image element to add graphics to web pages
- Configure images as backgrounds on web pages
- Configure images as hyperlinks
- Configure image maps
- Configure bullets in unordered lists with images
- Configure multiple background images with CSS3

From Chapter 5 of *Basics of Web Design HTML5 & CSS3*, Second Edition. Terry Ann Felke-Morris. Copyright © 2014 by Pearson Education, Inc. All rights reserved.

Web Graphics

Graphics can make web pages compelling and engaging. This section discusses types and features of graphic files used on the Web: **GIF**, **JPEG**, and **PNG**. Table 1 lists these graphic file types and their characteristics.

FIGURE 1 *This logo is a GIF.*

Graphic Interchange Format (GIF) Images

GIF images are best used for flat line drawings containing mostly solid tones and simple images such as clip art. The maximum number of colors in a GIF file is 256. GIF images have a .gif file extension. Figure 1 shows a logo image created in GIF format. **Lossless compression** is used when a GIF is saved. This means that nothing in the original image is lost and that the compressed image, when rendered by a browser, will contain the same pixels as the original. An **animated GIF** consists of several images or frames, each of which is slightly different. When the frames flash on the screen in order, the image appears animated.

The format GIF89A used by GIF images supports image **transparency**. In a graphics application, such as the open-source GIMP, one color (typically the background color) of the image can be set to be transparent. The background color (or background image) of the web page shows through the transparent area in the image. Figure 2 displays two GIF images on a blue texture background.

GIF saved with Transparency   GIF saved without Transparency

FIGURE 2 *Comparison of transparent and nontransparent GIFs.*

To avoid slow-loading web pages, graphic files should be optimized for the Web. Image **optimization** is the process of creating an image with the lowest file size that still renders a good-quality image—balancing image quality and file size. GIF images are typically optimized by reducing the number of colors in the image using a graphics application, such as Adobe Photoshop.

Joint Photographic Experts Group (JPEG) Images

JPEG images are best used for photographs. In contrast to a GIF image, a JPEG image can contain 16.7 million colors. However, JPEG images cannot be made transparent and they cannot be animated. JPEG images usually have a .jpg or .jpeg file extension. JPEG images are saved using **lossy compression**. This means that some pixels in the original image are lost or removed from the compressed file. When a browser renders the compressed image, the display is similar to but not exactly the same as the original image.

Web Graphics Styling Basics

There are trade-offs between the quality of the image and the amount of compression. An image with less compression will have higher quality and result in a larger file size. An image with more compression will have lower quality and result in a smaller file size.

When you take a photo with a digital camera, the file size is too large for optimal display on a web page. Figure 3 shows an optimized version of a digital photo with an original file size of 250KB. The image was optimized using a graphics application set to 80 percent quality, is now only 55KB, and displays well on a web page.

FIGURE 3 *JPEG saved at 80 percent quality (55KB file size) displays well on a web page.*

Figure 4 was saved with 20 percent quality and is only 19KB, but its quality is unacceptable. The quality of the image degrades as the file size decreases. The square blockiness you see in Figure 4 is called **pixelation** and should be avoided.

Adobe Photoshop and Adobe Fireworks are often used by web professionals to optimize images for the Web. GIMP (www.gimp.org) is a popular open-source image editor that supports multiple platforms. Pixlr offers a free, easy-to-use, online photo editor at http://pixlr.com/editor.

Another technique used with web graphics is to display a small version of the image, called a **thumbnail image**. Often the thumbnail is configured as an image hyperlink to display the larger image. Figure 5 shows a thumbnail image.

FIGURE 4 *JPEG saved at 20 percent quality (19KB file size).*

Portable Network Graphic (PNG) Images

PNG images combine the best of GIF and JPEG images and will be a replacement for GIF in the future. PNG graphics can support millions of colors, support variable transparency levels, and use lossless compression.

New WebP Image Format

Google's new WebP image format offers improved compression and smaller image file sizes, but it's not ready for use in commercial websites. WebP (pronounced "weppy") graphics are currently supported only by the Google Chrome Browser. More information about this new image format is available at http://developers.google.com/speed/webp.

FIGURE 5
This small thumbnail image is only 5KB.

TABLE 1 *Overview of Image File Types*

Image Type	Extension	Compression	Transparency	Animation	Colors
GIF	.gif	Lossless	Yes	Yes	256
JPEG	.jpg or .jpeg	Lossy	No	No	Millions
PNG	.png	Lossless	Yes	No	Millions

Web Graphics Styling Basics

Image Element

The **image element** configures graphics on a web page. These graphics can be photographs, banners, company logos, navigation buttons—you are limited only by your creativity and imagination. The image element is a void element and is not coded as a pair of opening and closing tags. The following code example configures an image named logo.gif, which is located in the same folder as the web page:

```
<img src="logo.gif" height="200" width="500" alt="My Company Name">
```

The **src attribute** specifies the file name of the image. The **alt attribute** provides a text replacement, typically a text description, of the image. The browser reserves the correct amount of space for your image if you use the height and width attributes with values either equal to or approximately the size of the image. Table 2 lists `<img>` tag attributes and their values. Commonly used attributes are shown in bold.

Review Table 2 and notice that several attributes are marked as obsolete. Although obsolete in HTML5, they are still valid in XHTML, so you'll see them coded in existing web pages. You'll learn to use CSS to recreate the functions of these now-obsolete attributes.

TABLE 2 *Attributes of the `<img>` Tag*

Attribute	Value
align	right, left (default) top, middle, bottom; (obsolete)
alt	Text phrase that describes the image; required
height	Height of image in pixels
hspace	Number in pixels of empty space to the left and right of the image; (obsolete)
id	Text name, alphanumeric, beginning with a letter, no spaces—the value must be unique and not used for other id values on the same web page document
name	Text name, alphanumeric, beginning with a letter, no spaces—this attribute names the image so that it can be easily accessed by client-side scripting languages such as JavaScript; (obsolete)
src	The URL or file name of the image; required
title	A text phrase containing advisory information about the image—typically more descriptive than the alt text
vspace	Number in pixels of empty space above and below the image; (obsolete)
width	Width of image in pixels

Web Graphics Styling Basics

In this Hands-On Practice you will place a logo graphic on a web page. Create a new folder called trilliumch5. The graphic used in this Hands-On Practice is located in the student files chapter5/ starters folder on the companion website at www.pearsonhighered.com/felke-morris. Copy the trilliumbanner.jpg file into your trilliumch5 folder. A starter version of the Trillium Media Design Home page is ready for you in the student files. Copy the chapter5/starter.html file into your trilliumch5 folder. Launch a browser to display the starter.html web page—notice that a mono-chromatic green color scheme has been configured with CSS. When you are finished with this Hands-On Practice, your page will look similar to the one shown in Figure 6—with a logo banner.

Launch a text editor and open the starter.html file. Notice that the h1 selector in the CSS has been configured with a height of 86px, which is the same as the height of the logo graphic.

Configure the logo graphic as follows:

Delete the text contained between the h1 opening and closing tags. Code an `<img>` tag to display trilliumbanner.jpg in this area. Remember to include the `src`, `alt`, `height`, and `width` attributes. Sample code follows:

```
<img src="trilliumbanner.jpg"
alt="Trillium Media Design" width="700"
height="86">
```

FIGURE 6 *Color swatches are shown at the left of the new Trillium Home page with a logo banner.*

Save your page as index.html in the trilliumch5 folder. Launch a browser and test your page. It should look similar to the one shown in Figure 6.

Note: If the image did not display on your web page, verify that you have saved the trilliumbanner.jpg file inside the trilliumch5 folder and that you have spelled the file name correctly in the `<img>` tag. The student files contain a sample solution in the chapter5/ trillium folder. Isn't it interesting how just one image can add visual interest to a web page?

Accessibility and the alt Attribute

Use the `alt` attribute to provide accessibility. Section 508 of the Rehabilitation Act requires the use of accessibility features for information technology (including websites) associated with the federal government. The alt attribute configures an alternative text description of the image. This alt text may be used by the browser in two ways: The browser will show the alt text in the image area before the graphic is downloaded and displayed. Some browsers will also show the alt text as a tool tip whenever the web page visitor places a mouse over the image area.

Standard browsers such as Internet Explorer and Mozilla Firefox are not the only type of application or user agent that can access your website. Major search engines run programs called spiders or robots; these programs index and categorize websites. They cannot process images, but some process the value of the alt attributes in image tags. Applications such as screen readers will read the text in the alt attribute out loud. A mobile browser may display the alt text instead of the image.

Image Hyperlinks

Writing the code to make an image function as a hyperlink is very easy. To create an **image link** all you need to do is surround your `<img>` tag with anchor tags. For example, to place a link around an image called home.gif, use the following code:

```
<a href="index.html"><img src="home.gif" height="19" width="85"
alt="Home"></a>
```

When an image is used as a hyperlink, some browsers display a blue outline (border) around the image. If you would prefer not to display this outline, use CSS to configure the border on the img element selector. The next Hands-On Practice will demonstrate this technique as you add image hyperlinks to a web page.

 Hands-On Practice 2

You will add image links to the Trillium Media Design Home page in this Hands-On Practice. You should already have the index.html and trilliumbanner.jpg files in your trilliumch5 folder. The graphics used in this Hands-On Practice are located in the student files in the chapter5/starters folder. Copy the home.gif, services.gif, and contact.gif files into your trilliumch5 folder. View Figure 7 to see how your page should look after you are done with this Hands-On Practice.

Let's get started. Launch a text editor and open index.html. Notice that the anchor tags are already coded—you'll just need to convert the text links to image links!

1. Whenever the main navigation consists of media, such as an image, some individuals may not be able to see the images (or may have images turned off in their browser). To provide navigation that is accessible to all, configure a set of plain text navigation links in the page footer area. Copy the `<nav>` element containing the navigation area to the lower portion of the page and paste it within the footer element, above the copyright line.

2. Now, focus on the top navigation area. Replace the text contained between each pair of anchor tags with an image element. Use home.gif for the link to index.html, services.gif for the link to services.html, and contact.gif for the link to contact.html. Be careful not to leave any extra spaces between the img tag and the opening and closing anchor tags. A sample follows:

```
<a href="index.html"><img src="home.gif" alt="Home" width="120"
height="40"></a>
```

Web Graphics Styling Basics

3. Here's a quick preview of borders. To eliminate the borders on the image hyperlinks, create a new style rule in the embedded CSS that configures no border for the img element selector. The code follows:

```
img { border-style: none; }
```

4. Save your page as index.html. Launch a browser and test your page. It should look similar to the one shown in Figure 7.

The student files contain a sample solution in the chapter5/trillium2 folder.

FIGURE 7 *The new Trillium Home page navigation with image links.*

Accessibility and Image Hyperlinks

When using an image for main navigation, there are two methods to provide for accessibility:

1. Add a row of plain text navigation hyperlinks in the page footer. These won't be noticed by most people but could be helpful to a person using a screen reader to visit your web page.

2. Configure the `alt` attribute for each image to contain the exact text that displays in the image. For example, code `alt="Home"` in the `<img>` tag for the Home button.

 What if my images don't display?

The following are common reasons for an image to not display on a web page:

▶ Is your image *really* in the website folder? Use Windows Explorer or the Mac Finder to double-check.

▶ Did you code the HTML and CSS correctly? Perform W3C CSS and HTML validation testing to find syntax errors that could prevent the image from displaying.

▶ Does your image have the exact file name that you have used in the CSS or HTML code? Attention to detail and consistency will be very helpful here.

Web Graphics Styling Basics

Configure Background Images

You can configure background color with the CSS `background-color` property. In addition to a background color, you can also choose to use an image for the background of an element.

The `background-image` Property

Use the CSS **`background-image`** property to configure a background image. For example, the following CSS code configures the HTML body selector with a background using the graphic texture1.png, located in the same folder as the web page file:

```
body { background-image: url(texture1.png); }
```

Using Both Background Color and a Background Image

You can configure both a background color and a background image. The background color (specified by the `background-color` property) will display first. Next, the image specified as the background will be displayed as it is loaded by the browser.

By coding both a background color and a background image you provide your visitor with a more pleasing visual experience. If the background image does not load for some reason, the background color will still have the expected contrast with your text color. If the background image is smaller than the web browser window and the web page is configured with CSS to not automatically tile (repeat), the page background color will display in areas not covered by the background image. The CSS for a page with both a background color and a background image is as follows:

```
body { background-color: #99cccc;
       background-image: url(background.jpg); }
```

Browser Display of a Background Image

You may think that a graphic created to be the background of a web page would always be about the size of the browser window viewport. However, the dimensions of the background image are often much smaller than the typical viewport. The shape of a background image is typically either a long thin rectangle or a small rectangular block. Unless otherwise specified in a style rule, browsers repeat, or tile, these images to cover the page background, as shown in Figures 8 and 9. The images have small file sizes so that they download quickly.

Web Graphics Styling Basics

Background Image

Web Page with Background Image

FIGURE 8 *A long, thin background image tiles down the page.*

Background Image

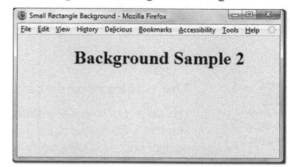

Web Page with Background Image

FIGURE 9 *A small rectangular background is repeated to fill the web page window.*

The `background-attachment` Property

Use the **`background-attachment` property** to configure whether the background image remains fixed in place or scrolls along with the page in the browser viewport. Valid values for the `background-attachment` property include `fixed` and `scroll` (the default).

 FAQ   What if my images are in their own folder?

It's a good idea to organize your website by placing all your images in a folder separate from your web pages. Notice that the CircleSoft website shown in Figure 10 has a folder called images, which contains GIF and JPEG files. To refer to these files in code, you also need to refer to the images folder. The following are some examples:

▶ The CSS code to configure the background.gif file from the images folder as the page background is as follows:

```
body { background-image: url(images/background.gif); }
```

▶ To configure a web page to display the logo.jpg file from the images folder, use the following code:

```
<img src="images/logo.jpg" alt="CircleSoft" width="588" height="120">
```

FIGURE 10 *A folder named "images"*

Position Background Images

The `background-repeat` Property

The default behavior of a browser is to repeat, or tile, background images to cover the entire element's background. Figures 8 and 9 display examples of this type of tiling for a web page background. This tiling behavior also applies to other elements, such as backgrounds for headings, paragraphs, and so on. You can change automatic tiling of a background image with the CSS **`background-repeat`** property. The values for the `background-repeat` property include `repeat` (default), `repeat-y` (vertical repeat), `repeat-x` (horizontal repeat), and `no-repeat` (image does not repeat). For example, configure `background-repeat: no-repeat;` to display the background image only once. Figure 11 provides examples of the actual background image and the result of applying various `background-repeat` property values. CSS3 provides for additional values for the `background-repeat` property are not yet well supported by browsers:

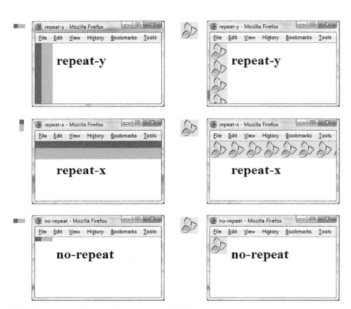

FIGURE 11 *Examples of the CSS* `background-repeat` *property.*

- `background-repeat: space;` Repeats the image in the background without clipping (or cutting off) parts of the image by adjusting empty space around the repeated images.

- `background-repeat: round;` Repeats the image in the background and scales (adjusts) the dimensions of the image to avoid clipping.

Positioning the Background Image

You can specify other locations for the background image besides the default top left location using the `background-position` property. Valid values for the `background-position` property include percentages; pixel values; or `left`, `top`, `center`, `bottom`, and `right`. The first value indicates horizontal position. The second value indicates vertical position. If only one value is provided, the second value defaults to center. In Figure 12, the background image has been placed on the right side of the element using the style rule

```
h2 { background-image: url(trilliumbg.gif);
     background-position: right;
     background-repeat: no-repeat; }
```

New Media and Web Design

FIGURE 12 *The flower background image was configured to display on the right side with CSS.*

Hands-On Practice 3

Let's practice using a background image. You will update the index.html file from Hands-On Practice 2 (shown in Figure 7). In this Hands-On Practice you will configure the h2 element selector with a background image that does not repeat. Obtain the trilliumbg.gif image from the student files chapter5/starters folder. Copy the image into your trilliumch5 folder. When you have completed this exercise, your page should look similar to the one shown in Figure 13. Launch a text editor and open index.html.

1. Modify the style rule for the h2 element selector to configure the `background-image` and `background-repeat` properties. Set the background image to be trilliumbg.gif. Set the background not to repeat. The h2 element selector style rules follow:

```
h2 { background-color: #d5edb3;
     color: #5c743d;
     background-image: url(trilliumbg.gif);
     background-repeat: no-repeat; }
```

2. Save your page as index.html. Launch a browser, and test your page. You may notice that the text in the h2 element is displayed over the background image. In this case, the page would look more appealing if there were more space, or padding, before the beginning of the text displayed by the h2 elements. A quick way to adjust this is to code the ` ` nonbreaking space special character about five times just after each opening `<h2>` tag. However, a more modern technique is to use the CSS `padding-left` property to add empty space within the left side of the element. Add the following declaration to the h2 element selector to add empty space before the text:

```
padding-left: 30px;
```

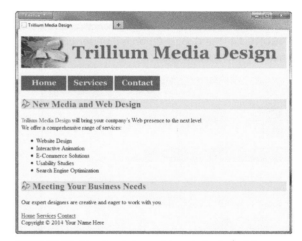

3. Save and test your page again. It should look similar to the one shown in Figure 13. The student files contain a sample solution in the chapter5/trillium3 folder.

FIGURE 13 *The background image in the* `<h2>` *areas is configured with* `background-repeat: no-repeat.`

Web Graphics Styling Basics

CSS3 Multiple Background Images

Now that you are familiar with background images, let's explore applying multiple background images to a web page. Although the CSS3 Backgrounds and Borders module is still in candidate recommendation status, current versions of most popular web browsers support the use of multiple background images.

Figure 14 shows a web page with two background images configured on the body selector: a green gradient image that repeats across the entire browser viewport and a flower image that displays once in the right footer area. Use the CSS3 **background property** to configure multiple background images. Each image declaration is separated by a comma. You can optionally add property values to indicate the image's position and whether the image repeats. The `background` property uses a shorthand notation—just list the values that are needed for relevant properties such as `background-position` and `background-repeat`.

FIGURE 14 *The Google Chrome browser displays multiple background images.*

FIGURE 15 *Progressive enhancement in action. Although only one background image displays, the web page has a similar display to Figure 14.*

Progressive Enhancement

Multiple background images are currently supported by recent versions of Firefox, Chrome, Safari, and Opera. Although supported in Internet Explorer 9, multiple background images are not supported by earlier versions of Internet Explorer. You'll use the technique of **progressive enhancement**, which is defined by web developer and HTML5 evangelist, Christian Heilmann, as "Starting with a baseline of usable functionality, then increasing the richness of the user experience step by step by testing for support for enhancements before applying them." In other words, start with a web page that displays well in most browsers and then add new design techniques, such as multiple background images, in a way that enhances the display for visitors using browsers that support the new technique.

To provide for progressive enhancement when using multiple background images, first configure a separate `background-image` property with a single image (rendered by browsers that do not support multiple background images) prior to the `background` property configured for multiple images (to be rendered by supporting browsers and ignored by nonsupporting browsers). Figure 15 shows the page displayed in Internet Explorer 8, which rendered the standard `background-image` property.

Web Graphics Styling Basics

Hands-On Practice 4

Let's practice configuring multiple background images. In this Hands-On Practice you will configure the body element selector to display multiple background images on the web page. Obtain the trilliumfoot.gif and the trilliumgradient.png images from the student files in the chapter5/starters folder. Copy the images into your trilliumch5 folder. You'll update the index.html file from the previous Hands-On Practice (shown in Figure 13). Launch a text editor and open index.html.

1. Modify the style rule for the body element selector. Configure the `background-image` property to display trilliumgradient.png. This style rule will be applied by browsers that do not support multiple background images. Configure a `background` property to display both the trilliumfoot.gif image and the trilliumgradient.png image. The trilliumfoot.gif image should not repeat and should be displayed in the lower right corner. The body selector style rules are as follows:

```
body { background-color: #f4ffe4; color: #333333;
      background-image: url(trilliumgradient.png);
      background: url(trilliumfoot.gif) no-repeat right bottom,
                  url(trilliumgradient.png); }
```

2. Save your page as index.html. Launch a browser and test your page. It will look different, depending on which browser you use—similar to either Figure 14 (a browser that supports multiple background images) or Figure 15 (a browser that does not support multiple background images).

3. There is usually more than one way to design a web page. Let's consider the placement of the flower image in the footer area of the web page. Why not configure the gradient image as the body element selector background and the flower image as the footer element selector background? This will provide for a similar display on all currently popular browsers. Let's try this out. Edit the index.html file. Remove the `background` property from the body element selector. A code sample is

```
body { background-color: #f4ffe4; color: #333333;
      background-image: url(trilliumgradient.png); }
```

Next, configure the trilliumfoot.gif image as the background for the footer element selector. Configure a height value that will be large enough to display the image. The code is

```
footer { background-image: url(trilliumfoot.gif);
        background-repeat: no-repeat;
        background-position: right top;
        height: 75px; }
```

4. Save your page as index2.html. Launch a browser and test your page. It should look similar to Figure 14 on all popular modern browsers. See the chapter5/trillium4 folder in the student files for solutions to this Hands-On Practice.

Web Graphics Styling Basics

The Favorites Icon

Ever wonder about the small icon you sometimes see in the address bar or tab of a browser? That's a **favorites icon**, often referred to as a **favicon**, which is a square image (either 16 × 16 pixels or 32 × 32 pixels) associated with a web page. The favicon shown in Figure 16 may display in the browser address bar, tab, or the favorites/bookmarks list.

Configuring a Favorites Icon

While earlier versions of Internet Explorer (such as versions 5 and 6) expected the file to be named favicon.ico and to reside in the root directory of the web server, a more modern approach is to associate the favicon.ico file with a web page using the link element. You can code the `<link>` tag in the head section of a web page to associate an external style sheet file with a web page file. You can also use the `<link>` tag to associate a favorites icon with a web page. Three attributes are used to associate a web page with a favorites icon: `rel`, `href`, and `type`. The value of the `rel` attribute is `icon`. The value of the `href` attribute is the name of the image file. The value of the `type` attribute describes the MIME type of the image—which defaults to `image/x-icon` for .ico files. The code to associate a favorites icon named favicon.ico to a web page is as follows:

```
<link rel="icon" href="favicon.ico" type="image/x-icon">
```

Be aware that Internet Explorer's support of the favorites icon is somewhat "buggy." You may need to publish your files to the Web in order for the favicon to display in even current versions of Internet Explorer. Other browsers, such as Firefox, display favicons more reliably and also support GIF and PNG image formats.

FIGURE 16 *The favorites icon displays in the browser tab and address bar.*

Web Graphics Styling Basics

Hands-On Practice 5

Let's practice using a favorites icon. Obtain the favicon.ico file from the student files in the chapter5/starters folder. In this exercise you will use your files from Hands-On Practice 4 (see the student files chapter5/trillium4 folder) as a starting point.

1. Launch a text editor and open index.html. Add the following link tag to the head section of the web page:

   ```
   <link rel="icon" href="favicon.ico" type="image/x-icon">
   ```

2. Save your page as index.html. Launch the Firefox browser and test your page. You should notice the small trillium flower in the Firefox browser tab as shown in Figure 17. The student files contain a sample solution in the chapter5/trillium5 folder.

FIGURE 17 *The favorites icon displays in the Firefox browser location and tab.*

 How can I create my own favorites icon?

You can create your own favicon with a graphics application, such as Adobe Fireworks, or with one of the following online tools:

▶ http://favicon.cc
▶ www.favicongenerator.com
▶ www.freefavicon.com
▶ www.xiconeditor.com

Web Graphics Styling Basics

Configure List Markers with CSS

The default display for an unordered list is to show a disc marker (often referred to as a bullet) in front of each list item. The default display for an ordered list is to show a decimal number in front of each list item. Use the `list-style-type` property to configure the marker for an unordered or ordered list. See Table 3 for common property values.

TABLE 3 *CSS Properties for Ordered and Unordered List Markers*

Property	Description	Value	List Marker Display
`list-style-type`	Configures the style of the list marker	`none`	No list markers display
		`disc`	Circle ("bullet")
		`circle`	Open circle
		`square`	Square
		`decimal`	Decimal numbers
		`upper-alpha`	Uppercase letters
		`lower-alpha`	Lowercase letters
		`lower-roman`	Lowercase Roman numerals
`list-style-image`	Image replacement for the list marker	The `url` keyword with parentheses surrounding the file name or path for the image	The image displays in front of each list item
`list-style-position`	Configures placement of markers	`inside`	Markers are indented, text wraps under the markers
		`outside` (default)	Markers have default placement

The property `list-style-type: none` prevents the browser from displaying the list markers (you'll see a use for this when configuring navigation hyperlinks). Figure 18 shows an unordered list configured with square markers using the following CSS:

```
ul { list-style-type: square; }
```

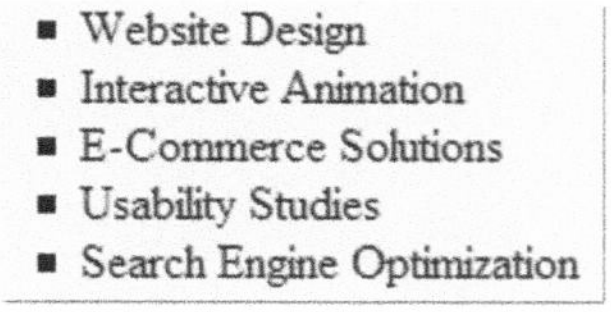

FIGURE 18

The unordered list markers are square.

- Website Design
- Interactive Animation
- E-Commerce Solutions
- Usability Studies
- Search Engine Optimization

Web Graphics Styling Basics

Figure 19 shows an ordered list configured with uppercase letter markers using the following CSS:

```
ol { list-style-type: upper-alpha; }
```

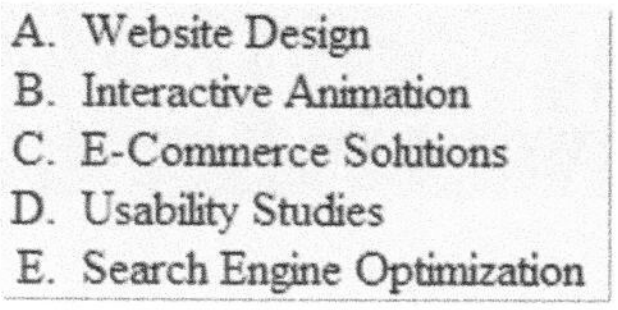

Configure an Image as a List Marker

Use the `list-style-image` property to configure an image as the marker in an unordered or ordered list. In Figure 20 an image named trillium.gif was configured to replace the list markers using the following CSS:

```
ul {list-style-image: url(trillium.gif); }
```

FIGURE 19
The ordered list markers use uppercase letters.

A. Website Design
B. Interactive Animation
C. E-Commerce Solutions
D. Usability Studies
E. Search Engine Optimization

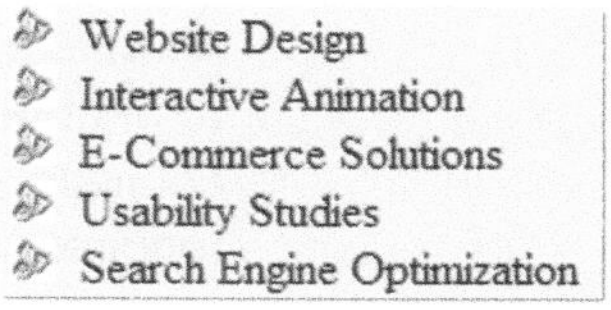

FIGURE 20
The list markers are replaced with an image.

- Website Design
- Interactive Animation
- E-Commerce Solutions
- Usability Studies
- Search Engine Optimization

Hands-On Practice 6

In this Hands-On Practice you'll replace the list markers on the Trillium Media Design home page with an image. Obtain the trillium.gif file from the student files in the chapter5/starters folder. In this exercise you will use your files from Hands-On Practice 5 (see the student files chapter5/trillium5 folder) as a starting point.

1. Launch a text editor and open index.html. Add the following style rule to the embedded CSS in the head section to configure the ul element selector with the `list-style-image` property:

```
ul { list-style-image: url(trillium.gif); }
```

2. Save your page as index.html. Launch in a browser and test your page. You should see the small trillium flower before each item in the unordered list as shown in Figure 20. The student files contain a sample solution in the chapter5/trillium6 folder.

Web Graphics Styling Basics

Image Maps

An **image map** is an image configured with multiple clickable or selectable areas that link to another web page or website. The selectable areas are called **hotspots**. Image maps can configure clickable areas in three shapes: rectangles, circles, and polygons. An image map requires the use of the image element, map element, and one or more area elements.

Map Element

The **map element** is a container tag that indicates the beginning and ending of the image map description. The **name attribute** is coded to associate the `<map>` tag with its corresponding image. The `id` attribute must have the same value as the `name` attribute. To associate a map element with an image, configure the image tag with the **usemap attribute** to indicate which `<map>` to use.

Area Element

The **area element** defines the coordinates or edges of the clickable area. It is a void tag that uses the `href`, `alt`, `title`, `shape`, and `coords` attributes. The `href` attribute identifies the web page to display when the area is clicked. The `alt` attribute provides a text description for screen readers. Use the **title attribute** to specify text that some browsers may display as a tooltip when the mouse is placed over the area. The **coords attriubte** indicates the coordinate position of the clickable area. Table 4 describes the type of coordinates needed for each `shape` attribute value.

TABLE 4 *Shape coordinates*

Shape	Coordinates	Meaning
rect	"x1,y1,x2,y2"	The coordinates at point (x1,y1) represent the upper-left corner of the rectangle. The coordinates at point (x2,y2) represent the lower-right corner of the rectangle.
circle	"x,y,r"	The coordinates at point (x,y) indicate the center of the circle. The value of r is the radius of the circle, in pixels.
polygon	"x1,y1,x2,y2,x3,y3", etc.	The values of each (x,y) pair represent the coordinates of a corner point of the polygon.

Web Graphics Styling Basics

Exploring a Rectangular Image Map

We'll focus on a rectangular image map. For a rectangular image map, the value of the `shape` attribute is `rect`, and the coordinates indicate the pixel positions as follows:

- distance of the upper-left corner from the left side of the image
- distance of the upper-left corner from the top of the image
- distance of the lower-right corner from the left edge of the image
- distance to the lower-right corner from the top of the image.

Figure 21 shows an image of a fishing boat. This example is in the student files at chapter5/map.html.

- The dotted rectangle around the fishing boat indicates the location of the hotspot.
- The coordinates shown (24, 188) indicate that the top-left corner is 24 pixels from the left edge of the image and 188 pixels from the top of the image.
- The pair of coordinates in the lower-right corner (339, 283) indicates that this corner is 339 pixels from the left edge of the image and 283 pixels from the top of the image.

FIGURE 21 *A sample image map.*

The HTML code to create this image map follows:

```
<map name="boat" id="boat">
<area href="http://www.fishingdoorcounty.com"
  shape="rect" coords="24,188,339,283"
  alt="Door County Fishing Charter"
  title="Door County Fishing Charter">
</map>
<img src="fishingboat.jpg" usemap="#boat"
  alt="Door County" width="416" height="350">
```

Note the use of the `alt` attribute on the area element in the previous code sample. Configure a descriptive `alt` attribute for each area element associated with an image map to provide for accessibility.

Most web developers do not hand-code image maps. Web authoring tools, such as Adobe Dreamweaver, have features that help you to generate image maps. There are also free online image map generators available at:

- www.maschek.hu/imagemap/imgmap
- http://image-maps.com
- http://mobilefish.com/services/image_map/image_map.php

Web Graphics Styling Basics

Review and Apply

Review Questions

1. Which declaration configures an unordered list item with a square list marker?

   a. `list-bullet: none;`

   b. `list-style-type: square;`

   c. `list-style-image: square;`

   d. `list-marker: square;`

2. Which of the following creates an image link to the index.html page when the home.gif graphic is clicked?

   a. `<a href="index.html" src="home.gif" alt="Home"></a>`

   b. `<a href="index.html"><img src="home.gif" alt="Home"></a>`

   c. `<img src="home.gif" href="index.html" alt="Home">`

   d. `<a src="home.gif"><img src="home.gif" alt="Home"></a>`

3. Why should you include `height` and `width` attributes on an `<img>` tag?

   a. They are required attributes and must always be included.

   b. They help the browser reserve the appropriate space for the image.

   c. They help the browser display the image in its own window.

   d. none of the above

4. Which attribute specifies text that is available to browsers and other user agents that do not support graphics?

   a. `alt`

   b. `text`

   c. `src`

   d. none of the above

5. What is the term used to describe a square icon that is associated with a web page and is displayed in the browser address bar or tab?

   a. background

   b. bookmark icon

   c. favicon

   d. logo

6. Which of the following graphic types is best suited to photographs?

   a. GIF

   b. photo

   c. BMP

   d. JPEG

7. Which of the following configures a graphic to repeat vertically down the side of a web page?

   a. `background-repeat: repeat-x;`

   b. `background-repeat: repeat;`

   c. `valign="left"`

   d. `background-repeat: repeat-y;`

8. Which CSS property configures the background image of an element?

   a. `background-color`

   b. `bgcolor`

   c. `favicon`

   d. `background-image`

Web Graphics Styling Basics

9. What is the process of creating an image with the lowest file size that still renders a good-quality image—balancing image quality and file size?

   a. progressive enhancement

   b. optimization

   c. usability

   d. image validation

10. What is the process of ensuring that web pages that are coded with new or advanced techniques are still usable in browsers that do not support the new techniques?

    a. validation

    b. progressive enhancement

    c. valid enhancement

    d. optimization

Hands-On Exercises

1. Write the code to place an image called primelogo.gif on a web page. The image is 100 pixels high by 650 pixels wide.

2. Write the code to create an image hyperlink. The image is called schaumburgthumb.jpg. It is 100 pixels high by 150 pixels wide. The image should link to a larger image called schaumburg.jpg. There should be no border on the image.

3. Write the code to create a `<div>` containing three images used as navigation links. Table 5 provides information about the images and their associated links.

TABLE 5

Image Name	Link Page Name	Image Height	Image Width
homebtn.gif	index.html	50	200
productsbtn.gif	products.html	50	200
orderbtn.gif	order.html	50	200

4. Experiment with background images.
   a. Locate the twocolor.gif file in the student files chapter5/starters folder. Design a web page that uses this file as a background image that repeats down the left side of the browser window. Save your file as bg1.html
   b. Locate the twocolor1.gif file in the student files chapter5/starters folder. Design a web page that uses this file as a background image that repeats across the top of the browser window. Save your file as bg2.html

5. Design a new web page about your favorite movie. Name the web page movie5.html. Configure a background color for the page and either background images or background colors for at least two sections of the page. Search the Web for a photo of a scene from the movie, an actress in the movie, or an actor in the movie. Include the following information on your web page:

   • Title of the movie

   • Director or producer

   • Leading actor

Web Graphics Styling Basics

- Leading actress
- Rating (R, PG-13, PG, G, NR)
- A brief description of the movie
- An absolute link to a review about the movie

It is unethical to steal an image from another website. Some websites have a link to their copyright policy. Most websites will give permission for you to use an image in a school assignment. If there is no available policy, e-mail the site's contact person and request permission to use the photo. If you are unable to obtain permission, you may substitute with clip art or an image from a free site instead.

Focus on Web Design

Providing access to the Web for all people is an important issue. Visit the W3C's Web Accessibility Initiative and explore their WCAG 2.0 Quick Reference at http://w3.org/WAI/WCAG20/quickref. View additional pages at the W3C's site as necessary. Explore the checkpoints that are related to the use of color and images on web pages. Create a web page that uses color, uses images, and includes the information that you discovered.

Answers to Review Questions

1. b	**2.** b	**3.** b
4. a	**5.** c	**6.** d
7. d	**8.** d	**9.** b
10. b		

Credits

Figures 3–5, 12–17, 21 © Terry Ann Morris, Ed.D. Reprinted with permission.

Figure 10 © Microsoft Corporation

Figures 6–9, 11, 22–27 © Terry Ann Morris, Ed.D. | Mozilla Foundation

Figure 21 © www.nerrs.noaa.gov

Web Graphics Styling Basics

More CSS Basics

You'll add to your CSS skill set in this chapter. In addition to configuring text with CSS, you'll be introduced to the CSS box model and configure margin, border, and padding. You'll also explore new CSS3 properties to round corners, apply shadow, adjust display of background images, and configure color and opacity.

You'll learn how to...

- Configure text typeface, size, weight, and style with CSS
- Align and indent text with CSS
- Describe and apply the CSS box model
- Configure width and height with CSS
- Configure margin, border, and padding with CSS

- Center web page content with CSS
- Apply shadows with CSS3
- Configure rounded corners with CSS3
- Apply CSS3 properties to background images
- Configure opacity, RGBA color, HSLA color, and gradients with CSS3

From Chapter 6 of *Basics of Web Design HTML5 & CSS3*, Second Edition. Terry Ann Felke-Morris. Copyright © 2014 by Pearson Education, Inc. All rights reserved.

Fonts with CSS

The `font-family` Property

The **`font-family` property** configures font typefaces. A web browser displays text with the fonts that have been installed on the user's computer. When a font is specified that is not installed on your web visitor's computer, the default font is substituted. Times New Roman is the default font displayed by most web browsers. Figure 1 shows font family categories and some common font typefaces.

Font Family Category	Font Family Description	Font Typeface Examples
serif	Serif fonts have small embellishments on the end of letter strokes; often used for headings.	Times New Roman, Georgia, Palatino
sans-serif	Sans-serif fonts do not have serifs; often used for web page text.	Arial, Tahoma, Helvetica, Verdana
monospace	Fixed-width font; often used for code samples.	Courier New, Lucida Console
cursive	Hand-written style; use with caution; may be difficult to read on a web page.	Lucida Handwriting, Brush Script, Comic Sans MS
fantasy	Exaggerated style; use with caution; sometimes used for headings; may be difficult to read on a web page.	Jokerman, Impact, Papyrus

FIGURE 1 *Common fonts.*

The Verdana, Tahoma, and Georgia font typefaces were specifically designed to display well on computer monitors. A common practice is to use a serif font (such as Georgia or Times New Roman) for headings and a sans-serif font (such as Verdana or Arial) for detailed text content. Not every computer has the same fonts installed. See www.ampsoft.net/webdesign-l/WindowsMacFonts.html for a list of "web-safe" fonts. Create a built-in backup plan by listing multiple fonts and categories for the value of the `font-family` property. The browser will attempt to use the fonts in the order listed. The following CSS configures the p element selector to display text in Verdana (if installed) or Arial (if installed) or the default installed sans-serif font.

```
p { font-family: Verdana, Arial, sans-serif; }
```

 Hands-On Practice 1

In this Hands-On Practice you will configure the `font-family` property. Create a new folder called trilliumch6. A starter version of the Trillium Media Design Home page is ready for you in the student files on the companion website at www.pearsonhighered.com/felke-morris. Copy the chapter6/starter.html file into your trilliumch6 folder. Launch a browser to display the starter.html web page—notice that the default browser font (typically Times New Roman) is used. When you are finished with this Hands-On Practice, your page will look similar to the one shown in Figure 2.

More CSS Basics

Launch a text editor and open the starter.html file. Configure the embedded CSS as follows:

1. Configure the body element selector to set global styles to use a sans-serif font typeface, such as Verdana or Arial. An example is

```
body { background-color: #f4ffe4;
       color: #333333;
       font-family: Verdana, Arial, sans-serif; }
```

2. Configure h1 and h2 element selectors to use a serif font typeface, such as Georgia or Times New Roman. Notice that "Times New Roman" is enclosed within quotation marks because the font name is more than a single word. Add the following style declaration to both the h1 and h2 element selectors.

```
font-family: Georgia, "Times New Roman", serif;
```

3. Configure a footer element selector to use a serif font typeface, such as Georgia or Times New Roman. An example is

```
footer { font-family: Georgia, "Times New Roman", serif; }
```

FIGURE 2 *The new Trillium home page.*

Save your page as index.html in the trilliumch6 folder. Launch a browser and test your page. It should look similar to the one shown in Figure 2. A sample solution is in the chapter6/trillium folder.

For many years, web designers have been limited to a set of common fonts for text on web pages. CSS3 introduced `@font-face`, which can be used to "embed" other fonts within web pages although you actually provide the location of the font and the browser downloads it. For example, if you own the rights to freely distribute the font named MyAwesomeFont and it is stored in a file myawesomefont.woff in the same folder as your web page, the following CSS will make it available to your web page visitors:

```
@font-face { font-family: MyAwesomeFont;
             src: url(myawesomefont.woff) format("woff"); }
```

After you code the `@font-face` rule, you can apply that font to a selector in the usual way, such as in the following example that configures h1 elements:

```
h1 { font-family: MyAwesomeFont, Georgia, serif; }
```

Current browsers support `@font-face` but there can be copyright issues. When you purchase a font for use on your own computer you do not necessarily purchase the right to freely distribute it. Visit www.fontsquirrel.com to browse a selection of commercial-use free fonts available for download and use.

Google Web Fonts provides a collection of free hosted embeddable web fonts. Explore the fonts available at www.google.com/webfonts. Once you choose a font, all you need to do is:

1. Copy and paste the link tag provided by Google in your web page document. (The link tag associates your web page with a CSS file that contains the appropriate `@font-face` rule.)

2. Configure your CSS `font-family` property with the Google web font name.

See the Getting Started guide at https://developers.google.com/webfonts/docs/getting_started for more information. Use web fonts judiciously to conserve bandwidth and avoid applying multiple web fonts to a web page. It's a good idea to use just one web font on a web page along with your typical fonts. This can provide you a way to use an uncommon font typeface in page headings and/or navigation without the need to create graphics for these page areas.

More CSS Basics

Text Properties with CSS

CSS provides you with lots of options for configuring the text on your web pages. In this section, you'll explore the `font-size`, `font-weight`, `font-style`, `text-transform`, and `line-height` properties.

The `font-size` Property

The **`font-size` property** sets the size of the font. Table 1 lists font size values, characteristics, and recommended usage.

TABLE 1 *Configuring Font Size*

Value Category	Values	Notes
Text Value	`xx-small`, `x-small`, `small`, `medium` (default), `large`, `x-large`, `xx-large`	Scales well when text is resized; limited options for text size.
Pixel Unit (px)	Numeric value with unit, such as `10px`	Pixel-perfect display depends on screen resolution; may not scale in every browser when text is resized.
Point Unit (pt)	Numeric value with unit, such as `10pt`	Use to configure print version of web page; may not scale in every browser when text is resized.
Em Unit (em)	Numeric value with unit, such as `.75em`	Recommended by W3C; scales well when text is resized in browser; many options for text size.
Percentage Value	Numeric value with percentage, such as `75%`	Recommended by W3C; scales well when text is resized in browser; many options for text size.

The **em unit** is a relative font unit that has its roots in the print industry back in the day when printers set type manually with blocks of characters. An em unit is the width of a square block of type (typically the uppercase M) for a particular font and type size. On web pages, an em unit corresponds to the width of the font and size used in the parent element (typically the body element). With this in mind, the size of an em unit is relative to the font typeface and default size. Percentage values work in a similar manner to em units. For example, `font-size: 100%;` and `font-size: 1em;` should render the same in a browser. To compare font sizes on your computer, launch a browser and view chapter6/fonts.html in the student files.

The `font-weight` Property

The **`font-weight` property** configures the boldness of the text. Configuring the CSS declaration `font-weight: bold;` has an effect similar to the `<b>` or `<strong>` HTML element.

More CSS Basics

The `font-style` Property

The **`font-style` property** typically is used to configure text displayed in italics. Valid values for `font-style` are `normal` (the default), `italic`, and `oblique`. The CSS `font-style: italic;` declaration has the same visual effect in the browser as an `<i>` or `<em>` HTML element.

The `text-transform` Property

The **`text-transform` property** configures the capitalization of text. Valid values for `text-transform` are `none` (default), `capitalize`, `uppercase`, or `lowercase`.

The `line-height` Property

The **`line-height` property** modifies the default height of a line of text and is often configured using a percentage value. For example, code `line-height: 200%;` to configure text to display double spaced.

Hands-On Practice 2

Let's try out those new CSS properties. When complete, your web page will look similar to the one shown in Figure 3. You should already have the index.html file in your trilliumch6 folder. Copy the trilliumlogo.jpg file from the chapter6/starters folder into your trilliumch6 folder. You'll code additional CSS style rules to configure the text and image on the page.

Launch a text editor and open the index.html file. Configure the embedded CSS as follows:

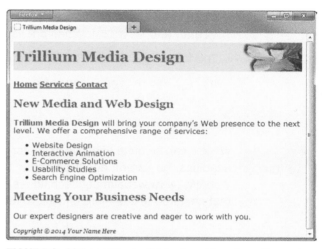

FIGURE 3 *CSS configures the text and image on the web page.*

1. Code style declarations for the h1 element selector that configure the trilliumlogo.jpg background image to display on the right without repeating:

```
background-image: url(trilliumlogo.jpg);
background-position: right;
background-repeat: no-repeat;
```

2. Add a style declaration to the h1 element selector that sets the `line-height` property to 200%. For example, `line-height: 200%;`

3. Configure the nav element selector to display text in bold font:

```
nav { font-weight bold; }
```

4. Add a style rule to the `companyname` class to display the text in bold font.

```
.companyname { color: #5c743d; font-weight: bold; }
```

5. Add style rules to the footer element selector to configure small text (use .80em) that is in italics.

```
footer { font-family: Georgia, "Times New Roman", serif;
         font-size: .80em; font-style: italic; }
```

Save your page as index.html in the trilliumch6 folder. Launch a browser and test your page. A sample solution is in the chapter6/trillium2 folder.

Align and Indent Text with CSS

HTML elements are left-aligned by default—they begin at the left margin. In this section you'll work with CSS properties to align and indent text.

The text-align Property

The CSS **text-align property** configures the alignment of text and inline elements within block elements such as headings, paragraphs, and divs. The left (default), center, right, and justify values are valid for the text-align property.

The following CSS code sample configures an h1 element to have centered text:

```
h1 { text-align: center; }
```

While it can be quite effective to center the text displayed in web page headings, be careful about centering text in paragraphs. According to WebAIM (www.webaim.org/techniques/textlayout), studies have shown that centered text is more difficult to read than left-aligned text.

The text-indent Property

The CSS **text-indent property** configures the indentation of the first line of text within an element. The value can be numeric (with a px, pt, or em unit) or a percentage. The following CSS code sample configures the first line of all paragraphs to be indented by 5 em units:

```
p { text-indent: 5em; }
```

 Hands-On Practice 3

You'll work with text-align and text-indent properties in this Hands-On Practice. You should already have the index.html file in your trilliumch6 folder. Copy the trilliumlogo.gif file from the chapter6/starters folder into your trilliumch6 folder.

Launch a text editor and open index.html. You'll code additional CSS style rules to configure the text and image on the page. When complete, your web page will look similar to the one shown in Figure 4.

FIGURE 4 *CSS has been used to indent text and center the footer.*

Configure the embedded CSS as follows:

1. Change the declarations for the background image on the h1 selector. Instead of configuring the trilliumlogo.jpg image to display on the right, configure the trilliumlogo.gif image to display one time on the left. Also configure a `text-indent` property set to 140 pixels for the h1 element selector, as follows:

    ```
    text-indent: 140px;
    ```

2. Configure the p element selector to indent the text on the first line (use the value 3em) as follows:

    ```
    p { text-indent: 3em; }
    ```

3. Add a style rule to the footer element selector to configure center alignment.

    ```
    footer { font-family: Georgia, "Times New Roman", serif;
             font-size: .80em;
             font-style: italic;
             text-align: center; }
    ```

Save your page as index.html in the trilliumch6 folder. Launch a browser and test your page. It should look similar to the one shown in Figure 4. A sample solution is in the chapter6/trillium3 folder.

FAQ Is there a way to place a comment within CSS?

Comments are ignored by browsers and can be helpful to document or annotate (in human terms) the purpose of the code. An easy way to add a comment to CSS is to type "/*" before your comment and "*/" after your comment. For example,

```
/* Configure Footer */
footer { font-size: .80em; font-style: italic; text-align: center; }
```

More CSS Basics

Width and Height with CSS

The `width` Property

The **`width` property** configures the width of an element's content in the browser viewport with either a numeric value unit (such as `100px` or `20em`) or percentage (such as `80%`, as shown in Figure 5) of the parent element. The actual width of an element displayed in the browser viewport includes the width of the element's content, padding, border, and margin—it is not the same as the value of the `width` property, which only configures the width of the element's *content*.

FIGURE 5 *The web page is set to 80% width.*

The `min-width` Property

The **`min-width` property** sets the minimum width of an element's content in the browser viewport with either a numeric value unit (such as `700px` or `20em`) or percentage (such as `75%`) of the parent element. This minimum width value can prevent content from jumping around when a browser is resized. Scrollbars appear if the browser viewport is resized below the minimum width (see Figures 6 and 7).

FIGURE 6 *As the browser is resized, the text wraps.*

FIGURE 7 *The* `min-width` *property avoids display issues.*

More CSS Basics

The max-width Property

The **max-width property** sets the maximum width of an element's content in the browser viewport with either a numeric value unit (such as 960px) or percentage (such as 90%) of the parent element. This maximum width value can reduce the possibility of text stretching across large expanses of the screen by a high-resolution monitor.

The height Property

The **height property** configures the height of an element's content in the browser viewport with either a numeric value unit (such as 900px) or percentage (such as 60%) of the parent element. Figure 8 shows a web page with an h1 area without a height or line-height property configured. Notice how part of the background image is truncated, or cut off. In Figure 9, the h1 area is configured with the height property. Notice the improved display of the background image.

FIGURE 8 *The background image is truncated.*

FIGURE 9 *The* height *property value corresponds to the height of the background image.*

 Hands-On Practice 4

You'll work with the height and width properties in this Hands-On Practice. When complete, your web page will look similar to the one shown in Figure 5.

You should already have the index.html and trilliumlogo.gif files in your trilliumch6 folder. Launch a text editor and open the index.html file.

1. Edit the embedded CSS to configure the document to take up 80% of the browser window but with a minimum width of 600px. Add the following style rules to the body element selector:

   ```
   width: 80%; min-width: 600px;
   ```

2. Add style declarations to the h1 element selector to configure height as 86px (the height of the background image) and line height as 250%.

   ```
   height: 86px; line-height: 250%;
   ```

Save your file. Launch a browser and test your page. A sample solution is in the chapter6/trillium4 folder.

More CSS Basics

The Box Model

Each element in a document is considered to be a rectangular box. As shown in Figure 10, this box consists of a content area surrounded by padding, a border, and margins. This is known as the box model.

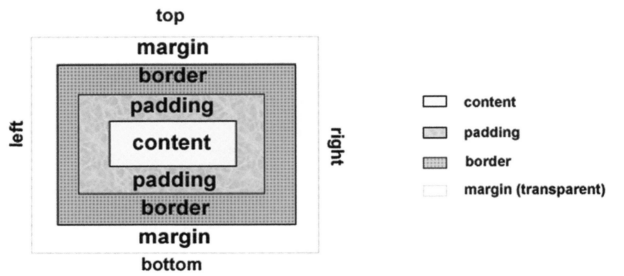

FIGURE 10 *The CSS box model.*

Content

The content area can consist of a combination of text and web page elements such as images, paragraphs, headings, lists, and so on. The visible width of the element on a web page is the total of the content width, the padding width, and the border width. However, the width property only configures the actual width of the content—not including any padding, border, or margin.

Padding

The padding area is between the content and the border. The default padding value is zero. When the background of an element is configured, the background is applied to both the padding and the content areas.

Border

The border area is between the padding and the margin. The default border has a value of 0 and does not display.

Margin

The margin determines the empty space between the element and any adjacent elements. The margin is always transparent—the background color of the web page or container element (such as a div) shows in this area. The solid line in Figure 10 that contains the margin area does not display on a web page. Browsers often have default margin values set for the web page document and for certain elements such as paragraphs, headings, forms, and so on. Use the margin property to override the default browser values.

The Box Model in Action

The web page shown in Figure 11 (student files chapter6/box.html) depicts the box model in action with an h1 and a div element.

> The h1 element is configured to have a light blue background, 20 pixels of padding (the space between the content and the border), and a black, 1-pixel border.

> The empty space where the white web page background shows through is the margin. When two vertical margins meet (such as between the h1 element and the div element), the browser collapses the margin size to be the larger of the two margin values instead of applying both margins.

> The div element has a medium-blue background, the browser default padding (which is no padding), and a black, 5-pixel border.

You will get more practice using the box model in this chapter. Feel free to experiment with the box model and the chapter6/box.html file.

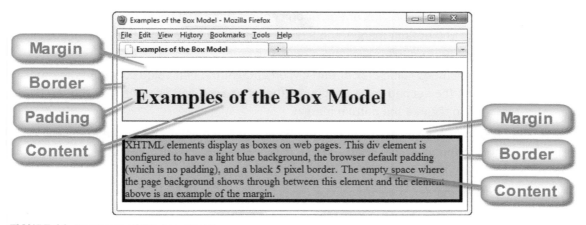

FIGURE 11 *Examples of the box model.*

Margin and Padding with CSS

The `margin` Property

Use the **`margin` property** to configure margins on all sides of an element. The margin determines the empty space between the element and any adjacent elements. The margin is always transparent—the background color of the web page or parent element shows in this area.

To configure the size of the margin, use a numeric value (px or em). To eliminate the margin, configure it to 0 (with no unit). Use the value `auto` to indicate that the browser should calculate the margin (more on this later in the chapter). You can also configure individual settings for `margin-top`, `margin-right`, `margin-bottom`, and `margin-left`. Table 2 shows CSS properties that configure margin.

TABLE 2 *Configuring* `margin` *with CSS*

Property	Description and Common Values
`margin`	Shorthand notation to configure the margin surrounding an element
	A numeric value (px or em) or percentage; for example: `margin: 10px;` if you set a value to 0, omit the unit
	The value `auto` is used to cause the browser to automatically calculate the margin for the element
	Two numeric values (px or em) or percentages; the first value configures the top margin and bottom margin, the second value configures the left margin and right margin; for example: `margin: 20px 10px;`
	Three numeric values (px or em) or percentage; the first value configures the top margin, the second value configures the left margin and right margin, and the third value configures the bottom margin
	Four numeric values (px or em) or percentages; the values configure the margins in the following order: `margin-top`, `margin-right`, `margin-bottom`, `margin-left`
`margin-bottom`	Bottom margin; a numeric value (px or em), percentage, or `auto`
`margin-left`	Left margin; a numeric value (px or em), percentage, or `auto`
`margin-right`	Right margin; a numeric value (px or em), percentage, or `auto`
`margin-top`	Top margin; a numeric value (px or em), percentage, or `auto`

The `padding` Property

The **`padding` property** configures empty space between the content of the HTML element (such as text) and the border. By default, the padding is set to 0. If you configure a background color or background image for an element, it is applied to both the padding and the content areas. See Table 3 for CSS properties that configure padding.

TABLE 3 *Configuring* `padding` *with CSS*

Property	Description and Common Values
`padding`	Shorthand notation to configure the amount of padding—the empty space between the element's content and border
	A numeric value (px or em) or percentage; for example: `padding: 10px;` if you set a value to 0, omit the unit
	Two numeric values (px or em) or percentages; the first value configures the top padding and bottom padding, the second value configures the left padding and right padding; for example: `padding: 20px 10px;`
	Three numeric values (px or em) or percentage; the first value configures the top padding, the second value configures the left padding and right padding, and the third value configures the bottom padding
	Four numeric values (px or em) or percentages; the values configure the padding in the following order: `padding-top`, `padding-right`, `padding-bottom`, `padding-left`
`padding-bottom`	Empty space between the content and bottom border; a numeric value (px or em) or percentage
`padding-left`	Empty space between the content and left border; a numeric value (px or em) or percentage
`padding-right`	Empty space between the content and right border; a numeric value (px or em) or percentage
`padding-top`	Empty space between the content and top border; a numeric value (px or em) or percentage

The web page shown in Figure 12 demonstrates use of the margin and padding properties. The example is in the student files at chapter6/box2.html.

The CSS is shown below:

```
body { background-color: #FFFFFF; }
h1   { background-color: #D1ECFF;
       padding-left: 60px; }
#box { background-color: #74C0FF;
       margin-left: 60px;
       padding: 5px 10px; }
```

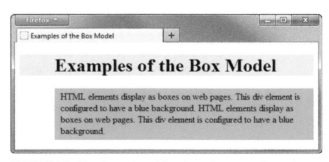

FIGURE 12 *Margin and padding have been configured.*

More CSS Basics

Borders with CSS

The **border property** configures the border, or boundary, around an element. By default, the border has a width set to 0 and does not display. See Table 4 for commonly used CSS properties that configure border.

TABLE 4 *Configuring* border *with CSS*

Property	Description and Common Values
border	Shorthand notation to configure the `border-width, border-style,` and `border-color` of an element; the values for `border-width, border-style,` and `border-color` separated by spaces; for example, `border: 1px solid #000000;`
border-bottom	Bottom border; the values for `border-width, border-style,` and `border-color` separated by spaces
border-left	Left border; the values for `border-width, border-style,` and `border-color` separated by spaces
border-right	Right border; the values for `border-width, border-style,` and `border-color` separated by spaces
border-top	Top border; the values for `border-width, border-style,` and `border-color` separated by spaces
border-width	Width of the border; a numeric pixel value (such as 1px) or the values `thin, medium, thick`
border-style	Style of the border; `none, inset, outset, double, groove, ridge, solid, dashed, dotted`
border-color	Color of the border; a valid color value

The **border-style property** offers a variety of formatting options. Be aware that these property values are not all uniformly applied by browsers. Figure 13 shows how recent versions of Firefox and Internet Explorer render various `border-style` values.

The CSS to configure the borders shown in Figure 13 uses a `border-width` of 3 pixels, `border-color` of #000033, and the value indicated for the `border-style` property. For example, the style rule to configure the dashed border is

```
.dashedborder { border-width: 3px;
                border-style: dashed;
                border-color: #000033; }
```

More CSS Basics

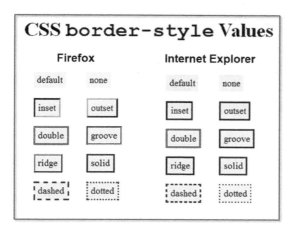

FIGURE 13 *Not all* border-style *values are rendered the same way by popular browsers.*

A shorthand notation allows you to configure all the border properties in one style rule by listing the values of border-width, border-style, and border-color. An example is

.dashedborder { border: 3px dashed #000033; }

 Hands-On Practice 5

You'll work with the border property in this Hands-On Practice. When complete, your web page will look similar to the one shown in Figure 14. You will use the box2.html file in the chapter6 folder of the student files as a starter file.

Launch a text editor and open the box2.html file. Configure the embedded CSS as follows:

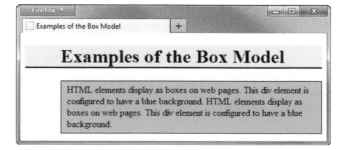

1. Configure the h1 to display a 3-pixel ridged bottom border in a dark gray color. Add the following style rule to the h1 element selector:

   border-bottom: 3px ridge #330000;

2. Configure the box id to display a 1-pixel solid black border. Add the following style rule to the #box selector:

   border: 1px solid #000000;

FIGURE 14 *The* border *property has been configured.*

3. Save your page as boxborder.html. Launch a browser and test your page. Compare your work with the sample solution at chapter6/box3.html.

More CSS Basics

CSS3 Rounded Corners

VideoNote
CSS Rounded Corners

Now that you have worked with borders and the box model, you may have begun to notice a lot of rectangles on your web pages! CSS3 introduced the **border-radius property**, which can be used to create rounded corners and soften up those rectangles. The `border-radius` property is supported by current versions of major browsers, including Internet Explorer (version 9 and later).

Valid values for the `border-radius` property include one to four numeric values (using pixel or em units) or percentages that configure the radius of the corner. If a single value is provided, it configures all four corners. If four values are provided the corners are configured in order of top left, top right, bottom right, and bottom left. You can configure corners individually with the `border-bottom-left-radius`, `border-bottom-right-radius`, `border-top-left-radius`, and `border-top-right-radius` properties.

CSS declarations to set a border with rounded corners are shown below. If you would like a visible border to display, configure the border property. Then set the value of the `border-radius` property to a value below 20px for best results.

```
border: 1px solid #000000;
border-radius: 15px;
```

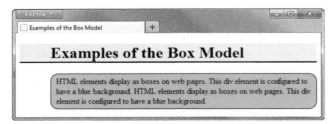

FIGURE 15 *Rounded corners were configured with CSS.*

See Figure 15 (chapter6/box4.html in the student files) for an example of this code in action.

Figure 16 (see chapter6/box5.html) shows a div element with only the top and left corners rounded. In this case, the `border-top-left-radius` and `border-bottom-left-radius` properties were used. The code follows.

```
#box { background-color: #74C0FF;
       margin-left: 60px;
       padding: 5px 20px;
       border-top-left-radius: 90px;
       border-bottom-left-radius: 90px; }
```

You can use your creativity to configure one, two, three, or four corners of an element when using `border-radius`. With progressive enhancement in mind, note that visitors to your site that are using older versions of Internet Explorer (versions 8 and

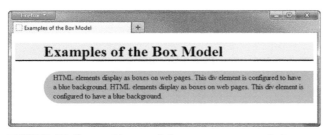

FIGURE 16 *Top and bottom left corners are rounded.*

earlier) will see only right-angle rather than rounded corners. However, the functionality and usability of the web page will not be affected. Keep in mind that another approach to getting a rounded look is to create a rounded rectangle background image with a graphics application.

 Hands-On Practice 6

You'll configure a logo header area that uses a background image and rounded borders in this Hands-On Practice.

1. Create a new folder called borderch6. Copy the lighthouselogo.jpg and background.jpg files in the chapter6/starters folder to your borderch6 folder. A starter file is ready for you in the student files. Copy the chapter6/starter1.html file into your borderch6 folder. Launch a browser to display the starter1.html web page shown in Figure 17.

2. Launch a text editor and open the starter1.html file. Save the file as index.html. Edit the embedded CSS and code an h1 element selector with style declarations that will configure the lighthouselogo.jpg image as a background image that does not repeat: height of 100px, width of 700px, font size of 3em, 150px of left padding, 30px of top padding, and a border radius of 15px. The style declarations are as follows:

FIGURE 17 *The starter1.html file.*

```
h1 { background-image: url(lighthouselogo.jpg);
     background-repeat: no-repeat;
     height: 100px; width: 700px; font-size: 3em;
     padding-left: 150px; padding-top: 30px;
     border-radius: 15px; }
```

3. Save the file. When you test your index.html file in a browser, it should look similar to the one shown in Figure 18 if you are using a browser that supports rounded corners. Otherwise the logo will have right-angle corners, but the web page will still be usable. Compare your work with the solution in the student files (chapter6/lighthouse/index.html).

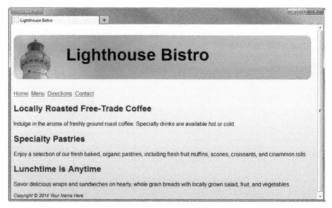

FIGURE 18 *The web page with the logo area configured.*

Center Page
Content with CSS

You learned how to center text on a web page earlier in this chapter—but what about centering the entire web page itself within the browser viewport? A popular page layout design that is easy to accomplish with just a few lines of CSS is to center the entire content of a web page within a browser viewport. The key is to configure a div element that contains or "wraps" the entire page content. The HTML is

```
<body>
<div id="wrapper">
... page content goes here ...
</div>
</body>
```

Next, configure CSS style rules for this container. Set the `width` property to an appropriate value. Set the `margin-left` and `margin-right` CSS properties to the value `auto`. This tells the browser to automatically divide the amount of space available for the left and right margins. The CSS is

```
#wrapper { width: 700px;
           margin-left: auto;
           margin-right: auto; }
```

You'll practice this technique in the next Hands-On Practice.

 Hands-On Practice 7

You'll center a web page in this Hands-On Practice. When complete, your web page will look similar to the one shown in Figure 19.

FIGURE 19 *The web page is centered with CSS.*

More CSS Basics

You should already have the index.html and trilliumlogo.gif files in your trilliumch6 folder. If not, obtain these files from the chapter6/trillium4 folder.

Launch a text editor and open the index.html file.

1. Edit the embedded CSS, and remove the `width` and `min-width` style declarations from the body selector.

2. Edit the embedded CSS, and configure a new selector, an id named `container`. Add style declarations for the `width`, `min-width`, `margin-left`, and `margin-right` properties as follows:

```
#container { margin-left: auto;
             margin-right: auto;
             width: 80%;
             min-width: 700px; }
```

3. Edit the HTML. Configure a div element assigned to the id `container` that "wraps" or contains the code within the body section. Code an opening div tag on a new line after the opening body tag. Assign the div to the id named `container`. Code the closing div tag on a new line before the closing body tag. Save the file. When you test your index.html file in a browser, it should look similar to the one shown in Figure 19. The student files contain a sample solution in the chapter6/trillium5 folder.

A common design practice is to configure the background color of the wrapper or container to be a light, neutral color that provides good contrast with text. Figure 20 (found in the student files, chapter6/lighthouse/lcenter.html) shows a web page with a background image along with centered page content (in a div assigned to the `container` id) with a neutral background. The example uses shorthand notation to set all margins for #container to the value `auto`. The padding is configured with three values setting 0 top padding, 20px left and right padding, and 10px bottom padding. The CSS is as follows:

```
#container { margin: auto;
             background-color: #ffffff;
             width: 850px;
             padding: 0 20px 10px; }
```

FIGURE 20 *The centered* #container *has a neutral background.*

CSS3 Box Shadow and Text Shadow

The CSS3 shadow properties **box-shadow** and **text-shadow** add depth and dimension to the visual display of a web page, as shown in Figure 21.

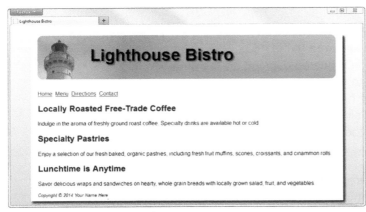

FIGURE 21 *Shadow properties add dimension.*

CSS3 `box-shadow` Property

CSS3 introduced the **box-shadow** property, which can be used to create a shadow effect on the box model. The box-shadow property is supported by current versions of major browsers, including Internet Explorer (version 9 and later). Configure a box shadow by coding values for the shadow's horizontal offset, vertical offset, blur radius (optional), spread distance (optional), and color:

- **Horizontal offset.** Use a numeric pixel value. Positive value configures a shadow on the right. Negative value configures a shadow on the left.
- **Vertical offset.** Use a numeric pixel value. Positive value configures a shadow below. Negative value configures a shadow above.
- **Blur radius (optional).** Configure a numeric pixel value. If omitted, defaults to the value 0 which configures a sharp shadow. Higher values configure more blur.
- **Spread distance (optional).** Configure a numeric pixel value. If omitted, defaults to the value 0. Positive values configure the shadow to expand. Negative values configure the shadow to contract.
- **Color value.** Configure a valid color value for the shadow.

Here's an example that configures a dark gray shadow with 5px horizontal offset, 5px vertical offset, 5px blur radius, and default spread distance:

```
box-shadow: 5px 5px 5px #828282;
```

Inner Shadow Effect. To configure an inner shadow, include the optional `inset` value. For example:

```
box-shadow: inset 5px 5px 5px #828282;
```

More CSS Basics

CSS3 `text-shadow` Property

The CSS3 **text-shadow property** is supported by current versions of modern browsers, including Internet Explorer (version 10 and later). Configure a text shadow by coding values for the shadow's horizontal offset, vertical offset, blur radius (optional), and color:

- **Horizontal offset.** Use a numeric pixel value. Positive value configures a shadow on the right. Negative value configures a shadow on the left.
- **Vertical offset.** Use a numeric pixel value. Positive value configures a shadow below. Negative value configures a shadow above.
- **Blur radius (optional).** Configure a numeric pixel value. If omitted, defaults to the value 0 which configures a sharp shadow. Higher values configure more blur.
- **Color value.** Configure a valid color value for the shadow.

Here's an example that configures a dark gray shadow with 3px horizontal offset, 3px vertical offset, and 5px blur radius.:

```
text-shadow: 3px 3px 5px #666;
```

 Hands-On Practice 8

You'll configure `text-shadow` and `box-shadow` in this Hands-On Practice. When complete, your web page will look similar to the one shown in Figure 21. Create a new folder called shadowch6. Copy the lighthouselogo.jpg and the background.jpg files from the chapter6/starters folder to your shadowch6 folder. Launch a text editor and open the chapter6/lighthouse/lcenter.html file (shown in Figure 20). Save the file in your shadowch6 folder with the name index.html.

1. Edit the embedded CSS and add the following style declarations to the `#container` selector to configure a box shadow:

   ```
   box-shadow: 5px 5px 5px #1e1e1e;
   ```

2. Add the following style declaration to the h1 element selector to configure a dark gray text shadow:

   ```
   text-shadow: 3px 3px 3px #666;
   ```

3. Add the following style declaration to the h2 element selector to configure a light gray text shadow with no blur: `text-shadow: 1px 1px 0 #ccc;`

4. Save the file. When you test your index.html file in a browser, it should look similar to the one shown in Figure 21 if you are using a browser that supports the `box-shadow` and `text-shadow` properties. Otherwise the shadows will not display, but the web page will still be usable. See the student files for a solution (chapter6/lighthouse/shadow.html).

 Browser support changes with each new browser version. There is no substitute for thoroughly testing your web pages. However, several resources are available with support lists: www.findmebyip.com/litmus, www.quirksmode.org/css/contents.html, and www.browsersupport.net/CSS.

CSS3 Background Clip and Origin

You're already familiar with how to configure a background image on a web page. This section introduces two CSS3 properties related to background images that provide you with options for clipping and sizing background images: `background-clip` and `background-origin`. As you work with these properties, keep in mind that block display elements such as div, header, and paragraph elements are rendered by the browser using the box model (refer to Figure 10), which surrounds the content of an element with padding, border, and margin.

CSS3 `background-clip` Property

The **`background-clip` property** confines the display of the background image with the following values:

- `content-box` clips off the image's display to fit the area behind the content
- `padding-box` clips off the image's display to fit the area behind the content and padding
- `border-box` (default) clips off the image's display to fit the area behind the content, padding, and border

The `background-clip` property is supported by current versions of modern browsers, including Internet Explorer 9. Figure 22 shows div elements configured with different values

FIGURE 22 The CSS3 `background-clip` property.

More CSS Basics

136

of the `background-clip` property. Note that the dashed border is intentionally large in these examples. The sample page is located in the student files (chapter6/clip folder). The CSS for the first div follows:

```
.test { background-image: url(myislandback.jpg);
       background-clip: content-box;
       width: 400px; padding: 20px; margin-bottom: 10px;
       border: 10px dashed #000; }
```

CSS3 `background-origin` Property

The CSS3 **`background-origin` property** positions the background image using the following values:

- ▶ `content-box` positions relative to the content area
- ▶ `padding-box` (default) positions relative to the padding area
- ▶ `border-box` positions relative to the border area

The `background-origin` property is supported by current versions of modern browsers, including Internet Explorer 9. Figure 23 shows div elements configured with different values of the `background-origin` property. The sample page is located in the student files (chapter6/origin folder). The CSS for the first div follows:

```
.test { background-image: url(trilliumsolo.jpg);
       background-origin: content-box;
       background-repeat: no-repeat; background-position: right top;
       width: 200px; padding: 20px; margin-bottom: 10px;
       border: 1px solid #000; }
```

You may have noticed that it's common to use several CSS properties when configuring background images. These properties typically work together. However, be aware that the `background-origin` property has no effect if the `background-attachment` property is set to the value `fixed`.

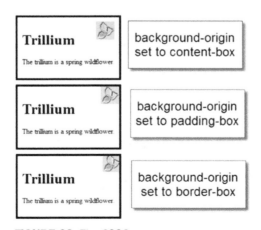

FIGURE 23 *The CSS3* `background-origin` *property.*

CSS3 Background Resize and Scale

The CSS3 **background-size** property can be used to resize or scale the background image. The background-size property is supported by current versions of modern browsers, including Internet Explorer 9. Valid values for the background-size property can be:

▶ a pair of percentage values (width, height)

If only one percentage value is provided, the second value defaults to auto and is determined by the browser.

▶ a pair of pixel values (width, height)

If only one numeric value is provided, the second value defaults to auto and is determined by the browser.

▶ cover

The value cover will preserve the aspect ratio of the image as it scales the background image to the *smallest* size for which both the height and width of the image can completely cover the area.

▶ contain

The value contain will preserve the aspect ratio of the image as it scales the background image to the *largest* size for which both the height and width of the image will fit within the area.

Figure 24 shows two div elements that are each configured with the same background image to display without repeating.

FIGURE 24 *The CSS3* background-size *property set to 100% 100%.*

The background image of the first div element is not configured with the `background-size` property and the image only partially fills the space. The CSS for the second div configures the `background-size` to be 100% 100% so the browser scales and resizes the background image to fill the space. The sample page is located in the student files (chapter6/size/sedona.html). The CSS for the second div follows:

```
#test1 {  background-image: url(sedonabackground.jpg);
          background-repeat: no-repeat;
          background-size: 100% 100%;  }
```

Figure 25 demonstrates use of the `cover` and `contain` values to configure the display of a 500×500 background image within a 200 pixel wide area on a web page. The web page on the left uses `background-size: cover;` to scale and resize the image to completely cover the area while keeping the aspect ratio of the image intact. The web page on the right uses `background-size: contain;` to scale and resize the image so that both the height and width of the image will fit within the area. Review the sample pages in the student files (chapter6/size/cover.html and chapter6/size/contain.html).

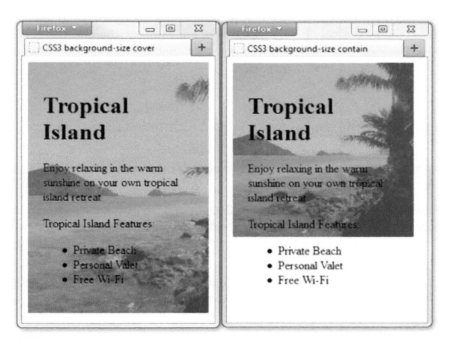

FIGURE 25 *Examples of* `background-size: cover;` *and* `background-size: contain;`

CSS3 Opacity

The CSS3 **opacity property** configures the transparency of an element. The opacity property is supported by current versions of major browsers, including Internet Explorer (version 9 and later). Opacity values range from 0 (which is completely transparent) to 1 (which is completely opaque and has no transparency). An important consideration when using the opacity property is that this property applies to both the text and the background. If you configure a semi-transparent opacity value for an element with the opacity property, both the background and the text displayed will be semi-transparent. See Figure 26 for an example of using the opacity property to configure an h1 element that is 60% opaque.

If you look very closely at Figure 26 or view the actual web page (student files chapter6/opacity/index.html), you'll see that both the white background and the black text in the h1 element are semi-transparent. The opacity property was applied to both the background color and to the text color.

FIGURE 26 *The background and text of the h1 area is transparent.*

Hands-On Practice 9

In this Hands-On Practice you'll work with the opacity property as you configure the web page shown in Figure 26.

1. Create a new folder called opacitych6. Copy fall.jpg file from the chapter6/starters folder to your opacitych6 folder. Launch a text editor and open the chapter1/template.html file. Save it in your opacitych6 folder with the name index.html. Change the page title to "Fall Nature Hikes".

2. Let's create the structure of the web page with a div that contains an h1 element. Add the following code to your web page in the body section:

```
<div id="content">
<h1>Fall Nature Hikes</h1>
</div>
```

3. Now, add style tags to the head section and configure the embedded CSS. You'll create an id named content to display the fall.jpg as a background image that does not repeat. The content id also has a width of 640 pixels, a height of 480 pixels,

More CSS Basics

auto margins (which will center the object horizontally in the browser viewport), and 20 pixels of top padding. The code is

```
#content { background-image: url(fall.jpg);
           background-repeat: no-repeat;
           margin: auto;
           width: 640px;
           height: 480px;
           padding-top: 20px; }
```

4. Now configure the h1 selector to have a white background color, opacity set to .6, font size set to 4em, 10 pixels of padding, and a 40-pixel left margin. Sample code is

```
h1 { background-color: #FFFFFF;
     opacity: 0.6;
     font-size: 4em;
     padding: 10px;
     margin-left: 40px; }
```

5. Save the file. When you test your index.html file in a browser that supports opacity (such as Chrome, Firefox, Safari, or Internet Explorer 9), it should look similar to the page shown in Figure 26. See the student files for a solution (chapter6/opacity/index.html).

6. Figure 27 shows the web page displayed in Internet Explorer 8, which does not support the `opacity` property. Notice that the visual aesthetic is not exactly the same, but the page is still usable. While Internet Explorer 9 supports opacity, earlier versions support the proprietary `filter` property with an opacity level configured between 1 (transparent) and 100 (opaque). A sample is found in the student files (chapter6/opacity/opacityie.html). The CSS for the IE-proprietary `filter` property is

```
filter: alpha(opacity=60);
```

FIGURE 27 *Internet Explorer 8 does not support the* opacity *property and displays an opaque background color.*

CSS3 RGBA Color

CSS3 supports new syntax for the color property that configures transparent color, called **RGBA color**. RGBA color is supported by current versions of major browsers, including Internet Explorer (version 9 and later). Four values are required: red, green, blue, and alpha (transparency). RGBA color does not use hexadecimal color values. Instead, decimal color values are configured—see the partial color chart in Figure 28 and the Web Safe Color Palette on the companion website for examples.

#FFFFFF
rgb (255, 255, 255)
	#FFFFCC
	rgb(255, 255, 204)
		#FFFF99
		rgb(255,255,153)
			#FFFF66
			rgb(255,255,102)

#FFFF33
rgb(255,255,51)
	#FFFF00
	rgb(255,255,0)
		#FFCCFF
		rgb(255, 204, 255)
			#FFCCCC
			rgb(255,204,204)

#FFCC99
rgb(255,204,153)
	#FFCC66
	rgb(255,204,102)
		#FFCC33
		rgb(255,204,51)
			#FFCC00
			rgb(255,204,0)

#FF99FF
rgb(255,153,255)
	#FF99CC
	rgb(255,153,204)
		#FF9999
		rgb(255,153,153)
			#FF9966
			rgb(255,153,102)

FIGURE 28 *Hexadecimal and RGB decimal color values.*

To configure RGBA color, the values for red, green, and blue must be decimal values from 0 to 255. The alpha value must be a number from 0 (transparent) to 1 (opaque). Figure 29 shows a web page with the text configured to be slightly transparent with RGBA color syntax.

How is using RGBA color different from using the opacity property?

The `opacity` property applies to both the background and the text within an element. If you'd like to specifically configure a semi-transparent background color, code the `background-color` h RGBA color or HSLA color (described in the next section) values. If you'd like to specifically ni-transparent text, code the `color` property with RGBA color or HSLA color values.

In this Hands-On Practice you'll configure white text with transparency as you configure the web page shown in Figure 29.

1. Launch a text editor and open the file you created in the previous Hands-On Practice (also located in the student files, chapter6/opacity/index.html). Save the file with the name rgba.html.

2. Delete the current style declarations for the h1 selector. You will create new style rules for the h1 selector to configure 10 pixels of right padding and right-aligned sans-serif white text that is 80% opaque with a font size of 5em. Since not all browsers support RBGA color, you'll configure the color property twice. The first instance will be the standard color value that is supported by all modern browsers; the second instance will configure the

FIGURE 29 *CSS3 RGBA color configures the transparent text.*

RGBA color. Older browsers will not understand the RGBA color and will ignore it. Newer browsers will "see" both of the color style declarations and will apply them in the order they are coded, so the result will be transparent color. The CSS for the h1 selector is

```
h1 { color: #ffffff;
     color: rgba(255, 255, 255, 0.8);
     font-family: Verdana, Helvetica, sans-serif;
     font-size: 5em;
     padding-right: 10px;
     text-align: right; }
```

3. Save the file. When you test your rgba.html file in a browser that supports RGBA color (such as Chrome, Firefox, Safari, or Internet Explorer 9), it should look similar to the page shown in Figure 29. See the student files for a solution (chapter6/opacity/rgba.html). If you are using a nonsupporting browser such as Internet Explorer 8 (or earlier), you'll see white text instead of transparent text. While Internet Explorer 9 supports RGBA color, earlier versions support the proprietary `filter` property; an example is in the student files (chapter6/opacity/rbgaie.html).

CSS3 HSLA Color

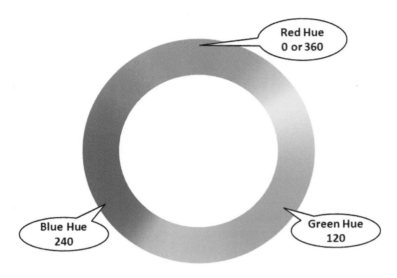

Red Hue
0 or 360

Blue Hue
240

Green Hue
120

FIGURE 30 *A color wheel.*

For many years web designers have configured RGB color using either hexadecimal or decimal values on web pages. Recall that RGB color is based on hardware—the red, green, and blue light that is emitted by computer monitors. CSS3 introduced a new color notation system called HSLA color, based on a color wheel model, which stands for hue, saturation, lightness, and alpha. HSLA color is supported in the most recent versions of all major browsers, including Internet Explorer 9.

Hue, Saturation, Lightness, and Alpha

When you work with HSLA color, think of a color wheel—a circle of color—with the color red at the top of the wheel as shown in Figure 30. **Hue** is the actual color which is represented by numeric values ranging from 0 to 360 (like the 360 degrees in a circle). For example, red is represented by both the values 0 and 360, green is represented by 120, and blue is represented by 240. Set hue to 0 when configuring black, gray, and white. **Saturation** configures the intensity of the color and is indicated by a percentage value (full color saturation= 100%, gray=0%). **Lightness** determines the brightness or darkness of the color and is indicated by a percentage value (normal color=50%, white=100%, black=0%). **Alpha** represents the transparency of the color and has a value from 0 (transparent) to 1 (opaque). Note that you can omit the alpha value and use the `hsl` keyword instead of the `hsla` keyword.

Red
hsla(360, 100%, 50%, 1.0);

Green
hsla(120, 100%, 50%, 1.0);

Blue
hsla(240, 100%, 50%, 1.0);

Black
hsla(0, 0%, 0%, 1.0);

Gray
hsla(0, 0%, 50%, 1.0);

White
hsla(0, 0%, 100%, 1.0);

FIGURE 31 *HSLA color examples.*

HSLA Color Examples

Configure HSLA color as shown in Figure 31 with the following syntax:

`hsla(`*hue value, saturation value, lightness value, alpha value*`)` ;

- Red: `hsla(360, 100%, 50%, 1.0);`
- Green: `hsla(120, 100%, 50%, 1.0);`
- Blue: `hsla(240, 100%, 50%, 1.0);`
- Black: `hsla(0, 0%, 0%, 1.0);`
- Gray: `hsla(0, 0%, 50%, 1.0);`
- White: `hsla(0, 0%, 100%, 1.0);`

According to the W3C, an advantage to using HSLA color is that it is more intuitive to work with than the hardware-oriented RGB color. You can use a color wheel model (remember your art classes in grade

More CSS Basics

school) to choose colors and generate the hue value from the degree placement on the circle. If you'd like to use a tone of a color, which is a color with gray added, vary the saturation value. If you'd like to use a shade or tint of a color, use the same hue value, but vary the lightness value to meet your needs. Figure 32 shows three shades of cyan blue configured using three different values for lightness: 25% (dark cyan blue), 50% (cyan blue), 75% (light cyan blue).

FIGURE 32 *Shades of cyan blue.*

▶ Dark Cyan Blue:
```
hsla(210, 100%, 25%, 1.0);
```
▶ Cyan Blue:
```
hsla(210, 100%, 50%, 1.0);
```
▶ Light Cyan Blue:
```
hsla(210, 100%, 75%, 1.0);
```

 Hands-On Practice 11

In this Hands-On Practice you'll configure light yellow transparent text as you configure the web page shown in Figure 33.

1. Launch a text editor and open the file you created in the previous Hands-On Practice (also located in the student files, chapter6/opacity/rgba.html). Save the file with the name hsla.html.

2. Delete the style declarations for the h1 selector. You will create new style rules for the h1 selector to configure 20 pixels of padding and serif light yellow text with a 0.8 alpha

FIGURE 33 *HSLA color.*

value and a font size of 6em. Since not all browsers support HSLA color, you'll configure the color property twice. The first instance will be the standard color value that is supported by all modern browsers; the second instance will configure the HSLA color. Older browsers will not understand the HSLA color and will ignore it. Newer browsers will "see" both of the color style declarations and will apply them in the order they are coded, so the result will be transparent color. The CSS for the h1 selector is

```
h1 { color: #ffcccc;
     color: hsla(60, 100%, 90%, 0.8);
     font-family: Georgia, "Times New Roman", serif;
     font-size: 6em;
     padding: 20px; }
```

3. Save the file. When you test your hsla.html file in a browser that supports HSLA color (such as Chrome, Firefox, Safari, or Internet Explorer 9), it should look similar to the page shown in Figure 33. See the student files for a solution (chapter6/opacity/hsla.html). If you are using a nonsupporting browser such as Internet Explorer 8 (or earlier), you'll see solid text instead of transparent text.

CSS3 Gradients

CSS3 provides a method to configure color as a **gradient**, which is a smooth blending of shades from one color to another color. A CSS3 gradient background color is defined purely with CSS—No image file is needed! This provides flexibility for web designers along with a savings in the bandwidth required to transfer gradient background image files.

The W3C has finalized gradients in the CSS Image Values and Replaced Content Module, but at the time this was written, this final syntax had not yet been adopted by all browsers. This section will provide an example of configuring a CSS3 linear gradient along with links to resources for further study.

Figure 21 displays a web page with a JPG gradient background image that was configured in a graphics application. The web page shown in Figure 34 (available at chapter6/lighthouse/gradient.html in the student files) does not use a JPG for the background—CSS3 gradient properties recreated the look of the linear gradient image.

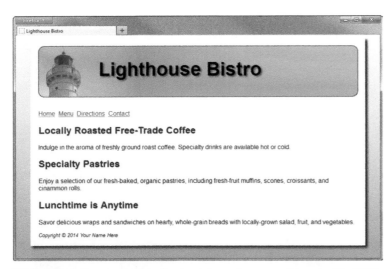

FIGURE 34 *The gradient in the background was configured with CSS3 without an image file.*

W3C Linear Gradient Syntax

To configure a basic linear gradient, code the `linear-gradient` function as the value of the `background-image` property. Indicate the direction of the gradient by coding the keyword phrase "to bottom", "to top", "to left" or "to right". Next, list the starting color and the ending color. The basic format for a two-color linear gradient that blends from white to green follows:

```
background-image: linear-gradient(to bottom, #FFFFFF, #00FF00);
```

CSS3 Gradients and Progressive Enhancement

It's very important to keep progressive enhancement in mind when using CSS3 gradients. Configure a "fallback" `background-color` property or `background-image` property, which will be rendered by browsers that do not support CSS3 gradients. In Figure 34 the background color was configured to be the same value as the ending gradient color.

More CSS Basics

Configuring CSS3 Gradients

Often when new CSS coding techniques are proposed by the W3C, browser vendors append an experimental browser-specific prefix (such as -webkit) to the beginning of the property or function and then later add support for the actual W3C property or function. The syntax for CSS3 gradients changed while it was in draft status. At the time this was written, Firefox was the only browser that supported the current W3C syntax. The other browsers still support an earlier version of the syntax. So, until browser support improves, code multiple style declarations for the background-image property to configure a gradient background:

◗ -webkit-linear-gradient (for Webkit browsers)

◗ -ms-linear-gradient (for Internet Explorer version 10)

◗ -o-linear-gradient (for Presto browsers)

◗ filter (for Internet Explorer version 9 and below, which uses the proprietary filter property instead of the linear-gradient function)

◗ linear-gradient (W3C syntax)

Configure the linear gradient function as the value of the background-image property. The following CSS code first configures a background color (for nonsupporting browsers) and then configures a linear gradient background that blends from white (#FFFFFF) to a medium blue (#8FA5CE):

```
body { background-color: #8FA5CE;
       background-image: -webkit-linear-gradient(#FFFFFF, #8FA5CE);
       background-image: -ms-linear-gradient(#FFFFFF, #8FA5CE);
       background-image: -o-linear-gradient(#FFFFFF, #8FA5CE);
       filter: progid:DXImageTransform.Microsoft.gradient
               (startColorstr=#FFFFFFFF, endColorstr=#FF8FA5CE);
       background-image: linear-gradient(to bottom, #FFFFFF, #8FA5CE); }
```

Since eventually all browsers will drop the browser prefixes and will support the W3C syntax, the linear-gradient declaration is coded last. The browser proprietary CSS syntax in this section is nonstandard. Your CSS code will not pass W3C validation when you use these properties. For more information on the syntax described above, visit the corresponding websites:

◗ **Webkit** (Chrome and Safari): http://webkit.org/blog/175/introducing-css-gradients

◗ **Gecko** (Mozilla): http://developer.mozilla.org/en/CSS/-moz-linear-gradient

◗ **Internet Explorer:** http://msdn.microsoft.com/en-us/library/ms532997

◗ **W3C:** http://dev.w3.org/csswg/css3-images/#gradients

Visit the following resources to delve deeper into CSS3 gradients:

◗ http://css-tricks.com/css3-gradients

◗ https://developer.mozilla.org/en/Using_gradients

◗ http://net.tutsplus.com/tutorials/html-css-techniques/quick-tip-understanding-css3-gradients

Experiment with generating CSS3 gradient code at www.colorzilla.com/gradient-editor, http://gradients.glrzad.com, and www.westciv.com/tools/gradients.

Review and Apply

Review Questions

1. Which CSS property will configure the font typeface?

   a. font-face   **b.** face

   c. font-family   **d.** size

2. Which CSS property will configure bold text?

   a. font-face   **b.** font-style

   c. font-weight   **d.** font-size

3. Which CSS property will configure italic text?

   a. font-face   **b.** font-style

   c. font-weight   **d.** font-size

4. Which configures a class called news with red text, large font, and Arial or a sans-serif font using CSS?

   a. news { color: red;
        font-size: large;
        font-family: Arial,
        sans-serif;}

   b. .news { color: red;
        font-size: large;
        font-family: Arial,
        sans-serif;}

   c. .news { text: red;
        font-size: large;
        font-family: Arial,
        sans-serif;}

   d. #news { text: red;
        font-size: large;
        font-family: Arial,
        sans-serif;}

5. Which of the following, from outermost to innermost, are components of the box model?

   a. margin, border, padding, content

   b. content, padding, border, margin

   c. content, margin, padding, border

   d. margin, padding, border, content

6. Which of the following is the CSS property that configures a drop shadow effect on text?

   a. box-shadow   **b.** text-shadow

   c. drop-shadow   **d.** shadow

7. Which of the following will configure padding that is 15 pixels on the top, 0 pixels on the left and right, and 5 pixels on the bottom?

   a. padding: 0px 5px 0px 15px;

   b. padding: top-15, left-0, right-0, bottom-5;

   c. padding: 15px 0 5px 0;

   d. padding: 0 0 15px 5px;

8. Which of the following is used along with the width property to configure centered page content?

   a. margin-left: auto;
   margin-right: auto

   b. margin: top-15, left-0, right-0, bottom-5;

   c. margin: 15px 0 5px 0;

   d. margin: 20px;

9. Which CSS property will center text within an element?

   a. center   **b.** text-align

   c. align   **d.** text-center

10. Which of the following will configure a border that is 5 pixels wide, the color #330000, and a solid line?

    a. border: 5px solid #330000;

    b. border-style: solid 5px;

    c. border: 5px, solid, #330000;

    d. border: 5px line #330000;

Hands-On Exercises

1. Write the CSS code for an external style sheet file named mystyle.css that configures the text to be brown, 1.2 em in size, and in Arial, Verdana, or a sans-serif font.

2. Write the HTML and CSS code for an embedded style sheet that configures a class called new, which has bold and italic text.

3. Write the CSS for a class named footer with the following characteristics: a light-blue background color, Arial or sans-serif font, dark-blue text color, 10 pixels of padding, and a narrow, dashed border in a dark-blue color.

4. Write the CSS for an id named notice that is configured with width set to 80% and centered.

5. Write the CSS to configure a class that will produce a headline with a dotted line underneath it. Choose a color that you like for the text and dotted line.

6. Write the CSS to configure an h1 selector with drop shadow text, a 50% transparent background color, and sans-serif font that is 4em in size.

7. Write the CSS to configure an id named section with small, red, Arial font, a white background, a width of 80%, and a drop shadow.

Focus on Web Design

This chapter expanded your capabilities to use CSS to configure web pages. Use a search engine to search for CSS resources. The following resources can help you get started:

- www.w3.org/Style/CSS
- www.noupe.com/design/40-css-reference-websites-and-resources.html
- www.css3.info

Create a web page that provides a list of at least five CSS resources on the Web. For each CSS resource provide the URL, website name, and a brief description. Your web page content should take up 80% of the browser viewport and be centered. Use at least five CSS properties from this chapter to configure the color and text. Place your name in the e-mail address at the bottom of the web page.

More CSS Basics

Answers to Review Questions

1. c	**2.** c	**3.** b
4. b	**5.** a	**6.** b
7. c	**8.** a	**9.** b
10. a		

Credits

Figure 10 © Terry Ann Morris, Ed.D. Reprinted with permission.

Figures 2–9, 11, 12, 14, 15–23, 29, 33, 34, 36–40 © Terry Ann Morris, Ed.D. | Mozilla Foundation

Figure 30 color wheel © Ken Perkins. Reprinted with permission

Page Layout Basics

We'll add to your toolbox of CSS page layout techniques in this chapter. You'll explore floating and positioning elements with CSS. You'll be introduced to a technique for configuring images called CSS sprites. You will also learn to use CSS to add interactivity to hyperlinks with pseudo-classes.

You'll learn how to...

- Configure float with CSS
- Configure fixed positioning with CSS
- Configure relative positioning with CSS
- Configure absolute positioning with CSS
- Create two-column page layouts with CSS
- Configure navigation in unordered lists and style with CSS
- Add interactivity to hyperlinks with CSS pseudo-classes
- Configure CSS sprites

From Chapter 7 of *Basics of Web Design HTML5 & CSS3*, Second Edition. Terry Ann Felke-Morris. Copyright © 2014 by Pearson Education, Inc. All rights reserved.

Normal Flow

Browsers render your web page code line by line in the order it appears in the .html document. This processing is called normal flow. **Normal flow** displays the elements on the page in the order they appear in the web page source code.

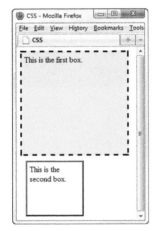

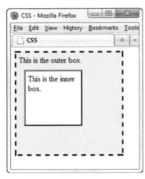

Figures 1 and 2 each display two div elements that contain text content. Let's take a closer look. Figure 1 shows a screenshot of two div elements placed one after another on a web page. In Figure 2 the boxes are nested inside each other. In both cases, the browser used normal flow (the default) and displayed the elements in the order in which they appeared in the source code. You can create web pages that the browser renders using normal flow.

You'll practice normal flow in the next Hands-On Practice. Then, later in the chapter, you'll experiment with CSS positioning and float to configure the flow, or placement, of elements on a web page.

FIGURE 1 *The div elements.*

FIGURE 2 *Nested elements.*

Hands-On Practice 1

You will explore the box model and normal flow in this Hands-On Practice as you work with the web pages shown in Figures 1 and 2.

Practice with Normal Flow

Launch a text editor and open the chapter7/starter1.html file from the student files on the companion website at www.pearsonhighered.com/felke-morris. Save the file with the name box1.html. Add the following code in the body of the web page to configure the two div elements:

```
<div class="div1">
This is the first box.
</div>
<div class="div2">
This is the second box.
</div>
```

Page Layout Basics

Now let's add embedded CSS in the head section to configure the "boxes." Add a new style rule for a class named `div1` to configure a light blue background, dashed border, width of 200 pixels, height of 200 pixels, and 5 pixels of padding. The code is

```
.div1 { width: 200px;
        height: 200px;
        background-color: #D1ECFF;
        border: 3px dashed #000000;
        padding: 5px; }
```

Create a style rule for a class named `div2` to configure a width and height of 100 pixels, white background color, ridged border, 10 pixel margin, and 5 pixels of padding. The code is

```
.div2 { width: 100px;
        height: 100px;
        background-color: #ffffff;
        border: 3px ridge #000000;
        padding: 5px;
        margin: 10px; }
```

Save the file. Launch a browser and test your page. It should look similar to the one shown in Figure 1. The student files contain a sample solution at chapter7/box1.html.

Practice with Normal Flow and Nested Elements

Launch a text editor and open the box1.html file from the student files (chapter7/box1.html). Save the file with the name box2.html. Delete the content from the body section of the web page. Add the following code to configure two div elements—one nested inside the other:

```
<div class="div1">
This is the outer box.
  <div class="div2">
  This is the inner box.
  </div>
</div>
```

Save the file. Launch a browser and test your page. It should look similar to the one shown in Figure 2. Notice how the browser renders the nested div elements—the second box is nested within the first box because it is coded inside the first div element in the web page source code. This is an example of normal flow. The student files contain a sample solution at chapter7/box2.html.

A Look Ahead—CSS Layout Properties

You've seen how normal flow causes the browser to render the elements in the order that they appear in the HTML source code. When using CSS for page layout there are situations in which you will want to specify the location of an element on the page—either the absolute pixel location, the location relative to where the element would normally display, or floating on the page. The CSS properties that configure the placement of elements on a web page are introduced in this chapter.

Float

The `float` Property

Elements that seem to float on the right or left side of either the browser window or another element are often configured using the `float` property. The browser renders these elements using normal flow and then shifts them to either the right or left as far as possible within their container (usually either the browser viewport or a div element).

- Use `float: right;` to float the element on the right side of the container.
- Use `float: left;` to float the element on the left side of the container.
- Specify a width for a floated element unless the element already has an implicit width—such as an img element.
- Other elements and web page content will flow around the floated element.

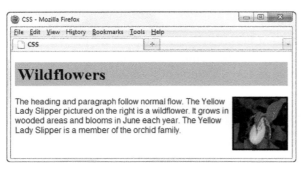

FIGURE 3 *The image is configured to float.*

Figure 3 shows a web page with an image configured with `float: right;` to float on the right side of the browser viewport (see the student files, chapter7/float.html). When floating an image, the `margin` property is useful to configure empty space between the image and text on the page.

View Figure 3 and notice how the image stays on the right side of the browser viewport. An id called `yls` was created that applies the `float`, `margin`, and `border` properties. The attribute `id="yls"` was placed on the image tag. The CSS is

```
h1 { background-color: #A8C682;
     padding: 5px;
     color: #000000; }
p { font-family: Arial, sans-serif; }
#yls { float: right;
       margin: 0 0 5px 5px;
       border: 1px solid #000000; }
```

The HTML source code is

```
<h1>Wildflowers</h1>
<img id="yls" src="yls.jpg" alt="Yellow Lady Slipper" height="100"
width="100">
<p>The heading and paragraph follow normal flow. The Yellow Lady
Slipper pictured on the right is a wildflower. It grows in wooded
areas and blooms in June each year. The Yellow Lady Slipper is
a member of the orchid family.</p>
```

Page Layout Basics

In this Hands-On Practice you'll practice using the CSS `float` property as you configure the web page shown in Figure 4.

Create a folder named ch7float. Copy the files starter2.html and yls.jpg from the chapter7 folder in the student files into your ch7float folder. Launch a text editor and open the starter2.html file. Notice the order of the images and paragraphs. Notice that there is no CSS to float the image. Display starter2.html in a browser. The browser renders the page using normal flow and displays the elements in the order they are coded.

Let's add CSS to float the image. Save the file with the name floatyls.html. With floatyls.html open in a text editor, modify the code as follows:

1. Add a style rule for a class named `float` that configures float, margin, and border properties:

```
.float { float: left;
         margin-right: 10px;
         border: 3px ridge #000000; }
```

2. Assign the image element to the class named `float` (use `class="float"`).

Save the file. Launch a browser and test your page. It should look similar to the web page shown in Figure 4. The student files contain a sample solution at chapter7/floatyls.html.

The Floated Element and Normal Flow

Take a moment to examine your file in a browser (see Figure 4) and consider how the browser rendered the page. The div element is configured with a light background color to demonstrate how floated elements are rendered outside of normal flow. Observe that the floated image and the first paragraph are contained within the div element. The h2 element follows the div. If all the elements were rendered using normal flow, the area with the light background color would contain both the child elements of the div: the image and the first paragraph. In addition, the h2 element would be placed on its own line under the div element.

However, once the image is placed vertically on the page, it is floated *outside of normal flow*—that's why the light background color only appears behind the first paragraph and why the h2 element's text begins immediately after the first paragraph and appears next to the floated image.

FIGURE 4 *The CSS* `float` *property left-aligns the image.*

Clear a Float

The `clear` Property

The `clear` property is often used to terminate, or "clear," a float. You can set the value of the `clear` property to `left`, `right`, or `both`—depending on the type of float you need to clear.

Review Figure 5 and the code sample in the student files at chapter7/floatyls.html. Notice that although the div element contains both an image and the first paragraph, the light background color of the div only displays behind the screen area occupied by the first paragraph—it stops a bit earlier than expected. Clearing the float will help take care of this display issue.

FIGURE 5 *The float needs to be cleared to improve the display.*

Clearing a Float with a Line Break

A common technique to clear a float within a container element is to add a line break element configured with the `clear` property. See the example in the student files at chapter7/floatylsclear1.html.

Observe that a CSS class is configured to clear the left float:

```
.clearleft { clear: left; }
```

Also, a line break tag assigned to the `clearleft` class is coded before the closing `</div>` tag. The code snippet for the div element is

```
<div>
<img class="float" src="yls.jpg" alt="Yellow Lady Slipper"
height="100" width="100">
<p>The Yellow Lady Slipper grows in wooded areas and blooms in June
each year. The flower is a member of the orchid family.</p>
<br class="clearleft">
</div>
```

Figure 6 displays a screen shot of this page. Note that the light background color of the div element extends farther down the page and the h2 element's text begins on its own line under the image.

FIGURE 6 *The* `clear` *property is applied to a line break tag.*

If you are not concerned about the light background color display, another option is to omit the line break tag and instead apply the `clearleft` class to the h2 element. This does not change the display of the light background color, but it does force the h2 element's text to begin on its own line, as shown in Figure 7 (see the student files at chapter7/floatylsclear2.html).

FIGURE 7 *The* `clear` *property is applied to the h2 element.*

Overflow

The `overflow` Property

The `overflow` property is often used to clear a float, although its intended purpose is to configure how content should display if it is too large for the area allocated. See Table 1 for a list of commonly used values for the `overflow` property.

TABLE 1 *The `overflow` Property*

Value	Purpose
visible	Default value; the content is displayed, and if it's too large, the content will "overflow" outside the area allocated to it
hidden	The content is clipped to fit the room allocated to the element in the browser viewport
auto	The content fills the area allocated to it and, if needed, scroll bars are displayed to allow access to the remaining content
scroll	The content is rendered in the area allocated to it and scroll bars are displayed

Clearing a Float with the `overflow` Property

Review Figure 8 and the code sample in the student files at chapter7/floatyls.html. Observe the div element, which contains the floated image and first paragraph on the page. Notice that although the div element contains both an image and the first paragraph, the div element's light background color does not extend as far as expected; it is only visible in the area occupied by the first paragraph. You can use the `overflow` property assigned to the container element to resolve this display issue and clear the float. In this case we'll apply the `overflow` and `width` properties to the div element selector. The CSS to configure the div in this manner is

```
div { background-color: #F3F1BF;
      overflow: auto;
      width: 100%; }
```

This CSS is all that is needed to be added to the code to clear the float and cause the web page to display similar to Figure 9 (see the student files at chapter7/floatylsoverflow.html).

FIGURE 8 *The display can be improved by clearing the float with overflow.*

Page Layout Basics

The `clear` Property Versus the `overflow` Property

Notice that Figure 9 (using the `overflow` property) and Figure 6 (applying the `clear` property to a line break tag) result in a similar web page display. You may be wondering about which CSS property (`clear` or `overflow`) is the best to use when you need to clear a float.

Although the `clear` property is widely used, in this example it is more efficient to apply the `overflow` property to the container element (for example, a div element). This will clear the float, avoid adding an extra line break tag, and ensure that the container element expands to enclose the entire floated element. Floating elements is a key technique in designing multicolumn page layouts with CSS.

FIGURE 9 *The `overflow` property is applied to the div element selector.*

Configuring Scrollbars with the `overflow` Property

The web page in Figure 10 demonstrates the use of `overflow: auto;` to automatically display scroll bars if the content exceeds the space allocated to it. In this case, the div that contains the paragraph and the floated image was configured with a width of 300px and a height of 100px. See the example web page in the student files at chapter7/floatylsscroll.html. The CSS for the div is shown below:

```
div { background-color: #F3F1BF;
      overflow: scroll;
      width: 300px;
      height: 100px;
}
```

FIGURE 10 *The browser displays scrollbars.*

? FAQ

Why aren't we using external styles?

Since we are only creating sample pages to practice new coding techniques, it is practical to work with a single file. However, if this were an actual website, you would be using an external style sheet for maximum productivity and efficiency.

Page Layout Basics

CSS Two-Column Page Layout

A common design for a web page is a two-column layout. This is accomplished with CSS by configuring one of the columns to float on the web page. This section introduces you to two formats of the two-column page layout.

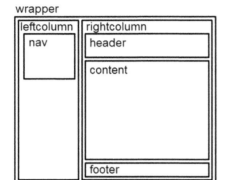

FIGURE 11 *The wireframe for a two-column layout with left navigation.*

Two-Column Layout with Left Navigation

See Figure 11 for a wireframe of a web page that has two columns.

The left column will contain navigation. The HTML template for the page layout is

```html
<div id="wrapper">
  <div id="leftcolumn">
    <nav>
    </nav>
  </div>
  <div id="rightcolumn">
    <header>
    </header>
    <div id="content">
    </div>
    <footer>
    </footer>
  </div>
</div>
```

The web page shown in Figure 12 implements the two columns with left navigation layout. An example is in the student files, chapter7/twocolumn1.html. The key to this layout is that the left column is coded to float to the left with the `float` property. The browser renders the other content on the page using normal flow.

▷ The wrapper is centered and takes up 80% of the web page width. The minimum width of the wrapper is 850 pixels. This area is assigned a medium-blue background color that will display behind the left column:

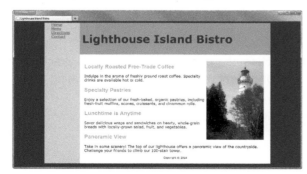

FIGURE 12 *A two-column page layout with left navigation.*

```css
#wrapper { width: 80%;
           margin: auto;
           min-width: 850px;
           background-color: #b3c7e6; }
```

▷ The left column is assigned a fixed width configured to float to the left. Since no background color is configured, the background color of the container element (the wrapper div) displays:

```css
#leftcolumn { float: left;
              width: 150px; }
```

Page Layout Basics

160

The right column is assigned a margin on the left that is equal to or greater than the width of the left column. This margin creates the look of two columns (often called "faux" columns). A white background color is assigned to the right column, which overrides the background color configured in the wrapper:

```
#rightcolumn { margin-left: 155px;
                background-color: #ffffff; }
```

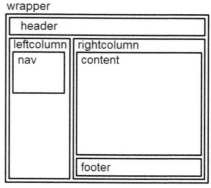

Two-Column Layout with Top Logo Header and Left Navigation

See Figure 13 for a wireframe of a web page with that has a top logo header spanning two columns with a navigation area in the left column. The HTML template for the page layout is

```
<div id="wrapper">
  <header>
  </header>
  <div id="leftcolumn">
    <nav>
    </nav>
  </div>
  <div id="rightcolumn">
    <div id="content">
    </div>
    <footer>
    </footer>
  </div>
</div>
```

FIGURE 13 *The wireframe for a two-column layout with a top logo area.*

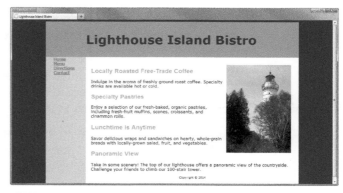

FIGURE 14 *A two-column page layout with a top logo and left navigation.*

The web page shown in Figure 14 implements the two columns with top logo layout. An example is in the student files, chapter7/twocolumn2.html. The CSS that configures the `wrapper`, `leftcolumn`, and `rightcolumn` areas is the same as for the web page shown in Figure 12. However, notice that the location of the `header` is different. It is now coded as the first element within the wrapper and displays before the left and right columns.

> **? FAQ**
>
> **Do I have to use a wrapper?**
>
> No, you are not required to use a wrapper or container for a web page layout. However, it does make it easier to get the two-column look because the background color of the wrapper div will display behind any of its child elements that do not have their own background color configured.

Not Yet Ready for Prime Time

There is one more aspect of the two-column layout web page design before it is ready for "prime time." The navigation area is a list of hyperlinks. In order to more closely semantically describe the navigation area, the hyperlinks should be configured in an unordered list. In the next section you'll learn techniques to configure vertical and horizontal navigation hyperlinks in unordered lists.

Vertical Navigation with an Unordered List

One of the advantages of using CSS for page layout involves the use of semantically correct code. Writing semantically correct code means using the markup tag that most accurately reflects the purpose of the content. Using the various levels of heading tags for content headings and subheadings or placing paragraphs of text within paragraph tags (rather than using line breaks) are examples of writing semantically correct code. This type of coding is a step in the direction to support the Semantic Web.

Leading Web developers such as Eric Meyer, Mark Newhouse, Jeffrey Zeldman, and others have promoted the idea of using unordered lists to configure navigation menus. After all, a navigation menu is a list of hyperlinks. You can configure an unordered list to omit the display of the list markers, or even display an image instead of a standard list marker.

 Configuring navigation with a list also helps to provide for accessibility. Screen reader applications offer easy keyboard access and verbal cues for information organized in lists, such as the number of items in the list.

Figure 15 shows the navigation area of a web page (found in the student files chapter7/twocolumn3.html) that uses an unordered list to organize the navigation links. The HTML is

```
<ul>
  <li><a href="index.html">Home</a></li>
  <li><a href="menu.html">Menu</a></li>
  <li><a href="directions.html">Directions</a></li>
  <li><a href="contact.html">Contact</a></li>
</ul>
```

- Home
- Menu
- Directions
- Contact

FIGURE 15
Navigation in an unordered list.

Configure an Unordered List with CSS

Home
Menu
Directions
Contact

FIGURE 16 *The list markers have been eliminated with CSS.*

OK, so now that we're semantically correct, how about improving the visual aesthetic? Let's use CSS to eliminate the list marker. We also need to make sure that our special styles only apply to the unordered lists in the navigation area (within the nav element) so we'll use a descendant selector. The CSS to configure the list in Figure 16 is

```
nav ul { list-style-type: none; }
```

Remove the Underline with the CSS `text-decoration` Property

The **`text-decoration` property** modifies the display of text in the browser and is most often used to eliminate the underline from the hyperlinks. As shown in Figure 17, the navigation hyperlinks are configured without an underline by coding:

```
text-decoration: none;
```

FIGURE 17 *The CSS* `text-decoration` *property has been applied.*

 Hands-On Practice 3

You will configure vertical navigation with an unordered list in this Hands-On Practice. Create a folder named ch7vert. Copy the files lighthouseisland.jpg, lighthouselogo.jpg, and starter3.html from the chapter7 folder in the student files into your ch7vert folder. Display the web page in a browser. It should look similar to Figure 18—notice that the navigation area needs to be configured.

Launch a text editor and open the starter3.html file. Save the file as index.html in your ch7vert folder.

FIGURE 18 *Notice that the navigation area needs to be configured.*

1. Review the code for this page, which uses a two-column layout. Examine the nav element within the `leftcolumn` div and modify the code surrounding the hyperlinks to configure the navigation in an unordered list.

```
<nav>
  <ul>
    <li><a href="index.html">Home</a></li>
    <li><a href="menu.html">Menu</a></li>
    <li><a href="directions.html">Directions</a></li>
    <li><a href="contact.html">Contact</a></li>
  </ul>
</nav>
```

2. Let's add CSS to the embedded styles to configure the unordered list elements only within the nav element: eliminate the list marker and set the padding to 10 pixels.

```
nav ul { list-style-type: none;
         padding: 10px; }
```

3. Next, configure the anchor tags within the nav element to have 10 pixels of padding, use bold font, and display no underline.

```
nav a { text-decoration: none;
        padding: 10px;
        font-weight: bold; }
```

FIGURE 19 *Two-column layout with vertical navigation.*

Save your page and test it in a browser. Your page should look similar to Figure 19. A sample is found in the student files (chapter7/vert/index.html).

Horizontal Navigation with an Unordered List

You may be wondering how to use an unordered list for a horizontal navigation menu. The answer is CSS! List item elements are block display elements. They need to be configured as inline display to appear in a horizontal line. The CSS `display` property makes this possible.

CSS `display` Property

The CSS **`display` property** configures the way that browsers render elements. See Table 2 for a list of commonly used values.

TABLE 2 *The* `display` *Property*

Value	Purpose
`none`	The element will not display
`inline`	The element will display as an inline display element without whitespace above and below
`inline-block`	The element will display as an inline display element adjacent to other inline display elements but also can be configured with properties of block display elements including width and height
`block`	The element will display as a block display element with whitespace above and below

Home   Menu   Directions   Contact

FIGURE 20 *Navigation in an unordered list.*

Figure 20 shows the navigation area of a web page (found in the student files chapter7/navigation.html) with a horizontal navigation area organized by an unordered list. The HTML is

```
<nav>
  <ul>
    <li><a href="index.html">Home</a></li>
    <li><a href="menu.html">Menu</a></li>
    <li><a href="directions.html">Directions</a></li>
    <li><a href="contact.html">Contact</a></li>
  </ul>
</nav>
```

Configure with CSS

The following CSS was applied in this example:

▶ To eliminate the list marker from unordered lists within the nav element, apply `list-style-type: none;` to the ul element selector:

```
nav ul { list-style-type: none; }
```

Page Layout Basics

- To render the list items within the nav element horizontally instead of vertically, apply `display: inline;` to the `nav li` selector:

  `nav li { display: inline; }`

- To eliminate the underline from the hyperlinks within the nav element, apply `text-decoration: none;` to the `nav a` selector. Also, configure right padding to add some space between the hyperlinks:

  `nav a { text-decoration: none; padding-right: 10px; }`

Hands-On Practice 4

You will configure horizontal navigation with an unordered list in this Hands-On Practice. Create a folder named ch7hort. Copy the files lighthouseisland.jpg, lighthouselogo.jpg, and starter4.html from the chapter7 folder in the student files into your ch7hort folder. Display the web page in a browser. It should look similar to Figure 21—notice that the navigation area needs to be configured to display in a single line.

Launch a text editor and open the starter4.html file. Save the file as index.html in your ch7hort folder.

FIGURE 21 *Notice that the navigation area needs to be configured.*

1. Examine the nav element and notice that it contains an unordered list with navigation hyperlinks. Let's add CSS to the embedded styles to configure the unordered list element within the nav element: eliminate the list marker, center the text, set the font size to 1.5em, and set the margin to 5 pixels.

   ```
   nav ul { list-style-type: none;
            text-align: center;
            font-size: 1.5em;
            margin: 5px; }
   ```

2. Configure the list item elements within the nav element to display as inline elements.

   ```
   nav li { display: inline; }
   ```

3. Configure the anchor elements within the nav element to display no underline. Also set the left and right padding to 10 pixels.

   ```
   nav a { text-decoration: none;
           padding-left: 10px;
           padding-right: 10px; }
   ```

Save your page and test it in a browser. Your page should look similar to Figure 22. A sample is found in the student files (chapter7/hort/index.html).

FIGURE 22 *Horizontal navigation within an unordered list.*

CSS Interactivity with Pseudo-Classes

VideoNote
Interactivity with CSS Pseudo-Classes

Have you ever visited a website and found that the text hyperlinks changed color when you moved the mouse pointer over them? Often, this is accomplished using a CSS **pseudo-class**, which can be used to apply a special effect to a selector. The five pseudo-classes that can be applied to the anchor element are shown in Table 3.

TABLE 3 *Commonly Used CSS Pseudo-Classes*

Pseudo-Class	When Applied
:link	Default state for a hyperlink that has not been clicked (visited)
:visited	Default state for a visited hyperlink
:focus	Triggered when the hyperlink has keyboard focus
:hover	Triggered when the mouse moves over the hyperlink
:active	Triggered when the hyperlink is actually clicked

Notice the order in which the pseudo-classes are listed in Table 3. Anchor element pseudo-classes *must be coded in this order* (although it's OK to omit one or more of those listed). If you code the pseudo-classes in a different order, the styles will not be reliably applied. It's common practice to configure the :focus and :active pseudo-classes with the same styles.

To apply a pseudo-class, write it after the selector. The following code sample will configure text hyperlinks to be red initially. The sample also uses the :hover pseudo-class to configure the hyperlinks to change their appearance when the visitor places the mouse pointer over them so that the underline disappears and the color changes.

1. Text hyperlinks are underlined by default.

🖨 Print This Page

2. The hover pseudo-class is triggered by the mouse. The browser no longer displays the underline below the hyperlink.

🖨 Print This Page

FIGURE 23 *Using the hover pseudo-class.*

```
a:link { color: #ff0000; }
a:hover { text-decoration: none;
        color: #000066; }
```

Figure 23 shows part of a web page that uses a similar technique. Note the position of the mouse pointer over the "Print This Page" hyperlink—the text color has changed and has no underline. Most modern browsers support CSS pseudo-classes.

Page Layout Basics

You will use pseudo-classes to create interactive hyperlinks in this Hands-On Practice. Create a folder named ch7hover. Copy the lighthouseisland.jpg, lighthouselogo.jpg, and starter3.html files from the chapter7 folder in the student files into your ch7hover folder. Display the web page in a browser. It should look similar to Figure 24—notice that the navigation area needs to be configured. Launch a text editor and open the starter3.html file. Save the file as index.html in your ch7hover folder.

FIGURE 24 *The navigation area needs to be styled in this two-column page layout.*

1. Review the code for this page, which uses a two-column layout. Examine the `leftcolumn` id and modify the code within the nav element to configure the navigation in an unordered list.

```
<nav>
  <ul>
    <li><a href="index.html">Home</a></li>
    <li><a href="menu.html">Menu</a></li>
    <li><a href="directions.html">Directions</a></li>
    <li><a href="contact.html">Contact</a></li>
  </ul>
</nav>
```

2. Let's add CSS to the embedded styles to configure the unordered list element within the nav element: eliminate the list marker and set the padding to 10 pixels.

```
nav ul { list-style-type: none; padding: 10px; }
```

3. Next, configure basic interactivity with pseudo-classes.

   ▶ Configure the anchor elements within the nav element to have 10 pixels of padding, use bold font, and display no underline.

   ```
   nav a { text-decoration: none; padding: 10px;
           font-weight: bold; }
   ```

   ▶ Use pseudo-classes to configure anchor tags within the nav element to display white (#ffffff) text for unvisited hyperlinks, light-gray (#eaeaea) text for visited hyperlinks, and dark blue (#000066) text when the mouse hovers over hyperlinks:

   ```
   nav a:link { color: #ffffff; }
   nav a:visited { color: #eaeaea; }
   nav a:hover { color: #000066; }
   ```

FIGURE 25 *CSS pseudo-classes add interactivity to the navigation.*

Save your page and test it in a browser. Move your mouse over the navigation area and notice the text color change. Your page should look similar to Figure 25. A sample is found in the student files (chapter7/hover/index.html).

Practice with CSS Two-Column Layout

Hands-On Practice 6

In this Hands-On Practice you'll create a new version of the Lighthouse Island Bistro home page with a top header section spanning two columns, content in the left column, navigation in the right column, and a footer section below the two columns. See Figure 26 for the wireframe. You will configure the CSS in an external style sheet. Create a new folder named ch7practice. Copy the starter5. html, lighthouseisland.jpg, and lighthouselogo.jpg files from the chapter7 folder in the student files into your ch7practice folder.

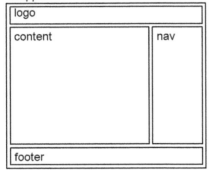

FIGURE 26 *The wireframe for a two-column layout with a top logo area.*

1. Launch a text editor and open the starter5.html file. Save the file as index.html. Add a link element to the head section of the web page that associates this file with an external style sheet named lighthouse.css. A code sample is

   `<link href="lighthouse.css" rel="stylesheet">`

   Save the index.html file.

2. Launch a text editor and create a new file named lighthouse.css in your ch7practice folder. Configure the CSS for the wireframe sections as follows:

▸ The body element selector: very dark blue background (#00005D) and Verdana, Arial, or the default sans-serif font typeface

```
body { background-color: #00005D;
       font-family: Verdana, Arial, sans-serif; }
```

▸ The wrapper id: centered, take up 80% of the browser viewport, a minimum width of 940px, display text in a dark-blue color (#000066), and display a medium-blue (#B3C7E6) background color (*this color will display behind the nav section*)

```
#wrapper { margin: 0 auto; width: 80%; min-width: 940px;
           background-color: #B3C7E6; color: #000066; }
```

▸ The header element selector: slate blue (#869DC7) background color, very dark blue (#00005D) text color, 150% font size, top, right, and bottom padding of 10px, 155 pixels of left padding, height set to 130 pixels, and the lighthouselogo.jpg background image

```
header { background-color: #869DC7; color: #00005D;
         font-size: 150%; padding: 10px 10px 10px 155px;
         height: 130px;
         background-repeat: no-repeat;
         background-image: url(lighthouselogo.jpg); }
```

Page Layout Basics

▶ The nav element selector: float on the right, width of 150px, display bold text, letter spacing of 0.1 em

```
nav { float: right; width: 150px; font-weight: bold;
      letter-spacing: 0.1em; }
```

▶ The content id: white background color (#FFFFFF), black text color (#000000), 10 pixels of padding on the top and bottom, and 20 pixels of padding on the left and right and overflow set to auto.

```
#content { background-color: #FFFFFF; color: #000000;
           padding: 10px 20px; overflow: auto; }
```

▶ The footer element selector: 70% font size, centered text, 10 pixels of padding, a slate blue background color (#869DC7) and clear set to both.

```
footer { font-size: 70%; text-align: center; padding: 10px;
         background-color: #869DC7; clear: both; }
```

Save the lighthouse.css file. Display index.html in a browser. Your page should look similar to Figure 27.

3. Continue editing the lighthouse.css file to style the h2 element selector and floating image. Configure the h2 element selector with slate blue text color (#869DC7) and Arial or sans-serif font typeface. Configure the floatright id to float on the right side with 10 pixels of margin.

```
h2 { color: #869DC7;
     font-family: Arial, sans-serif; }
floatright { float: right; margin: 10px; }
```

FIGURE 27 *The home page with major page sections configured using CSS.*

4. Continue editing the lighthouse.css file and configure the vertical navigation bar.

▶ Configure the unordered list: eliminate list markers, set zero margin and zero padding:

```
nav ul { list-style-type: none; margin: 0; padding: 0; }
```

▶ Configure hyperlinks: no underline, 20 pixels padding, medium-blue background color (#B3C7E6), and 1 pixel solid white bottom border. Use display: block; to allow the web page visitor to click anywhere in the anchor "button" to activate the hyperlink.

```
nav a { text-decoration: none;  padding: 20px; display: block;
        background-color: #B3C7E6;
        border-bottom: 1px solid #FFFFFF; }
```

▶ Configure the :link, :visited, and :hover pseudo-classes as follows:

```
nav a:link { color: #FFFFFF; }
nav a:visited { color: #EAEAEA; }
nav a:hover { color: #869DC7;
              background-color: #EAEAEA; }
```

Save your files. Display your index.html page in a browser. Move your mouse over the navigation area and notice the interactivity, as shown in Figure 28. A sample solution is in the chapter7/practice/index.html file.

FIGURE 28 *CSS pseudo-classes add interactivity to the page.*

Positioning with CSS

You've seen how normal flow causes the browser to render the elements in the order that they appear in the HTML source code. When using CSS for page layout there are situations when you may want more control over the position of an element. The **position property** configures the type of positioning used when the browser renders an element. Table 4 lists position property values and their purpose.

TABLE 4 *The* position *Property*

Value	Purpose
static	Default value; the element is rendered in normal flow
fixed	Configures the location of an element within the browser viewport; the element does not move when the page is scrolled
relative	Configures the location of an element relative to where it would otherwise render in normal flow
absolute	Precisely configures the location of an element outside of normal flow

Static Positioning

Static positioning is the default and causes the browser to render an element in normal flow. As you've worked through the exercises in this book, you have created web pages that the browser rendered using normal flow.

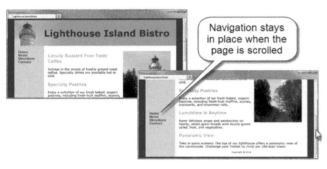

FIGURE 29 *The navigation is configured with fixed positioning.*

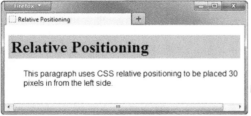

FIGURE 30 *The paragraph is configured using relative positioning.*

Fixed Positioning

Use **fixed positioning** to cause an element to be removed from normal flow and to remain stationary, or "fixed in place," when the web page is scrolled in the browser viewport. Figure 29 shows a web page (found in the student files chapter7/fixed.html) with a navigation area configured with fixed position. The navigation stays in place even though the user has scrolled down the page. The CSS follows:

```
nav { position: fixed; }
```

Relative Positioning

Use **relative positioning** to change the location of an element slightly, relative to where it would otherwise appear in normal flow. However, the area in normal flow is still reserved for the element and other elements will flow around that reserved space. Configure relative positioning with the position: relative; property along with one or more of the following offset properties: left, right, top, bottom. Table 5 lists the offset properties.

Figure 30 shows a web page (see the student files chapter7/relative.html) that uses relative positioning along with the left property to configure the placement of an element in relation to the normal flow. In this case, the container element is the body of the web page. The result is that the content of the element is rendered as being offset or shifted by 30 pixels from

Page Layout Basics

170

TABLE 5 *The Position Offset Properties*

Property	Value	Purpose
left	Numeric value or percentage	The position of the element offset from the left side of the container element
right	Numeric value or percentage	The position of the element offset from the right side of the container element
top	Numeric value or percentage	The position of the element offset from the top of the container element
bottom	Numeric value or percentage	The position of the element offset from the bottom of the container element

the left where it would normally be placed at the browser's left margin. Notice also how the padding and background-color properties configure the heading element. The CSS is

```
p { position: relative;
    left: 30px;
    font-family: Arial, sans-serif; }
h1 { background-color: #cccccc;
     padding: 5px;
     color: #000000; }
```

The HTML source code follows:

```
<h1>Relative Positioning</h1>
<p>This paragraph uses CSS relative positioning to be placed 30 pixels in from the
left side.</p>
```

Absolute Positioning

Use **absolute positioning** to precisely specify the location of an element outside of normal flow in relation to its first parent non-static element. If there is no non-static parent element, the absolute position is specified in relation to the body of the web page. Configure absolute positioning with the position: absolute; property along with one or more of the offset properties (left, right, top, bottom) listed in Table 5.

Figure 31 depicts a web page that configures an element with absolute positioning to display the content 200 pixels in from the left margin and 100 pixels down from the top of the web page document. An example is in the student files, chapter7/absolute.html).

The CSS is

```
p { position: absolute;
    left: 200px;
    top: 100px;
    font-family: Arial, sans-serif;
    width: 300px; }
```

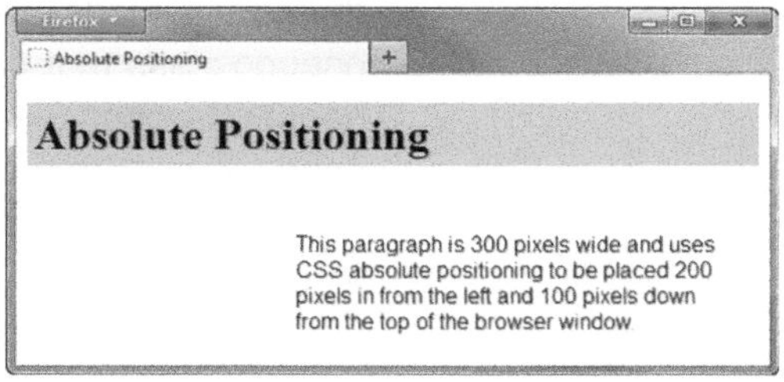

The HTML source code is

```
<h1>Absolute Positioning</h1>
<p>This paragraph is 300 pixels wide and uses CSS absolute positioning to be
placed 200 pixels in from the left and 100 pixels down from the top of the browser
window.</p>
```

FIGURE 31 *The paragraph is configured with absolute positioning.*

Practice with Positioning

Recall that the CSS `:hover` pseudo-class provides a way to configure styles to display when the web page visitor moves the mouse over an element. You'll use this basic interactivity along with CSS positioning and display properties to configure an interactive image gallery with CSS and HTML. Figure 32 shows the interactive image gallery in action (available in the student files, chapter7/gallery/gallery.html). When you place the mouse over a thumbnail image, the larger version of the image is displayed along with a caption. If you click on the thumbnail, the larger version of the image displays in its own browser window.

FIGURE 32 *An interactive image gallery with CSS.*

Hands-On Practice 7

In this Hands-On Practice you will create the interactive image gallery web page shown in Figure 32. Copy the following images located in the student files chapter7/starters folder into a folder named gallery: photo1.jpg, photo2.jpg, photo3.jpg, photo4.jpg, photo1thumb.jpg, photo2thumb.jpg, photo3thumb.jpg, and photo4thumb.jpg.

Launch a text editor and modify the chapter1/template.html file to configure a web page as indicated:

1. Configure the text, Image Gallery, within an h1 element and within the title element.

2. Code a div assigned to the id named `gallery`. This div will contain the thumbnail images, which will be configured within an unordered list.

3. Configure an unordered list within the div. Code four li elements, one for each thumbnail image. The thumbnail images will function as image links with a `:hover` pseudo-class that causes the larger image to display on the page. We'll make this all happen by configuring an anchor element containing both the thumbnail image and a span element that comprises the larger image along with descriptive text. An example of the first li element is

```
<li><a href="photo1.jpg"><img src="photo1thumb.jpg" width="100"
    height="75" alt="Golden Gate Bridge">
    <span><img src="photo1.jpg" width="250" height="150"
    alt="Golden Gate Bridge"><br>Golden Gate Bridge</span></a>
</li>
```

4. Configure all four li elements in a similar manner. Substitute the actual name of each image file for the href and src values in the code. Write your own descriptive text for

Page Layout Basics

each image. Use photo2.jpg and photo2thumb.jpg in the second li element. Use photo3.jpg and photo3thumb.jpg in the third li element. Use photo4.jpg and photo4thumb.jpg for the fourth li element. Save the file as index.html in the gallery folder. Display your page in a browser. You'll see an unordered list with the thumbnail images, the larger images, and the descriptive text. Figure 33 shows a partial screen capture.

5. Now, let's add embedded CSS. Open your index.html file in a text editor and code a style element in the head section. The `gallery` id will use relative positioning instead of the default static positioning. This does not change the location of the gallery but sets the stage to use absolute positioning on the span element in relation to its container (#gallery) instead of in relation to the entire web page document. This won't matter too much for our very simple example, but it would be very helpful if the gallery were part of a more complex web page. Configure embedded CSS as follows:

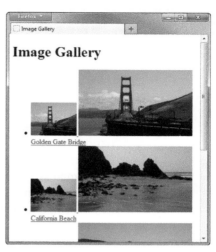

FIGURE 33 *The web page display before CSS.*

a. Set the gallery id to use relative positioning.
```
#gallery { position: relative; }
```

b. The unordered list in the gallery should have a width of 250 pixels and no list marker.
```
#gallery ul { width: 250px; list-style-type: none; }
```

c. Configure the list item elements in the gallery with inline display, left float, and 10 pixels of padding.
```
#gallery li { display: inline; float: left; padding: 10px; }
```

d. The images in the gallery should not display a border.
```
#gallery img { border-style: none; }
```

e. Configure anchor elements in the gallery to have no underline, #333 text color, and italic text.
```
#gallery a { text-decoration: none; color: #333; font-style: italic; }
```

f. Configure span elements in the gallery not to display initially.
```
#gallery span { display: none; }
```

g. Configure the span elements in the gallery to display *only* when the web visitor hovers the mouse over the thumbnail image link. Set the location of the span to use absolute positioning. Locate the span 10 pixels down from the top and 300 pixels in from the left. Center the text within the span:
```
#gallery a:hover span { display: block; position: absolute;
         top: 10px; left: 300px; text-align: center; }
```

Save your page and display it in a browser. Your interactive image gallery should work well in modern browsers. Compare your work to Figure 32 and the sample in the student files (chapter7/gallery/gallery.html).

CSS Sprites

When browsers display web pages, they must make a separate http request for every file used by the page, including .css files and image files such as .gif, .jpg, and .png files. Each http request takes time and resources. A **sprite** is an image file that contains multiple small graphics. The single graphics file saves download time because the browser only needs to make one http request for the combined image instead of many requests for the individual smaller images. Using CSS to configure the small graphics combined in the sprite as background images for various web page elements is called **CSS sprites**, a technique made popular by David Shea (www.alistapart.com/articles/sprites).

The CSS sprites technique uses the CSS `background-image`, `background-repeat`, and `background-position` properties to manipulate the placement of the background image.

Figure 34 shows a sprite with two lighthouse images on a transparent background. These images are configured as background images for the navigation hyperlinks with CSS as shown in Figure 35. You'll see this in action as you complete the next Hands-On Practice.

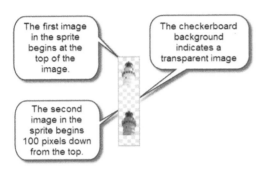

> The first image in the sprite begins at the top of the image.

> The checkerboard background indicates a transparent image

> The second image in the sprite begins 100 pixels down from the top.

FIGURE 34 *The sprite consists of two images.*

FIGURE 35 *Sprites in action.*

 Hands-On Practice 8

You will work with CSS sprites in this Hands-On Practice as you create the web page shown in Figure 35. Create a new folder named sprites. Copy the following files from the chapter 7 folder into your sprites folder: starter6.html, lighthouseisland.jpg, lighthouselogo.jpg, and sprites. gif. The sprites.gif, shown in Figure 34, contains two lighthouse images. The first lighthouse image starts at the top of the graphics file. The second lighthouse image begins 100 pixels down from the top of the graphics file. We'll use this information about the location of the second image within the graphics file when we configure the display of the second image. Launch a text editor and open starter6.html. Save the file as index .html. You will edit the embedded styles to configure background images for the navigation hyperlinks.

1. Configure the background image for navigation hyperlinks. Add the following styles to the `nav a` selector to set the background image to the sprites.gif with no repeat. The value `right` in the `background-position` property configures the lighthouse image to display at the right of the navigation element. The value 0 in the `background-position` property configures the display at offset 0 from the top (at the very top) so the first lighthouse image displays.

```
nav a { text-decoration: none;
        display: block;
        padding: 20px;
        background-color: #B3C7E6;
        border-bottom: 1px solid #FFFFFF;
        background-image: url(sprites.gif);
        background-repeat: no-repeat;
        background-position: right 0; }
```

2. Configure the second lighthouse image to display when the mouse pointer passes over the hyperlink. Add the following styles to the `nav a:hover` selector to display the second lighthouse image. The value `right` in the `background-position` property configures the lighthouse image to display at the right of the navigation element. The value `-100px` in the `background-position` property configures the display at an offset of 100 pixels down from the top so the second lighthouse image appears.

```
nav a:hover { background-color: #EAEAEA;
              color: #869DC7;
              background-position: right -100px; }
```

Save the file and test it in a browser. Your page should look similar to Figure 35. Move your mouse pointer over the navigation hyperlinks to see the background images change. Compare your work with the sample found in the student files (chapter7/sprites/index.html).

? **FAQ** How can I create my own sprite graphics file?

Most web developers use a graphics application such as Adobe Photoshop, Adobe Fireworks, or GIMP to edit images and save them in a single graphics file for use as a sprite. Or, you could use a web-based sprite generator such as the ones listed below:

▶ CSS Sprites Generator: http://csssprites.com

▶ CSS Sprite Generator: http://spritegen.website-performance.org

▶ SpritePad: http://wearekiss.com/spritepad

If you already have a sprite graphic, check out the online tool at Sprite Cow (www.spritecow.com) that can generate pixel-perfect `background-position` property values for a sprite.

Review and Apply

Review Questions

1. Which of the following causes an element not to display?

   a. `display: block;`

   b. `display: 0px;`

   c. `display: none;`

   d. `display: inline;`

2. Which of the following is an image file that contains multiple small graphics?

   a. thumbnail

   b. snap

   c. sprite

   d. float

3. Which of the following properties can be used to clear a float?

   a. `float` or `clear`

   b. `clear` or `overflow`

   c. `position` or `clear`

   d. `overflow` or `float`

4. Which of the following causes an element to display without empty space above and below?

   a. `display: static;`

   b. `display: none;`

   c. `display: block;`

   d. `display: inline;`

5. Which of the following pseudo-classes is the default state for a hyperlink that has already been clicked?

   a. `:hover`

   b. `:link`

   c. `:onclick`

   d. `:visited`

6. Which of the following is used to change the location of an element slightly in relation to where it would otherwise appear on the page?

   a. relative positioning

   b. static positioning

   c. absolute positioning

   d. fixed positioning

7. Which of the following configures a class called `notes` to float to the left?

   a. `.notes { left: float; }`

   b. `.notes { float: left; }`

   c. `.notes { float-left: 200px; }`

   d. `.notes { position: float; }`

8. Which of the following is the rendering flow used by a browser by default?

   a. HTML flow

   b. normal display

   c. browser flow

   d. normal flow

9. Which of the following is an example of using a descendant selector to configure the anchor tags within the nav element?

   a. `nav. a`   **b.** `a nav`

   c. `nav a`   **d.** `#nav a`

10. Which of the following is used along with the `left`, `right`, and/or `top` property to precisely configure the position of an element outside of normal flow?

    a. `position: relative;`

    b. `position: absolute;`

    c. `position: float;`

    d. `absolute: position;`

Hands-On Exercises

1. Write the CSS for an id with the following characteristics: fixed position, light gray background color, bold font weight, and 10 pixels of padding.

2. Write the CSS for an id with the following characteristics: float to the left of the page, light-beige background, Verdana or sans-serif large font, and 20 pixels of padding.

3. Write the CSS for an id that will be absolutely positioned on a page 20 pixels from the top and 40 pixels from the right. This area should have a light-gray background and a solid border.

4. Write the CSS for a class that is relatively positioned. This class should appear 15 pixels in from the left. Configure the class to have a light-green background.

5. Create a web page about your favorite hobby, movie, or music group. Configure the text, color, and a two-column layout with CSS.

Focus on Web Design

There is still much for you to learn about CSS. A great place to learn about web technology is on the Web itself. Use a search engine to search for CSS page layout tutorials. Choose a tutorial that is easy to read. Select a section that discusses a CSS technique that was not covered in this chapter. Create a web page that uses this new technique. Consider how the suggested page layout follows (or does not follow) principles of design such as contrast, repetition, alignment, and proximity. The web page should provide the URL of your tutorial, the name of the website, a description of the new technique you discovered, and a discussion of how the technique follows (or does not follow) principles of design.

Answers to Review Questions

1. c	2. c	3. b
4. d	5. d	6. a
7. b	8. d	9. c
10. b		

Credits

Figure 23 © Terry Ann Morris, Ed.D. | Microsoft Corporation

Figures 1–10, 12, 14, 18, 19, 21, 22, 24, 25, 30–35, 37, 39, 40 © Terry Ann Morris, Ed.D. | Mozilla Foundation

More on Links, Layout, and Mobile

Now let's explore the topics in this chapter, including relative hyperlinks and named fragment hyperlinks, captioning a figure, more new HTML5 structural elements, ensuring compatibility with older browsers, styling for print, styling for mobile browsers, and responsive web design techniques as you configure CSS3 media queries to target mobile devices.

You'll learn how to...

▶ Code relative hyperlinks to web pages in folders within a website

▶ Configure a hyperlink to a named fragment internal to a web page

▶ Configure images with captions using the HTML5 figure and figcaption elements

▶ Configure a collection of images to float across a web page

▶ Configure web pages with new HTML5 section, hgroup, article, and time elements

▶ Apply techniques to ensure backward compatibility with older browsers

▶ Configure web pages for printing with CSS

▶ Describe mobile web design best practices

▶ Configure web pages for mobile display using the viewport meta tag

▶ Apply responsive web design techniques with CSS3 media queries and flexible images

From Chapter 8 of *Basics of Web Design HTML5 & CSS3*, Second Edition. Terry Ann Felke-Morris. Copyright © 2014 by Pearson Education, Inc. All rights reserved.

More on Relative Linking

A relative hyperlink is used to link to web pages within your site. You can code relative links to display web pages that are all inside the same folder. There are times when you need to link to files that are located in other folders on your website. Let's consider a website for a bed and breakfast that features rooms and events. The folder and file listing is shown in Figure 1. The main folder for this website is called casita, and the web developer has created separate subfolders—named images, rooms, and events—to organize the site.

casita
index.html
contact.html
casita.css

images
logo.gif
scenery.jpg

rooms
canyon.html
javelina.html

events
weekend.html
festival.html

FIGURE 1 *The web page files are organized in folders.*

Relative Link Examples

Recall that when linking to a file located in the same folder or directory, the value of the `href` attribute is the name of the file. For example, to link from the home page (index.html) to the contact.html page, code the anchor element as follows:

```
<a href="contact.html">Contact</a>
```

When linking to a file that is inside a folder within the current directory, use both the folder name and the file name in the relative link. For example, to link from the home page (indext.html) to the canyon.html page (located in the rooms folder), code the anchor element as follows:

```
<a href="rooms/canyon.html">Canyon</a>
```

As shown in Figure 1, the canyon.html page is located in the rooms subfolder of the casita folder. The home page for the site (index.html) is located in the casita folder. When linking to a file that is up one directory level from the current page, use the ".../" notation. To link to the home page for the site from the canyon.html page, code the anchor element as follows:

```
<a href="../index.html">Home</a>
```

When linking to a file that is in a folder on the same level as the current folder, the href value will use the ".../" notation to indicate moving up one level; then specify the desired folder. For example, to link to the weekend.html page in the events folder from the canyon.html page in the rooms folder, code the anchor element as follows:

```
<a href="../events/weekend.html">Weekend Events</a>
```

Don't worry if the use of ".../" notation and linking to files in different folders seems new and different. In most, you will code either absolute links to other websites or relative links to files in the same folder. You can explore the example of the bed and breakfast website located in the student files on the companion website www.pearsonhighered.com/felke-morris (see chapter8/CasitaExample) to become more familiar with coding references to files in different folders.

More on Links, Layout, and Mobile

Hands-On Practice 1

This hands-on practice provides an opportunity to practice coding hyperlinks to files in different folders. The website you'll be working with has pages in prototype form—the navigation and layout of the pages are configured, but the specific content has not yet been added. You'll focus on the navigation area in this Hands-On Practice. Figure 2 shows a partial screen shot of the bed and breakfast's prototype home page with a navigation area on the left side of the page.

Examine Figure 3 and notice the new juniper.html file listed within the rooms folder. You will create a new web page (Juniper Room) named juniper.html and save it in the rooms folder. Then, you will update the navigation area on each existing web page to link to the new Juniper Room page.

Let's get started.

1. Copy the CasitaExample folder (chapter8/CasitaExample) from the student files. Rename the folder casita.

2. Display the index.html file in a browser and click through the navigation links. View the source code of the pages and notice how the `href` values of the anchor tags are configured to link to and from files within different folders.

3. Launch a text editor and open the canyon.html file. You'll use this file as a starting point for your new Juniper Room page. Save the file as juniper.html in the rooms folder.

   a. Edit the page title and h2 text—change "Canyon" to "Juniper".

   b. Add a new li element in the navigation area that contains a hyperlink to the juniper.html file.

   ```
   <li><a href="juniper.html">Juniper Room</a></li>
   ```

   Place this hyperlink between the Javelina Room and Weekend Events navigation hyperlinks as shown in Figure 4. Save the file.

4. Use the coding for the Canyon and Javelina hyperlinks as a guide as you add the Juniper Room link to the navigation area on each of the following pages:

   index.html
   contact.html
   rooms/canyon.html
   rooms/javelina.html
   events/weekend.html
   events/festival.html

Save all the .html files and test your pages in a browser. The navigation hyperlink to the new Juniper Room page should work from every other page. The hyperlinks on the new Juniper Room page should function well and open other pages as expected. A solution is in the student files (chapter8/CasitaSolution folder).

FIGURE 2 *The navigation area.*

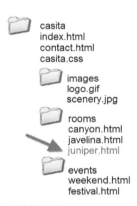

FIGURE 3 *New juniper. html file is in the rooms folder.*

FIGURE 4 *The new navigation area.*

More on Links, Layout, and Mobile

Fragment Identifiers

VideoNote
Linking to a Named Fragment

Browsers begin the display of a web page at the top of the document. However, there are times when you need to provide the capability to link to a specific portion of a web page instead of the top. You can accomplish this by coding a hyperlink to a **fragment identifier** (sometimes called a named fragment or fragment id), which is simply an HTML element with an `id` attribute.

There are two components to your coding when using fragment identifiers:

1. The tag that identifies the **named fragment** of a web page. This tag must be assigned to an id. For example: `<div id="content">`

2. The anchor tag that links to the named fragment on a web page.

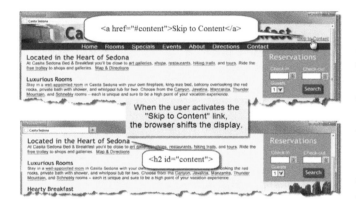

FIGURE 5 *The "skip to content" link in action.*

Lists of frequently asked questions (FAQs) often use fragment identifiers to jump to a specific part of the page and display the answer to a question. Linking to a named fragment is often seen on long web pages. You might see a "Back to top" hyperlink that a visitor can click to cause the browser to quickly scroll the page up to the top for easy site navigation. Another use of fragment identifiers helps to provide for accessibility. Web pages may have a fragment identifier to indicate the beginning of the actual page content. When the visitor clicks on the "Skip to content" hyperlink, the browser links to the named fragment and shifts focus to the content area of the page. This "Skip to content" or "Skip navigation" link provides a way for screen reader users to skip repetitive navigation links (see Figure 5).

This is accomplished in two steps:

1. **Establish the Target.** Create the "skip to content" fragment identifier by configuring an element that begins the page content with an id, for example, `<h2 id="content">`.

2. **Reference the Target.** At the point of the page where you want to place a hyperlink to the content, code an anchor element. Use the `href` attribute and place a # symbol (called a hash mark) before the name of the fragment identifier. The code for a hyperlink to the named fragment "content" is
`<a href="#content">Skip to Content</a>`.

The hash mark indicates that the browser should search for an id on the same page. If you forget to type the hash mark, the browser will not look on the same web page; it will look for an external file.

Legacy Alert. Older web pages may use the name attribute and refer to named anchors rather than fragment identifiers. This coding technique is obsolete and not valid in HTML5. Named anchors use the `name` attribute to identify or name the fragment. For example,

```
<a name="content" id="content"></a>.
```

Hands-On Practice 2

You will work with fragment identifiers in this Hands-On Practice. Launch a text editor and open the chapter8/starter1.html file from the student files. Save the file as favorites.html. Figure 6 shows a screenshot of this web page. Examine the source code and notice that the top portion of the page contains an unordered list with categories of interest (such as Hobbies, HTML5, and CSS) that correspond to the text displayed in the h2 elements below. Each h2 element is followed by a description list of topics and URLs related to that category. It might be helpful to web page visitors if they can click a category item and immediately jump to the page area that has information related to that item. This could be a useful application of linking to fragment identifiers!

FIGURE 6 *You will add hyperlinks to fragment identifiers.*

Modify the page as follows:

1. Code a named fragment for each h2 element. For example,

   ```
   <h2 id="hobbies">Hobbies</h2>
   ```

2. Add hyperlinks to the items in the unordered list so that each entry will link to its corresponding heading.

3. Add a named fragment near the top of the page.

4. Near the bottom of the favorites.html page, add a hyperlink to scroll to the top of the page.

Save the file and test it in a browser. Compare your work with the sample found in the student files (chapter8/favorites.html).

There may be times when you need to link to a named fragment on another web page. To accomplish this, place a "#" followed by the fragment identifier `id` value after the file name in the anchor tag. So, to link to "Hobbies" (given that it is a named fragment called "hobbies") from any other page on the same website, you could use the following HTML:

```
<a href="favorites.html#hobbies">Hobbies</a>
```

Why don't some of my hyperlinks to fragment identifiers work?

The web browser fills the browser viewport with the web page and will scroll to display the named fragment at the top of the viewport. However, if there is not enough "page" left below the named fragment, the content where the named fragment is located will not be displayed at the top of the browser viewport. The browser tries to do the best it can while still filling the viewport with the web page content. Try adding some blank lines (use the `<br>` tag) or padding to the lower portion of the web page. Save your work and retest your hyperlinks.

More on Links, Layout, and Mobile

Figure and Figcaption Elements

HTML5 introduces a number of elements that are useful to semantically describe the content. While you could use a generic div element to configure an area on a web page with an image and a caption, the figure and figcaption elements are more descriptive of the content. The div element is useful but very generic in nature. When the figure and figcaption elements are used, the structure of the content is well defined.

The Figure Element

The block display **figure element** comprises a unit of content that is self-contained, such as an image, along with one optional figcaption element.

The Figcaption Element

The block display **figcaption element** provides a caption for the figure content.

Captioning a Figure

The web page shown in Figure 7 demonstrates the use of the figure and figcaption elements. The example in the student files (chapter8/caption/caption.html) configures a text caption centered below the image. The HTML code is

```
<figure>
  <img src="lighthouseisland.jpg"
       width="250" height="355"
       alt="Lighthouse Island">
  <figcaption>
    Island Lighthouse, Built in 1870
  </figcaption>
</figure>
```

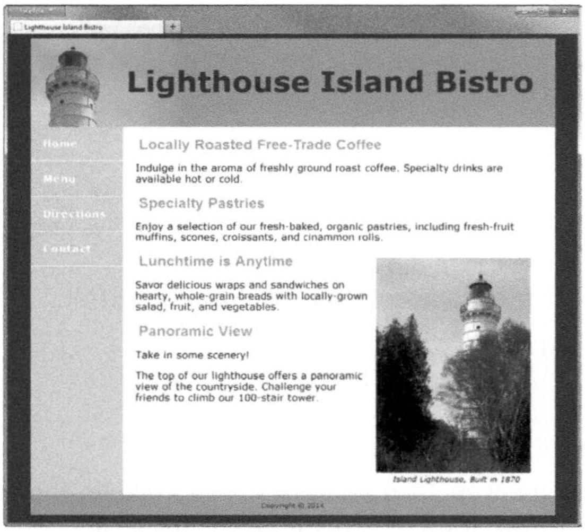

CSS is needed to configure the display. The figure element selector is set as follows: float to the right, 260 pixels in width, and a 10 pixel margin. The figcaption element selector is configured to render small, italic, centered text. The CSS is

```
figure { float: right;
         width: 260px;
         margin: 10px; }
```

FIGURE 7 *The figure and figcaption elements are used on this web page.*

More on Links, Layout, and Mobile

```
figcaption { text-align: center;
             font-size: .8em;
             font-style: italic; }
```

 Hands-On Practice 3

In this Hands-On Practice you will use the figure and figcaption elements to create the web page that displays an image element with a text caption, as shown in Figure 8. Create a new folder named mycaption. Copy the myisland.jpg file from the student files chapter8/starters folder into the mycaption folder.

1. Launch a text editor and open the template file located at chapter1/template.html in the student files. Modify the title element. Save the file as index.html in your mycaption folder.

2. With the file open in the text editor, code the following HTML to configure a figure element that contains an image with a text caption (using the figcaption element).

FIGURE 8 *The figure and figcaption elements in action.*

```
<figure>
  <img src="myisland.jpg" width="480"
       height="320" alt="Tropical Island">
  <figcaption>
    Tropical Island Getaway
  </figcaption>
</figure>
```

Save the file and test it in a browser. You should see the image and text caption display.

3. Next, you'll code embedded CSS to give this page a little style. Add embedded CSS to the head section that configures the figure element selector to be 480 pixels wide, with a border, and with padding set to 5px. Configure the figcaption element selector to have centered text using the Papyrus font typeface (or the default Fantasy Family font). The code follows:

```
<style>
  figure { width: 480px;
           border: 1px solid #000000;
           padding: 5px; }
  figcaption { text-align: center;
               font-family: Papyrus, fantasy; }
</style>
```

Save the file as index.html in the mycaption folder. Launch a browser to test your page. It should look similar to the page shown in Figure 8. The student files contain a sample solution in the chapter8/caption2 folder.

Practice with Floating Figures

FIGURE 9 *The images float in this web page.*

In this Hands-On Practice you will create the web page shown in Figure 9, which displays a group of images with captions.

You'll configure the images and their captions to float on the web page to fill the available space in the browser viewport. The display will change based on the size of the browser viewport.

FIGURE 10 *The floated images move as the browser is resized.*

Figure 10 shows the same web page displayed in a browser that has been resized to be smaller.

Create a new folder named float8. Copy the following images from the student files chapter8/starters folder into the float8 folder: photo1.jpg, photo2.jpg, photo3.jpg, photo4.jpg, photo5.jpg, and photo6.jpg.

Launch a text editor and open the template file located at chapter1/template.html in the student files. Save the file as index.html in your float8 folder. Modify the file to configure a web page as indicated:

1. Configure the text, Floating Images, within an h1 element and within the title element.

2. Code six figure elements, one for each image. Within the figure element, configure the image

element and a figcaption element with an appropriate text description of the image. An example of the first figure element is

```
<figure>
  <img src="photo1.jpg" alt="Golden Gate Bridge"
       width="225" height="168">
  <figcaption>Golden Gate Bridge</figcaption>
</figure>
```

3. Configure all six figure elements in a similar manner. Substitute the actual name of each image file for the src values in the code. Write your own descriptive text for each image. Use photo2.jpg in the second figure element, photo3.jpg in the third figure element, photo4.jpg in the fourth figure element, photo5.jpg in the fifth figure element, and photo6.jpg in the sixth figure element. Save the file. Display your page in a browser. Figure 11 shows a partial screen capture.

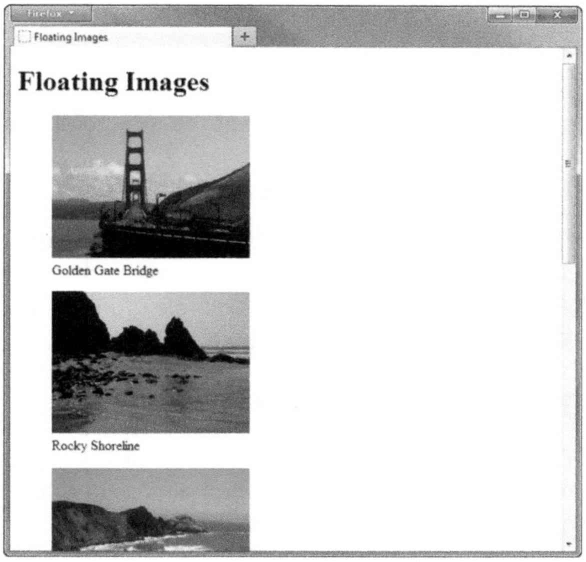

4. Now, let's add embedded CSS. Open your file in a text editor and code a style element in the head section. Configure the figure element selector to float to the left. Also set the width to 225 pixels, bottom padding to 10 pixels, and background color to light gray (#EAEAEA). Configure the figcaption element selector to display centered, italic text in the Georgia (or other serif) font. The CSS follows

FIGURE 11 *The web page before CSS.*

```
figure { float: left;
         width: 225px;
         padding-bottom: 10px;
         background-color: #EAEAEA; }
figcaption { text-align: center;
             font-style: italic;
             font-family: Georgia, serif; }
```

Save your page and display it in a browser. Experiment with resizing the browser window to see the display change. Compare your work to Figures 9 and 10. A sample solution is in the student files (chapter8/float).

More HTML5 Elements

You've worked with the HTML5 header, nav, and footer elements throughout this text. These HTML5 elements are used along with div and other elements to structure web page documents in a meaningful manner that defines the purpose of the structural areas. In this section you'll explore five more HTML5 elements.

The Hgroup Element

The block display **hgroup element** groups heading level tags and is useful if the logo header area of a web page contains both the website name and a **tagline**, which is a phrase that identifies and captures the essence of a business. For example, "unique and personalized gifts" is the tagline of e-commerce website RedEnvelope (www.redenvelope.com).

The Section Element

The purpose of a **section element** is to indicate a "section" of a document, such as a chapter or topic. This block display element could contain header, footer, section, article, aside, figure, div, and other elements needed to configure the content.

The Article Element

The **article element** is intended to present an independent entry, such as a blog posting, comment, or e-zine article that could stand on its own. This block display element could contain header, footer, section, aside, figure, div, and other elements needed to configure the content.

The Aside Element

The **aside element** indicates a sidebar or other tangential content. This block display element could contain header, footer, section, aside, figure, div, and other elements needed to configure the content.

The Time Element

The **time element** represents a date or a time. An optional `datetime` attribute can be used to specify a calendar date and/or time in machine-readable format. Use YYYY-MM-DD for a date. Use a 24-hour clock and HH:MM for time. See www.w3.org/TR/html-markup/time.html.

 Hands-On Practice 5

In this Hands-On Practice you'll begin with the two-column Lighthouse Island Bistro home page (shown in Figure 7) and apply the hgroup, section, article, aside, and time elements to create the page with blog postings shown in Figure 12.

Create a new folder named blog8. Copy the following files from the student files chapter8/caption folder into the blog8 folder: caption.html, lighthouseisland.jpg, and lighthouselogo.jpg.

More on Links, Layout, and Mobile

Launch a text editor, and open the caption.html file. Save the file as index.html. Examine the source code, and locate the header element.

1. Code hgroup tags within the header element to contain the h1 element. Add the tagline "the best coffee on the coast" with an h2 element within the hgroup element. Your code should look similar to the following

```
<header>
  <hgroup>
    <h1>Lighthouse Island
    Bistro</h1>
    <h2>the best coffee on
    the coast</h2>
  </hgroup>
</header>
```

2. Replace the contents of the div assigned to the id named content with the following code:

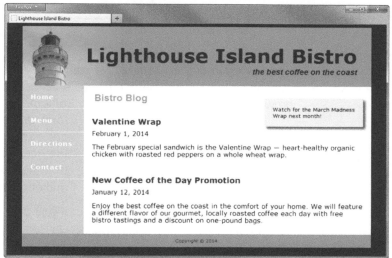

FIGURE 12 *This page utilizes the new elements.*

```
<h2>Bistro Blog</h2>
<aside>Watch for the
March Madness Wrap next
month!</aside>
<section>
  <article>
    <header><h1>Valentine Wrap</h1></header>
    <time datetime="2014-02-01">February 1, 2014</time>
    <p>The February special sandwich is the Valentine Wrap &mdash; heart-
    healthy organic chicken with roasted red peppers on a whole wheat wrap.</p>
  </article>
  <article>
    <header><h1>New Coffee of the Day Promotion</h1></header>
    <time datetime="2014-01-12">January 12, 2014</time>
    <p>Enjoy the best coffee on the coast in the comfort of your home. We will
    feature a different flavor of our gourmet, locally roasted coffee each day
    with free bistro tastings and a discount on one-pound bags.</p>
  </article>
</section>
```

3. Configure CSS for the h1 and h2 elements within the header element at the top of the page. Use descendant HTML selectors. Set the h1 bottom margin to 0. Set the h2 with 20 pixels of right padding, a top margin of 0, and .80em italic, right-aligned, #00005D color text.

4. Configure CSS for the header element contained within each article element. Use a descendant HTML selector. Set background color to #FFFFFF, no background image, 100% font size, 0 left padding, and auto height (use `height: auto;`).

5. The aside element contains content that is tangential to the main content. Configure CSS to display the aside element on the right (use float) with a 200 pixel width, light gray background color, 20 pixels of padding, 80% font size, and a 5px box shadow. Configure a relative position 20 pixels from the top (use `position: relative; top: -20px;`).

Save your file. Display your index.html page in a browser. It should look similar to the page shown in Figure 12. A sample solution is in the student files (chapter8/blog).

More on Links, Layout, and Mobile

HTML5 Compatibility with Older Browsers

Internet Explorer 9 and current versions of Safari, Chrome, Firefox, and Opera offer good support of the HTML5 elements you've been using. However, not everyone has a recent browser installed on their computer. Some people still use earlier versions of browsers for a variety of reasons. Although this issue will decrease in importance over time as people update their computers, your clients will most likely insist that their web pages are usable to as broad of an audience as possible.

FIGURE 13 *Outdated browsers do not support HTML5.*

Figure 13 shows the web page you created in Hands-On Practice 5 displayed in the outdated Internet Explorer 7—it's quite different from the modern display shown in Figure 12. The good news is that there are two easy methods to ensure backward compatibility of HTML5 with older, outdated browsers: configuring block display with CSS and the HTML5 Shim.

Configure CSS Block Display

Add one style rule to your CSS to inform older browsers to display HTML5 elements such as header, hgroup, nav, footer, section, article, figure, figcaption, and aside as block display (with empty space above and below). Example CSS follows:

```
header, hgroup, nav, footer, section, article, figure, figcaption,
aside { display: block; }
```

This technique will work well in all browsers except for Internet Explorer 8 and earlier versions. So, what's to be done about Internet Explorer 8 and earlier versions? That's where the HTML5 Shim (also called the HTML5 Shiv) is useful.

HTML5 Shim

Remy Sharp offers a solution to enhance the support of Internet Explorer 8 and earlier versions (see http://remysharp.com/2009/01/07/html5-enabling-script and http://code.google.com/p/html5shim). The technique uses conditional comments that are only supported by Internet Explorer and are ignored by other browsers. The conditional comments cause Internet Explorer to interpret JavaScript statements that configure it to recognize and process CSS for the new HTML5 element selectors. Sharp has uploaded the script to Google's code project and has made it available for anyone to use.

Add the following code to the head section of a web page after CSS to cause Internet Explorer 8 and earlier versions to correctly render your HTML5 code:

```
<!--[if lt IE 9]>
<script src="http://html5shim.googlecode.com/svn/trunk/html5.js">
</script>
<![endif]-->
```

What's the drawback to this approach? Be aware that your web page visitors using Internet Explorer 8 and earlier versions may see a warning message and must have JavaScript enabled for this method to work.

 Hands-On Practice 6

In this Hands-On Practice you'll modify the two-column Lighthouse Island Bistro home page (shown in Figure 12) to ensure backward compatibility with older browsers. Create a new folder named shim8. Copy the following files from the student files chapter8/blog folder into the shim8 folder: index.html, lighthouseisland.jpg, and lighthouselogo.jpg.

1. Launch a text editor, and open the index.html file. Examine the source code, and locate the head element and style element.

2. Add the following style declaration to the embedded styles:

   ```
   header, hgroup, nav, footer, section, article, figure, figcaption,
   aside { display: block; }
   ```

3. Add the following code below the closing style tag and above the closing head tag:

   ```
   <!--[if lt IE 9]>
   <script src="http://html5shim.googlecode.com/svn/trunk/html5.js">
   </script>
   <![endif]-->
   ```

4. Save your file. Display your index.html page in a modern browser. It should look similar to the page shown in Figure 12 in a modern browser.

5. Test in an outdated browser or in a simulation of an outdated browser.

   ▸ If you have access to a computer with an older version of Internet Explorer (such as IE7), use it to test your page.

   ▸ If you have Internet Explorer version 9 or later installed, you can simulate an older version of Internet Explorer by launching the page in the browser, pressing the F12 key to open the Developer Tools dialog box, and selecting Browser Mode > Internet Explorer 7. You may need to click through a message that requests you to provide permission for a script to run (that's the HTML5 Shim Javascript!).

When you test your page in either an older version of Internet Explorer or in the Internet Explorer 7 simulation you'll know that the HTML5 Shim has worked if the display is similar to Figure 12. The solution is in the student files chapter8/shim folder.

 Visit Modernizr at www.modernizr.com to explore a free open-source JavaScript library that enables backward compatibility for HTML5 and CSS3 in older browsers.

More on Links, Layout, and Mobile

CSS for Print

Even though the "paperless society" has been talked about for decades, the fact is that many people still love paper, and you can expect your web pages to be printed. CSS offers you some control over what gets printed and how the printouts are configured. This is easy to do using external style sheets. Create one external style sheet with the configurations for browser display and a second external style sheet with the special printing configurations. Associate both of the external style sheets to the web page using two link elements. Configure a **media attribute** on each link element. Table 1 describes the values of the media attribute.

TABLE 1 *The* media *Attribute*

Value	Purpose
screen	The default value; indicates the style sheet that configures typical browser viewport display on a color computer screen
print	Indicates the style sheet that configures the printed formatting
handheld	Although this value is intended by the W3C to indicate the style sheet that configures display on handheld mobile devices, in practice, the attribute value is not reliably applied (see Return of the Mobile Stylesheet at http://www.alistapart.com/articles/return-of-the-mobile-stylesheet for more information). Methods for configuring the design of mobile web pages will be introduced later in this chapter.

Modern browsers will use the correct style sheet depending on whether they are rendering a screen display or preparing to print a document. Configure the link element for your browser display with media="screen". Configure the link element for your printout with media="print". An example of the HTML is

```
<link rel="stylesheet" href="lighthouse.css" media="screen">
<link rel="stylesheet" href="lighthouseprint.css" media="print">
```

Print Styling Best Practices

You might be wondering how a print style sheet should differ from the CSS used to display the web page in a browser. Let's explore some commonly used techniques for styling printed web pages.

- **Hide Non-Essential Content.**   It's common practice to prevent banner ads, navigation, or other extraneous areas from appearing on the printout. Use the display: none; style declaration to hide content that is not needed on a printout of the web page.

- **Configure Font Size and Color for Printing.**   Another common practice is to configure the font sizes on the print style sheet to use pt units. This will better control the text on the printout. You might also consider configuring the text color to black (#000000) if you envision the need for visitors to print your pages often. The default setting on most browsers prevent background colors and background images from printing, but you can also prevent background image and background color display in your print style sheet.

▶ **Control Page Breaks.**   Use the CSS `page-break-before` or `page-break-after` properties to control page breaks when printing the web page. Well-supported values for these properties are `always` (the page break will always occur as designated), `avoid` (if possible, the page break will not occur before or after, as designated), and `auto` (default). For example, to configure a page break at a specific point in the document (in this case, right before an element assigned to the class named `newpage`), configure the CSS as shown below:

```
.newpage { page-break-before: always; }
```

 Hands-On Practice 7

In this Hands-On Practice you'll rework the Lighthouse Island Bistro home page (Figure 12) to use external style sheets and be configured for optimal screen display and printing. Create a new folder named print8. Copy the following files from the student files chapter8/blog folder into the print8 folder: index.html, lighthouseisland.jpg, and lighthouselogo.jpg.

1. Launch a text editor, and open the index.html file. Examine the source code and locate the style element. Copy the CSS contained between the style tags and paste into a new text document named bistro.css. Save the bistro.css file in the print8 folder.

2. Edit the index.html file, delete the style tags and CSS, and code a link tag in the head section that associates the web page with the bistro.css file for screen display (use `media="screen"`).

3. Edit the index.html file and add another link tag that associates the web page with a file named bistroprint.css for printing (use `media="print"`). Save the index.html file.

4. Launch a text editor and open bistro.css. Since you want to keep most of the styles for printing, you will start by creating a new version of the external style sheet. Save bistro.css with the name of bistroprint.css in the ch8print folder. You will modify three areas on this style sheet: the header selector, the `content` id selector, and the nav selector.

   ▶ Modify the header styles to print using black text in 20 point font size:
   ```
   header { color: #000000; font-size: 20pt; }
   ```
   ▶ Modify the `content` id to print using a serif typeface in a 12 point font size:
   ```
   #content { font-family: "Times New Roman", serif; font-size: 12pt; }
   ```
   ▶ Modify the navigation area to not display:
   ```
   nav { display: none; }
   ```
   Save your file in the print8 folder.

5. Test your work. Display your index.html file in a browser. Select Print > Preview. Your display should look similar to the page shown in Figure 14. The header and content font sizes have been configured. The navigation does not display. The student files contain a copy of index.html and bistroprint.css in the chapter8/print folder.

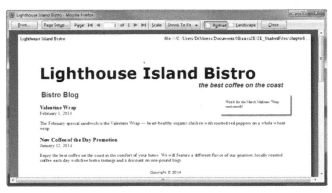

FIGURE 14 *The print preview display of the web page.*

More on Links, Layout, and Mobile

Mobile Web Design

Three methods can be used to provide access for website visitors who use mobile devices. One option is to design and publish a second website with a .mobi TLD. Visit **JCPenney** at http://jcp.com and http://jcp.mobi to see this in practice. Another option is to design and publish a separate website within your own domain that is optimized for mobile use. This technique is utilized by the White House website at www.whitehouse.gov (Figure 15) and http://m.whitehouse.gov (Figure 16).The third option is to configure one website with separate styles for mobile and desktop browser display. Before we focus on coding, let's consider design techniques for the mobile web.

FIGURE 15 *The regular White House website (www.whitehouse.gov) viewed in a browser.*

FIGURE 16
The mobile version of the White House website (http://m.whitehouse.gov).

Mobile Web Design Considerations

Mobile web users are typically on-the-go, need information quickly, and may be easily distracted. A web page that is optimized for mobile access should try to serve these needs. Take a moment to review Figures 15 and 16 and observe how the design of the mobile website addresses the following design considerations:

▶ **Small screen size.** The size of the header area is reduced to accommodate a small screen display.

▶ **Low bandwidth (slow connection speed).** Note that the large images visible in Figure 15 are not displayed on the mobile version of the web page.

▶ **Font, color, and media issues.** Common font typefaces are utilized. There is also good contrast between text and background color.

▶ **Awkward controls, and limited processor and memory.** The mobile website uses a single-column page layout that facilitates keyboard tabbing and will be easy to control by touch. The page is mostly text, which will be quickly rendered by a mobile browser.

▶ **Functionality.** Hyperlinks to popular site features are displayed directly under the header. A search feature is also provided.

Let's build on this base of design considerations and expand them.

Optimize Layout for Mobile Use

A single-column page layout (Figure 17) with a small header, key navigation links, content, and page footer works well for a mobile device display. Mobile screen resolutions vary greatly (for example, 320×240, 320×480, 360×640, 480×800, 640×690, and 1136×640). W3C recommendations include the following:

▶ Limit scrolling to one direction.

▶ Use heading elements.

▶ Use lists to organize information (such as unordered lists, ordered lists, and description lists).

More on Links, Layout, and Mobile

- Avoid using tables because they typically force both horizontal and vertical scrolling on mobile devices.
- Provide labels for form controls.
- Avoid using pixel units in style sheets.
- Avoid absolute positioning in style sheets.
- Hide content that is not essential for mobile use.

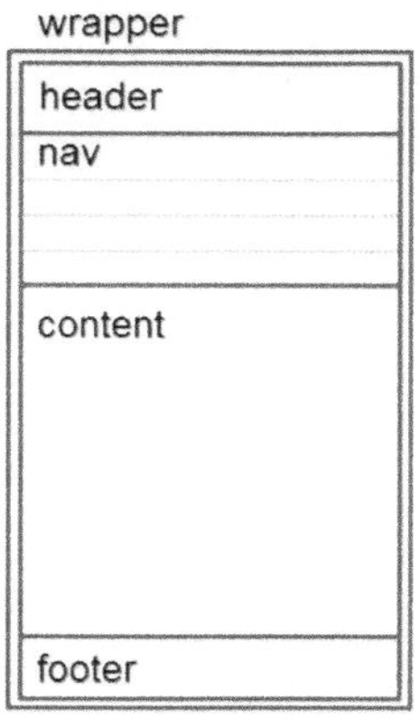

Optimize Navigation for Mobile Use

Easy-to-use navigation is crucial on a mobile device. The W3C recommends the following:

- Provide minimal navigation near the top of the page.
- Provide consistent navigation.
- Avoid hyperlinks that open files in new windows or pop-up windows.
- Try to balance both the number of hyperlinks on a page and the number of levels of links needed to access information.

Optimize Graphics for Mobile Use

Graphics can help to engage visitors, but be aware of the following W3C recommendations for mobile use:

- Avoid displaying images that are wider than the screen width (assume a 320 pixel screen width on a smartphone display).
- Configure alternate small, optimized background images.
- Some mobile browsers will downsize all images, so images with text can be difficult to read.
- Avoid the use of large graphic images.
- Specify the size of images.
- Provide alternate text for graphics and other non-text elements.

Optimize Text for Mobile Use

It can be difficult to read text on a small mobile device. The following W3C recommendations will aid your mobile visitors:

- Configure good contrast between text and background colors.
- Use common font typefaces.
- Configure font size with em units or percentages.
- Use a short, descriptive page title.

The W3C has published Mobile Web Best Practices 1.0, a list of 60 mobile web design best practices, at www.w3.org/TR/mobile-bp. Flipcards that summarize the Mobile Web Best Practices 1.0 document are available at www.w3.org/2007/02/mwbp_flip_cards.html.

Design for One Web

The W3C mission of building "**One Web**" refers to the concept of providing a single resource that is configured for optimal display on multiple types of devices. This is more efficient than creating multiple versions of a web document. With "One Web" in mind, the next sections introduce using the viewport meta tag and CSS media queries to target and deliver style sheets that are optimized for mobile display.

FIGURE 17

Wireframe for a typical single column page layout.

More on Links, Layout, and Mobile

Viewport Meta Tag

There are multiple uses for meta tags. You use the meta tag to configure the character encoding on a web page. In this section we'll explore the new **viewport meta tag**, which was created as an Apple extension that helps with displays on mobile devices such as iPhones and Android smartphones by setting the width and scale of the viewport. Figure 18 shows the display of a web page in a desktop browser.

FIGURE 18 *A web page displayed in a desktop browser.*

Figure 19 displays a screen shot of the same web page displayed on an Android device. Examine Figure 19 and notice that the mobile device zoomed out to display the entire web page on the tiny screen. The text on the web page is difficult to read.

Figure 20 shows the same web page after the viewport meta tag was added to the head section of the document. Setting the `initial-scale` directive to the value 1 caused the mobile browser to avoid zooming out on the web page and to display it in a more usable manner. The code is shown below:

```
<meta name="viewport"
content="width=device-width,
initial-scale=1.0">
```

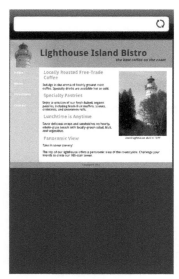

FIGURE 19 *Mobile display of a web page without the viewport meta tag.*

FIGURE 20 *The viewport meta tag helps with mobile display.*

More on Links, Layout, and Mobile

Code the viewport meta tag with the HTML `name="viewport"` and `content` attributes. The value of the HTML `content` attribute can be one or more **directives** (also referred to as properties by Apple), such as the `device-width` directive and directives that control zooming and scale. Table 2 lists viewport meta tag directives and their values.

Now that you've scaled the page to be readable, what about styling it for optimal mobile use? That's where CSS comes into play. You'll explore CSS Media Queries in the next section.

TABLE 2 *Viewport Meta Tag Directives.*

Directive	Values	Purpose
width	Numeric value or `device-width` which indicates actual width of the device screen	The width of the viewport in pixels
height	Numeric value or `device-height` which indicates actual height of the device screen	The height of the viewport in pixels
initial-scale	Numeric multiplier; Set to 1 for 100% initial scale	Initial scale of the viewport
minimum-scale	Numeric multiplier; Mobile Safari default is 0.25	Minimum scale of the viewport
maximum-scale	Numeric multiplier; Mobile Safari default is 1.6	Maximum scale of the viewport
user-scalable	yes allows scaling, no disables scaling	Determines whether a user can zoom in or out

 If a web page displays a phone number, wouldn't it be handy for a person using a smartphone to be able to tap on the phone number and place a call or send an SMS (Short Message Service) text message? It's very easy to configure a telephone hyperlink or SMS hyperlink for use by smartphones.

According to RFC 3966, you can configure a telephone hyperlink by using a telephone scheme: Begin the `href` value with `tel:` followed by the phone number. For example, to configure a telephone hyperlink on a web page for use by mobile browsers, code as follows:

```
<a href="tel:888-555-5555">Call 888-555-5555</a>
```

RFC 5724 indicates that an SMS scheme hyperlink intended to send a text message can be configured by beginning the `href` value with `sms:` followed by the phone number, as shown in the following code:

```
<a href="sms:888-555-5555">Text 888-555-5555</a>
```

Not all mobile browsers and devices support telephone and text hyperlinks, but expect increased use of this technology in the future.

More on Links, Layout, and Mobile

CSS3 Media Queries

The term **responsive web design** refers to progressively enhancing a web page for different viewing contexts (such as smartphones and tablets) through the use of coding techniques including fluid layouts, flexible images, and media queries.

For examples of the power of responsive web design techniques, review the Media Queries website at http://mediaqueri.es to view a gallery of sites that demonstrate responsive web design. The screen captures in the gallery show web pages displayed with the following browser viewport widths: 320px (smartphone display), 768px (tablet portrait display), 1024px (netbook display and tablet landscape display), and 1600px (large desktop display).

What's a Media Query?

According to the W3C (www.w3.org/TR/css3-mediaqueries) a **media query** is made up of a media type (such as screen) and a logical expression that determines the capability of the device that the browser is running on, such as screen resolution and orientation (portrait or landscape). When the media query evaluates as true, the media query directs browsers to CSS you have coded and configured specifically for those capabilities. Media queries are supported by current versions of major browsers, including Internet Explorer (version 9 and later).

FIGURE 21 *CSS media queries help to configure the page for mobile display.*

Media Query Example Using a Link Element

Figure 21 shows the same web page as Figure 20, but it looks quite different because of a link element that includes a media query and is associated with a style sheet configured for optimal mobile display on a popular smartphone. The HTML is shown below:

```
<link href="lighthousemobile.css" rel="stylesheet"
      media="only screen and (max-width: 480px)">
```

The code sample above will direct browsers to an external stylesheet that has been configured for optimal display on the most popular smartphones. The media type value `only` is a keyword that will hide the media query from outdated browsers. The media type value `screen` targets devices with screens. Commonly used media types and keywords are listed in Table 3.

The `max-width` media feature is set to 480px. While there are many different screen sizes for smartphones these days, a maximum width of 480px will target the landscape display size of many popular models. A media query may test for both minimum and maximum values. For example,

```
<link href="lighthousetablet.css" rel="stylesheet"
      media="only screen and (min-width: 768px) and (max-width: 1024px)">
```

More on Links, Layout, and Mobile

TABLE 3 *Media Types*

Media Type	Value Purpose
`all`	All devices
`screen`	Screen display of web page
`only`	Causes older nonsupporting browsers to ignore the media query
`print`	Print out of web page

Media Query Example Using an `@media` Rule

A second method of using media queries is to code them directly in your CSS using an **@media rule**. Begin by coding `@media` followed by the media type and logical expression. Then enclose the desired CSS selector(s) and declaration(s) within a pair of braces. The sample code below configures a different background image specifically for smartphone display.

```
@media only screen and (max-width: 480px) {
  header { background-image: url(mobile.gif);
  }
}
```

Table 4 lists commonly used media query features.

Visit the following resources for collections of media query examples that target various devices:

- http://css-tricks.com/snippets/css/media-queries-for-standard-devices
- http://webdesignerwall.com/tutorials/css3-media-queries

TABLE 4 *Commonly Used Media Query Features*

Features	Values	Criteria
`max-device-height`	Numeric value	The height of the screen size of the output device in pixels is smaller or equal to the value
`max-device-width`	Numeric value	The width of the screen size of the output device in pixels is smaller or equal to the value
`min-device-height`	Numeric value	The height of the screen size of the output device in pixels is greater than or equal to the value
`min-device-width`	Numeric value	The width of the screen size of the output device in pixels is greater than or equal to the value
`max-height`	Numeric value	The height of the viewport in pixels is smaller than or equal to the value; (reevaluated when screen is resized)
`min-height`	Numeric value	The height of the viewport in pixels is greater than or equal to the value; (reevaluated when screen is resized)
`max-width`	Numeric value	The width of the viewport in pixels is smaller than or equal to the value; (reevaluated when screen is resized)
`min-width`	Numeric value	The width of the viewport in pixels is greater than or equal to the value; (reevaluated when screen is resized)
`orientation`	portrait or landscape	The orientation of the device

Practice with Media Queries

In this Hands-On Practice you'll rework a version of the two-column Lighthouse Island Bistro home page (Figure 22) to display a single-column page when the viewport size is 768 pixels or smaller (a tablet portrait display) and display a page further optimized for smartphone display when the viewport size is 480 pixels or smaller. Create a folder named query8. Copy the starter2.html file from the chapter8 folder into the query8 folder and rename it as index.html. Copy the lighthouseisland.jpg file from the student files chapter8/starters folder into the query8 folder. Launch a browser and view index.html as shown in Figure 22. Open index.html in a text editor. Review the embedded CSS and note that the two-column layout is fluid—the width is set to 80% and there is no minimum width set. The two-column look is accomplished by configuring a nav element that floats to the left.

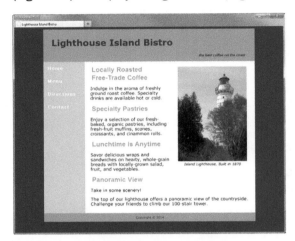

FIGURE 22 *The two-column desktop display.*

1. Edit the embedded CSS. Add the following @media rule before the ending style tag. The @media rule will change the float, width, and padding properties configured for the nav element selector when the viewport size is 768 pixels or smaller.

   ```
   @media only screen and (max-width: 768px) {
      nav { float: none; width: 100%;
            padding: 0.5em; }
   }
   ```

2. Save the index.html file. Test your index.html file in a desktop browser. When the browser is maximized, the page should look similar to Figure 22. When you resize the browser to be smaller (width less than or equal to 768 pixels), the page should look similar to Figure 23 with a single column layout. As you can see, we still have some work to do.

3. Edit the embedded CSS and add style rules within the media query that remove the margin, expand the wrapper id, and configure the nav area li elements with inline display and the nav area ul elements with centered text.

FIGURE 23 *The media query has been applied.*

More on Links, Layout, and Mobile

```
@media only screen and (max-width: 768px) {
  body { margin: 0; }
  #wrapper { margin: auto; }
  nav { float: none; width: auto; padding: 0.5em; }
  nav li { display: inline; }
  nav ul { text-align: center; }
}
```

4. Save the index.html file. Test your index.html file in a desktop browser. When the browser is maximized, the page should look similar to Figure 22. When you resize the browser to be smaller (a width less than or equal to 768 pixels), the page should look similar to Figure 24. Continue to resize the web page and notice that the hyperlinks will shift and are not well-aligned. We still have more work to do to optimize the page for display on small mobile devices.

5. Edit the embedded CSS. Add the following @media rule before the ending style tag. The @media rule will configure styles for the body element selector, wrapper id, content id, the figure element selector, and the li elements in the navigation area. The code follows:

```
@media only screen and (max-width: 480px) {
  body { margin: 0; }
  #wrapper { width: auto; }
  #content { margin-top: -.5em; }
  figure { float: none; padding: 0;
           margin: 0; text-align: center; }
  nav li { display: block; font-size: 120%; margin: 0;
           border-bottom: 2px ridge #00005D; }
}
```

6. Save the index.html file. Test your index.html file in a desktop browser. When the browser is maximized, the page should look similar to Figure 22. When you resize the browser to be smaller (width less than 769 pixels and greater than 480 pixels), the page should look similar to Figure 24 with a single column layout. When you resize the browser to be even smaller (width equal to or less than 480 pixels) the page should look similar to Figure 25. The web page you've created is an example of applying responsive web design techniques. The student files contain a suggested solution in the chapter8/query folder.

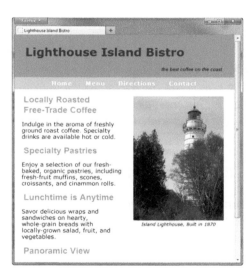

FIGURE 24 *The web page is configured for the width of a tablet in portrait mode.*

FIGURE 25 *The web page is configured for the width of a typical smartphone.*

Flexible Images

In his book, *Responsive Web Design*, Ethan Marcotte described a **flexible image** as a fluid image that will not break the page layout as the browser viewport is resized. Flexible images, along with fluid layouts and media queries, are the components of responsive web design.

The technique to configure an image as flexible requires a change to the HTML and additional CSS to style the flexible image.

1. Edit the img elements in the HTML. Remove the `height` and `width` attributes.
2. Configure the `max-width: 100%;` style declaration in the CSS. If the width of the image is less than the width of the container element, the image will display with its actual dimensions. If the width of the image is greater than the width of the container element, the image will be resized by the browser to fit in the container (instead of hanging out over the margin).
3. To keep the dimensions of the image in proportion and maintain the aspect ratio of the image, Bruce Lawson suggests to also set the `height: auto;` style declaration in the CSS (see http://brucelawson.co.uk/2012/responsive-web-design-preserving-images-aspect-ratio).

Background images can also be configured for a more fluid display at various viewport sizes. Although it's common to code a `height` property when configuring a background image with CSS, the result is a somewhat non-responsive background image. Explore configuring other CSS properties for the container such as `font-size`, `line-height`, and `padding` in percentage values. The `background-size: cover;` property can also be useful. You'll typically see a more pleasing display of the background image in various-sized viewports. Another option is to configure different image files to use for backgrounds and use media queries to determine which background image is displayed. A disadvantage to this option is that multiple files are downloaded although only one file is displayed. You'll apply flexible image techniques in the next Hands-On Practice.

 Hands-On Practice 9

In this Hands-On Practice you'll work with a web page that demonstrates responsive web design. Figure 26 depicts the three-column desktop browser display and demonstrates the effects of media queries which are configured to display a two-column page when the viewport size is 768 pixels or smaller (a tablet portrait display) and display a single-column page optimized for smartphone display when the viewport size is 480 pixels or smaller. You will edit the CSS to configure flexible images.

Create a folder named flexible8. Copy the starter3.html file from the chapter8 folder into the flexible8 folder and rename it index.html. Copy the following images from the student files chapter8/starters folder into the flexible8 folder: header.jpg and pools.jpg. Launch a browser and view index.html as shown in Figure 27. View the code in a text editor and

More on Links, Layout, and Mobile

notice that the `height` and `width` attributes have already been removed from the HTML. View the CSS and notice that the web page uses a fluid layout with percentage values for widths. Edit the embedded CSS.

Desktop Browser   Tablet Display Width   Smartphone Display Width

FIGURE 26 *The web page demonstrates responsive web design techniques.*

1. Locate the h1 element selector. Remove the height style declaration. Add declarations to set the font size to 300%, top padding 5%, bottom padding 5%, 0 left padding, and 0 right padding. The CSS follows:

```
h1 { text-align: center;
     font-size: 300%;
     padding: 5% 0;
     text-shadow: 3px 3px
     3px #F4E8BC; }
```

2. Locate the header element selector. Add the `background-size: cover;` declaration to cause the browser to scale the background image to fill the container. The CSS follows:

FIGURE 27 *The web page before the images are configured to be flexible.*

```
header { background-image: url(header.jpg);
         background-repeat: no-repeat;
         background-size: cover; }
```

3. Add a style rule for the img element selector that sets maximum width to 100% and height to the value auto. The CSS follows:

```
img { max-width: 100%;
      height: auto; }
```

4. Save the index.html file. Test your index.html file in a desktop browser. As you resize the browser window, you'll see your page respond and look similar to the screen captures in Figure 26. The web page demonstrates responsive web design with the following techniques: fluid layout, media queries, and flexible images. A suggested solution is in the student files chapter8/flexible folder.

Explore FURTHER

You learned basic techniques for configuring flexible, fluid images in this section. However, there are a number of responsive image techniques being discussed and tested on the Web which are intended to eliminate duplicate downloads and serve the most appropriate image for the device being used, including adaptive images for rendering on devices with high pixel density retina displays such as the iPhone and iPad. Visit the following resources to explore the topic of responsive images:

▶ http://alistapart.com/articles/responsive-images-and-web-standards-at-the-turning-point

▶ http://css-tricks.com/which-responsive-images-solution-should-you-use

▶ www.netmagazine.com/features/problem-adaptive-images

More on Links, Layout, and Mobile

Testing Mobile Display

The best way to test the mobile display of a web page is to publish it to the Web and access it from a mobile device. However, not everyone has access to a smartphone. Several options for emulating a mobile display are listed below:

FIGURE 28 *Testing a web page with the Opera Mobile Emulator.*

FIGURE 29

Approximating the mobile display with a desktop browser.

- ▶ **Opera Mobile Emulator** (shown in Figure 28)

  Windows only download; Supports media queries

  www.opera.com/developer/tools/mobile

- ▶ **Mobilizer**

  Windows and Mac download; Supports media queries

  www.springbox.com/mobilizer

- ▶ **Opera Mini Simulator**

  Runs in a browser window; Supports media queries

  www.opera.com/mobile/demo

- ▶ **iPhone Emulator**

  Runs in a browser window; Does not support media queries

  www.testiphone.com

- ▶ **iPhoney**

  Mac only download; Does not support media queries

  www.marketcircle.com/iphoney

- ▶ **iPadPeek**

  Runs in a browser window; Supports media queries

  http://ipadpeek.com

Testing with a Desktop Browser

If you don't have a smartphone and/or are unable to publish your files to the Web—no worries—as you've seen in this chapter (also see Figure 29) you can approximate the mobile display of your web page using a desktop browser. Verify the placement of your media queries.

- ▶ If you have coded media queries within your CSS, display your page in a desktop browser and then reduce the width and height of the viewport until it approximates a mobile screen size (such as 320×480).
- ▶ If you have coded media queries within a link tag, edit the web page and temporarily modify the link tag to point to your mobile CSS style sheet. Then,

display your page in a desktop browser and reduce the width and height of the viewport until it approximates a mobile screen size (such as 320×480).

While you can guess at the size of your browser viewport, the following tools can be helpful:

FIGURE 30 *Testing the web page with a smartphone.*

▶ **Chris Pederick's Web Developer Extension**

Available for Firefox and Chrome

http://chrispederick.com/work/web-developer

Select Resize > Display Window Size

▶ **Internet Explorer 9 Developer Tools**

Select Tools > F12 Developer Tools > Resize

For Serious Developers Only

If you are a software developer or information systems major, you may want to explore the SDKs (Software Developer Kits) for the iOS and Android platforms. Each SDK includes a mobile device emulator. Figure 30 shows an example screen capture.

▶ **iOS SDK** (Mac only)

http://developer.apple.com/programs/ios/develop.html

▶ **Android SDK**

http://developer.android.com/sdk/index.html

Keep in mind that Internet Explorer prior to version 9 does support media queries. The Google code repository offers a JavaScript workaround for this issue. Add the following code in the head section of your web page to make the script available for Internet Explorer version 8 and lower.

```
<!--[if lt IE 9]>
<script src=
"http://css3-mediaqueries-js.googlecode.com/svn/trunk/css3-mediaqueries.js">
</script>
<![endif]-->
```

This section provided an introduction to mobile web design. The styles for desktop browser viewing were coded and the media queries were constructed to adapt the layout for mobile devices. This is a typical workflow when you need to rework an existing website for mobile device display.

However, if you are designing a new website, there is an alternate approach that was first proposed by Luke Wroblewski. Design the mobile style sheet first and then develop alternate styles for tablet and/or desktop browsers that progressively enhance the design with multiple columns and larger images. You can find out more about this "Mobile First" approach at the following resources:

▶ www.lukew.com/ff/entry.asp?933

▶ www.lukew.com/ff/entry.asp?1137

▶ www.techradar.com/news/internet/mobile-web-design-tips-mobile-should-come-first-719677

Review and Apply

Review Questions

Multiple Choice. Choose the best answer for each item.

1. Which of the following causes an element not to display?

   a. `display: block;`

   b. `display: 0px;`

   c. `display: none;`

   d. this cannot be done with CSS

2. Which of the following is the attribute used to indicate whether the style sheet is for printing or for screen display?

   a. `rel`   **b.** `type`

   c. `media`   **d.** `content`

3. How would you link to the named fragment `#jobs` on the page employ.html from the home page of the site?

   a. `<a name="employ.html#jobs">Jobs</a>`

   b. `<a href="employ.html#jobs">Jobs</a>`

   c. `<a link="employ.html#jobs">Jobs</a>`

   d. `<a href="#jobs">Jobs</a>`

4. Which of the following is an HTML5 element used to indicate tangential content?

   a. `header`

   b. `sidebar`

   c. `nav`

   d. `aside`

5. Which of the following attributes define a fragment identifier on a page?

   a. `bookmark`

   b. `fragment`

   c. `href`

   d. `id`

6. Which meta tag is used to configure display for mobile devices?

   a. viewport

   b. handheld

   c. mobile

   d. screen

7. Which of the following is a mobile web design best practice?

   a. Embed text in images wherever possible.

   b. Configure a single-column page layout.

   c. Configure a multiple-column page layout.

   d. Avoid using lists to organize information.

8. Which of the following font units is recommended for mobile display?

   a. pt unit

   b. px unit

   c. cm unit

   d. em unit

9. When using CSS media queries, code the _____ keyword to hide the query from older nonsupporting browsers.

   a. `modern`

   b. `screen`

   c. `only`

   d. `print`

10. Which of the following is an HTML5 element used to present an independent entry, such as a blog posting or comment that could stand on its own?

    a. `section`

    b. `article`

    c. `aside`

    d. `content`

Hands-On Exercises

1. Write the HTML to create a fragment identifier at the beginning of a web page designated by `"top"`.

2. Write the HTML to create a hyperlink to the named fragment designated by `"top"`.

3. Write the HTML to associate a web page with an external style sheet named myprint.css to configure a printout.

4. Write the HTML to configure a header element that contains an hgroup element with an h1 element, h2 element, and h3 element. Configure your school name as the h1 element. Configure your major as the h2 element. Configure the name of your current web development course as the h3 element.

5. Create a web page about your favorite hobby, movie, or music group. Include the following HTML5 elements: header, nav, figure, figcaption, article, and footer. Configure the text, color, and layout with CSS.

6. Modify the web page you created in Hands-On Exercise 5 to apply components of responsive web design to display well on both desktop and smartphone browsers. *Hint*: Add the viewport meta tag, configure flexible images, and edit the CSS to configure a media query with appropriate style rules for typical smartphone device display.

Focus on Web Design

As you read about mobile web design best practices in this chapter, you may have noticed some overlap with techniques that provide for accessibility, such as alternate text and use of headings. Explore the Web Content Accessibility and Mobile Web document at www.w3.org/WAI/mobile. Explore related links that interest you. Write a one-page, double-spaced summary that describes areas of overlap and how web developers can support both accessibility and mobile devices.

Answers to Review Questions

1. c	**2.** c	**3.** b
4. d	**5.** d	**6.** a
7. b	**8.** d	**9.** c
10. b		

Credits

Figures 1, 3, © Microsoft Corporation

Figures 2, 4–14, 18–27, 29, 32–35, 36–38 © Terry Ann Morris, Ed.D. | Mozilla Foundation

Figures 15, 16 © Whitehouse.gov | Mozilla Foundation

Figure 28 Testing a web page with Opera Mobile Emulator screenshot. Copyright © Opera Software A/S. Reprinted with permission

Table Basics

Back in the day, tables were often used to format the layout of a web page. However, CSS is the page layout tool of choice for modern web designers. In this chapter, you'll become familiar with coding HTML tables to organize information on a web page.

You'll learn how to...

- Describe the recommended use of a table on a web page
- Configure a basic table with the table, table row, table header, and table cell elements
- Configure table sections with the thead, tbody, and tfoot elements

- Increase the accessibility of a table
- Style an HTML table with CSS
- Describe the purpose of CSS structural pseudo-classes

From Chapter 9 of *Basics of Web Design HTML5 & CSS3*, Second Edition. Terry Ann Felke-Morris. Copyright © 2014 by Pearson Education, Inc. All rights reserved.

Table Overview

The purpose of a table is to organize information. In the past, before CSS was well-supported by browsers, tables were also used to format web page layouts. An HTML table is composed of rows and columns, like a spreadsheet. Each individual table cell is at the intersection of a specific row and column.

- Each table begins with a `<table>` tag and ends with a `</table>` tag.
- Each table row begins with a `<tr>` tag and ends with a `</tr>` tag.
- Each cell (table data) begins with a `<td>` tag and ends with a `</td>` tag.
- Table cells can contain text, graphics, and other HTML elements.

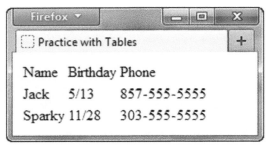

FIGURE 1 *Table with three rows and three columns.*

Figure 1 shows a sample table with three rows and three columns. The sample HTML for the table shown in Figure 1 is

```
<table>
  <tr>
    <td>Name</td>
    <td>Birthday</td>
    <td>Phone</td>
  </tr>
  <tr>
    <td>Jack</td>
    <td>5/13</td>
    <td>857-555-5555</td>
  </tr>
  <tr>
    <td>Sparky</td>
    <td>11/28</td>
    <td>303-555-5555</td>
  </tr>
</table>
```

Notice how the table is coded row by row. Also, each row is coded cell by cell. This attention to detail is crucial to the successful use of tables. An example can be found in the student files on the companion website at www.pearsonhighered.com/felke-morris (chapter9/table1.html).

The Table Element

Table elements are block display elements that contain tabular information. The table begins with a `<table>` tag and ends with a `</table>` tag.

The `border` Attribute

In HTML 4 and XHTML, the purpose of the `border` attribute was to indicate the presence and the width of a visible table border. The `border` attribute is used

Table Basics

differently in HTML5. When following HTML5 syntax, code `border="1"` to cause the browser to render default borders around the table and table cells. The web page in Figure 2 (student files chapter9/table1a.html) depicts a table with `border="1"`. If the `border` attribute is omitted, most browsers will not display a default border around the table and table cells (as shown in Figure 1). CSS is used to style the border of a table. You'll get practice styling a table with CSS later in the chapter.

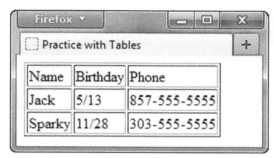

FIGURE 2 *A table rendered by the browser with a visible border.*

Table Captions

The **caption element** is often used with a data table to describe its contents. The table shown in Figure 3 uses `<caption>` tags to set the caption to "Bird Sightings". The caption element is coded on the line immediately after the opening `<table>` tag. An example can be found in the student files (chapter9/table2.html). The HTML for the table is

FIGURE 3 *The caption for this table is Bird Sightings.*

```
<table border="1">
  <caption>Bird Sightings</caption>
  <tr>
    <td>Name</td>
    <td>Date</td>
  </tr>
  <tr>
    <td>Bobolink</td>
    <td>5/25/10</td>
  </tr>
  <tr>
    <td>Upland Sandpiper</td>
    <td>6/03/10</td>
  </tr>
</table>
```

?FAQ What about other attributes that I've seen coded on table tags, like `cellpadding`, `cellspacing`, and `summary` attributes?

Earlier versions of HTML (such as HTML 4 and XHTML) provided a variety of attributes for configuring the table element, including `cellpadding`, `cellspacing`, `bgcolor`, `align`, `width`, and `summary`. These attributes are considered invalid and obsolete in HTML5. It is preferred to configure presentational display characteristics (such as alignment, width, cell padding, cell spacing, and background color) within CSS instead of with HTML attributes. Although the `summary` attribute supported accessibility and served to describe the table, the W3C suggests using one of the following techniques to replace the `summary` attribute and provide context for a table: configure descriptive text in the caption element, provide an explanatory paragraph directly on the web page, or simplify the table. You'll get practice configuring tables with CSS later in this chapter.

Table Basics

Table Rows, Cells, and Headers

VideoNote
Configure a Table

The **table row element** configures a row within a table on a web page. The table row begins with a `<tr>` tag and ends with a `</tr>` tag.

The **table data element** configures a cell within a row in a table on a web page. The table cell begins with a `<td>` tag and ends with a `</td>` tag. See Table 1 for common attributes of the table data cell element.

TABLE 1 *Commonly Used Attributes of the Table Data and Table Header Cell Elements*

Attribute	Value	Purpose
`colspan`	Numeric	The number of columns spanned by a cell
`headers`	The id value(s) of a column or row heading cell	Associates the table data cells with table header cells; may be accessed by screen readers
`rowspan`	Numeric	The number of rows spanned by a cell
`scope`	`row` or `column`	The scope of the table header cell contents (row or column); may be accessed by screen readers

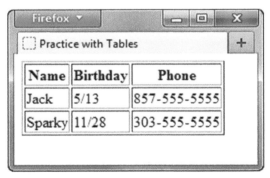

FIGURE 4 *Using `<th>` tags to indicate column headings.*

The **table header element** is similar to a table data element and configures a cell within a row in a table on a web page. Its special purpose is to configure column and row headings. Text displayed within a table header element is centered and bold. The table header element begins with a `<th>` tag and ends with a `</th>` tag. See Table 1 for common attributes of the table header element. Figure 4 shows a table with column headings configured by `<th>` tags. The HTML for the table shown in Figure 4 is as follows (also see chapter9/table3.html in the student files). Notice that the first row uses `<th>` instead of `<td>` tags:

Table Basics

```
<table border="1">
  <tr>
    <th>Name</th>
    <th>Birthday</th>
    <th>Phone</th>
  </tr>
  <tr>
    <td>Jack</td>
    <td>5/13</td>
    <td>857-555-5555</td>
  </tr>
  <tr>
    <td>Sparky</td>
    <td>11/28</td>
    <td>303-555-5555</td>
  </tr>
</table>
```

 Hands-On Practice 1

Create a web page similar to Figure 5 that describes two schools you have attended. Use the caption "School History Table". The table has three rows and three columns. The first row will have table header elements with the headings "School Attended", "Years", and "Degree Awarded". You will complete the second and third rows with your own information within table data elements.

To get started, launch a text editor and open the template.html file from the chapter1 folder in the student files. Modify the title element. Use table, table row, table header, table data, and caption elements to configure a table similar to Figure 5.

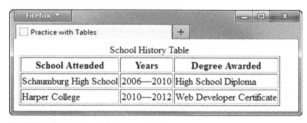

FIGURE 5 *School History Table.*

Hints: The table has three rows and three columns. To configure a border, use `border="1"` on the `<table>` tag. Use the table header element for the cells in the first row.

Save your file and display it in a browser. It should look similar to Figure 5. A sample solution is found in the student files (chapter9/table4.html).

Span Rows and Columns

You can alter the gridlike look of a table by applying the `colspan` and `rowspan` attributes to table data or table header elements. As you get into more complex table configurations like these, be sure to sketch the table on paper before you start typing the HTML.

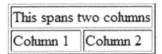

FIGURE 6 *Table with a row that spans two columns.*

The **`colspan` attribute** specifies the number of columns that a cell will occupy. Figure 6 shows a table cell that spans two columns.

The HTML for the table is

```
<table border="1">
  <tr>
    <td colspan="2">This spans two columns</td>
  </tr>
  <tr>
    <td>Column 1</td>
    <td>Column 2</td>
  </tr>
</table>
```

The `rowspan` **attribute** specifies the number of rows that a cell will occupy. An example of a table cell that spans two rows is shown in Figure 7.

FIGURE 7 *Table with a column that spans two rows.*

The HTML for the table is

```
<table border="1">
  <tr>
    <td rowspan="2">This spans two rows</td>
    <td>Row 1 Column 2</td>
  </tr>
  <tr>
    <td>Row 2 Column 2</td>
  </tr>
</table>
```

An example of the tables in Figures 6 and 7 can be found in the student files (chapter9/table5.html).

Table Basics

Hands-On Practice 2 ————————————————————

To create the web page shown in Figure 8, launch a text editor and open the template.html file from the chapter1 folder in the student files. Modify the title element. Use table, table row, table head, and table data elements to configure the table.

1. Code the opening `<table>` tag. Configure a border with `border="1"`.

2. Begin the first row with a `<tr>` tag.

3. The table data cell with "Cana Island Lighthouse" spans three rows. Code a table data element. Use the `rowspan="3"` attribute.

4. Code a table data element that contains the text "Built: 1869".

5. End the first row with a `</tr>` tag.

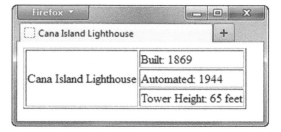

FIGURE 8 *Practice with the rowspan attribute.*

6. Begin the second row with a `<tr>` tag. This row will only have one table data element because the cell in the first column is already reserved for "Cana Island Lighthouse".

7. Code a table data element that contains the text "Automated: 1944".

8. End the second row with a `</tr>` tag.

9. Begin the third row with a `<tr>` tag. This row will only have one table data element because the cell in the first column is already reserved for "Cana Island Lighthouse".

10. Code a table data element that contains the text "Tower Height: 65 feet".

11. End the third row with a `</tr>` tag.

12. Code the closing `</table>` tag.

Save the file and view it in a browser. A sample solution is found in the student files (chapter9/table6.html). Notice how the "Cana Island Lighthouse" text is vertically aligned in the middle of the cell—this is the default vertical alignment. You can modify the vertical alignment using CSS—see the section "Style a Table with CSS" later in this chapter.

 Is there a way to create a table-like page layout with CSS?

Yes, if you'd like to explore using CSS to style table-like layouts on web pages, check out the CSS `display` property. The CSS `display` property configures whether and how an element is displayed. Internet Explorer 8 was the last major browser to add support for the `display: table` property values. Rachel Andrew's article, "Everything You Know About CSS Is Wrong" (www.digital-web.com/articles/everything_you_know_about_CSS_Is_wrong), encourages developers to embrace the `display: table` coding methods.

Be aware that this technique is still quite limited. For example, there is no built-in mechanism to emulate the rowspan or colspan attribute in HTML tables. However, this is in the works with the CSS3 draft recommendation at www.w3.org/Style/CSS/current-work, which includes new CSS specifications for working with multicolumn layouts and grid positioning.

Table Basics

Configure an Accessible Table

 Tables can be useful to organize information on a web page, but what if you couldn't see the table and were relying on assistive technology like a screen reader to read the table to you? You'd hear the contents of the table just the way it is coded—row by row, cell by cell. This might be difficult to understand. This section discusses coding techniques to improve the accessibility of tables.

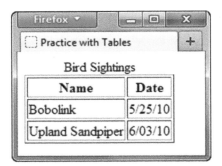

FIGURE 9 *This simple data table uses* <th> *tags and the caption element to provide for accessibility.*

For a simple informational data table like the one shown in Figure 9, the W3C recommends the following:

▶ Use table header elements (<th> tags) to indicate column or row headings.

▶ Use the caption element to provide a text title or caption for the table.

An example web page is in the student files (chapter9/table7.html). The HTML is

```
<table border="1">
<caption>Bird Sightings</caption>
  <tr>
    <th>Name</th>
    <th>Date</th>
  </tr>
  <tr>
    <td>Bobolink</td>
    <td>5/25/10</td>
  </tr>
  <tr>
    <td>Upland Sandpiper</td>
    <td>6/03/10</td>
  </tr>
</table>
```

Table Basics

However, for more complex tables the W3C recommends specifically associating the table data cell values with their corresponding headers. The technique that is recommended uses the id attribute (usually in a <th> tag) to identify a specific header cell and the **headers attribute** in a <td> tag. The code to configure the table in Figure 9 using headers and id attributes is as follows (also found in the student files chapter9/table8.html):

```
<table border="1">
<caption>Bird Sightings</caption>
  <tr>
    <th id="name">Name</th>
    <th id="date">Date</th>
  </tr>
  <tr>
    <td headers="name">Bobolink</td>
    <td headers="date">5/25/10</td>
  </tr>
  <tr>
    <td headers="name">Upland Sandpiper</td>
    <td headers="date">6/03/10</td>
  </tr>
</table>
```

? **FAQ** What about the scope attribute?

The scope attribute specifies the association of table cells and table row or column headers. It is used to indicate whether a table cell is a header for a column (scope="col") or row (scope="row"). An example of the code for the table in Figure 8 that uses this attribute is as follows (also see the student files chapter9/table9.html):

```
<table border="1">
<caption>Bird Sightings</caption>
  <tr>
    <th scope="col">Name</th>
    <th scope="col">Date</th>
  </tr>
  <tr>
    <td>Bobolink</td>
    <td>5/25/10</td>
  </tr>
  <tr>
    <td>Upland Sandpiper</td>
    <td>6/03/10</td>
  </tr>
</table>
```

As you review the code sample above, you may notice that using the scope attribute to provide for accessibility requires less coding than implementing the headers and id attributes. However, due to inconsistent screen reader support of the scope attribute, the WCAG 2.0 recommendations for coding techniques encourage the use of headers and id attributes rather than the scope attribute.

Table Basics

Style a Table with CSS

Before CSS was well-supported by browsers, it was common practice to configure the visual aesthetic of a table with HTML attributes. The modern approach is to use CSS to style a table. Table 2 lists corresponding CSS properties with HTML attributes used to style tables.

TABLE 2 *Configuring Tables with HTML Attributes and CSS Properties*

HTML Attribute	CSS Property
align	To align a table, configure the `width` and `margin` properties for the table element selector. To center a table, use `table { width: 75%; margin: auto; }`
	To align content within table cells, use `text-align`
width	width
height	height
cellpadding	padding
cellspacing	`border-spacing` configures space between cell borders with a numeric value (px or em) or percentage. If you set a value to 0, omit the unit. One value configures both horizontal and vertical spacing. When two values are used, the first value configures the horizontal spacing, and the second value configures the vertical spacing.
	`border-collapse` configures the border area. The values are `separate` (default) and `collapse` (removes extra space between table and cell borders).
bgcolor	background-color
valign	vertical-align
border	border, border-style, border-spacing
none	background-image
none	`caption-side` specifies caption placement. Values are `top` (default) and `bottom`

 Hands-On Practice 3

Lighthouse Island Bistro Specialty Coffee Menu

Specialty Coffee	Description	Price
Lite Latte	Indulge in a shot of locally roasted espresso with steamed, skim milk.	$3.50
Mocha Latte	Chocolate lovers will enjoy a shot of locally roasted espresso, steamed milk, and dark, milk, or white chocolate.	$4.00
MCP Latte	A luscious mocha latte with caramel and pecan syrup.	$4.50

FIGURE 10 *The table before CSS.*

In this Hands-On Practice you will code CSS style rules to configure an informational table on a web page. Create a folder named ch9table. Copy the starter.html file from the chapter9 folder in the student files to your ch9table folder. Display the starter.html file in a browser. The page should look similar to Figure 10.

Table Basics

Launch a text editor and open the starter.html file from your ch9table folder. Locate the style tags in the head section. You will code embedded CSS in this Hands-On Practice. Position your cursor on the blank line between the style tags.

1. Configure the table element selector to be centered, have a dark blue, 5 pixel border, and have a width of 600px:

```
table { margin: auto; border: 5px solid #000066; width: 600px; }
```

Save the file as menu.html and display your page in a browser. Notice that there is a dark blue border surrounding the entire table.

2. Configure the td and th element selectors with a border, padding, and Arial or the default sans-serif font typeface:

```
td, th { border: 1px solid #000066; padding: 5px;
         font-family: Arial, sans-serif; }
```

Save the file and display your page in a browser. Each table cell should now be outlined with a dark blue border and should display text in a sans serif font.

3. Eliminate the empty space between the borders of the table cells with the **border-spacing property**. Add a `border-spacing: 0;` declaration to the table element selector. Save the file and display your page in a browser.

4. Configure the caption to be displayed with Verdana or the default sans-serif font typeface, bold font weight, font size 1.2 em, and 5 pixels of bottom padding:

```
caption { font-family: Verdana, sans-serif; font-weight: bold;
          font-size: 1.2em; padding-bottom: 5px; }
```

5. Let's experiment and configure background colors for the rows instead of cell borders. Modify the style rule for the td and th element selectors, remove the border declaration, and set `border-style` to none:

```
td, th {  padding: 5px; font-family: Arial, sans-serif;
          border-style: none; }
```

6. Create a new class called `altrow` that sets a background color:

```
.altrow { background-color: #eaeaea; }
```

7. Modify the `<tr>` tags in the HTML: assign the second and fourth `<tr>` tags to the `altrow` class. Save the file. Display your page in a browser. The table area should look similar to the one shown in Figure 11.

Notice how the background color of the alternate rows adds subtle interest to the web page. Compare your work with the sample located in the student files (chapter9/menu.html).

Lighthouse Island Bistro Specialty Coffee Menu

Specialty Coffee	Description	Price
Lite Latte	Indulge in a shot of locally roasted espresso with steamed, skim milk.	$3.50
Mocha Latte	Chocolate lovers will enjoy a shot of locally roasted espresso, steamed milk, and dark, milk, or white chocolate.	$4.00
MCP Latte	A luscious mocha latte with caramel and pecan syrup.	$4.50

FIGURE 11 *Rows are configured with alternating background colors.*

CSS3 Structural Pseudo-classes

In the previous section you configured CSS and applied a class to every other table row to configure alternating background colors, often referred to as "zebra striping." You may have found this to be a bit inconvenient and wondered if there was a more efficient method. Well, there is! CSS3 **structural pseudo-class selectors** allow you to select and apply classes to elements based on their position in the structure of the document, such as every other row. CSS3 pseudo-classes are supported by current versions of Firefox, Opera, Chrome, Safari, and Internet Explorer 9. Earlier versions of Internet Explorer do not support CSS3 pseudo-classes, so consider using this coding technique only for enhancements to a web page. Table 3 lists common CSS3 structural pseudo-class selectors and their purpose.

To apply a pseudo-class, write it after the selector. The following code sample will configure the first item in an unordered list to display with red text.

```
li:first-of-type { color: #FF0000; }
```

TABLE 3 *Common CSS3 Structural Pseudo-classes*

Pseudo-class	Purpose
:first-of-type	Applies to the first element of the specified type
:first-child	Applies to the first child of an element (CSS2 selector)
:last-of-type	Applies to the last element of the specified type
:last-child	Applies to the last child of an element
:nth-of-type(n)	Applies to the "nth" element of the specified type
	Values: an integer, odd, or even

 Hands-On Practice 4

In this Hands-On Practice you will rework the table you configured in Hands-On Practice 3 to use CSS3 structural pseudo-class selectors to configure color.

1. Launch a text editor, and open the menu.html file in your ch9table folder (also found in the student files chapter9/menu.html). Save the file as menu2.html.

2. View the source code, and notice that the second and fourth tr elements are assigned to the altrow class. You won't need this class assignment when using CSS3 structural pseudo-class selectors. Delete class="altrow" from the tr elements.

Table Basics

3. Examine the embedded CSS and locate the `altrow` class. Change the selector to use a structural pseudo-class that will apply the style to the even-numbered table rows. Replace `.altrow` with `tr:nth-of-type (even)` as shown in the following CSS declaration:

```
tr:nth-of-type(even) { background-color: #eaeaea; }
```

4. Save the file. Display your page in a browser. The table area should look similar to the one shown in Figure 11.

5. Let's configure the first row to have a dark blue background (#006) and light gray text (#eaeaea) with the `:first-of-type` structural pseudo-class. Add the following to the embedded CSS:

```
tr:first-of-type { background-color: #006;
                   color: #eaeaea; }
```

6. Save the file. Display your page in a browser. The table area should look similar to the one shown in Figure 12. A sample solution is available in the student files (chapter9/menucss3.html).

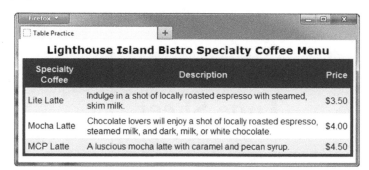

FIGURE 12 *CSS3 pseudo-class selectors style the table rows.*

Configuring the First Letter

Ever wonder how to easily style the first letter of a paragraph to be different from the rest? It's easy using the CSS2 `:first-letter` **pseudo-element.** Use the following code to configure the text as shown in Figure 13:

```
p:first-letter { font-size: 3em;
                 font-weight: bold; color: #F00; }
```

An example is available the student files (chapter9/letter.html).

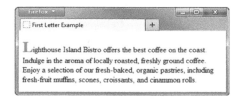

FIGURE 13 *Configure the first letter with CSS.*

Explore the topic of pseudo-elements further. Find out about the `:before`, `:after`, and `:first-line` pseudo-elements at the following resources:

▶ http://css-tricks.com/pseudo-element-roundup
▶ http://coding.smashingmagazine.com/2011/07/13/
learning-to-use-the-before-and-after-pseudo-elements-in-css/

Configure Table Sections

There are many configuration options when coding tables. Table rows can be put together into three types of table row groups: table head with `<thead>`, table body with `<tbody>`, and table footer with `<tfoot>`.

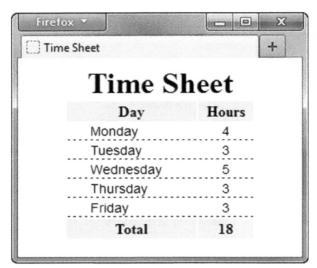

FIGURE 14 *CSS configures the thead, tbody, and tfoot element selectors.*

These groups can be useful when you need to configure the areas in the table in different ways, using either attributes or CSS. The `<tbody>` tag is required if you configure a `<thead>` or `<tfoot>` area, although you can omit either the table head or table footer if you like.

The following code sample (see chapter9/tfoot.html in the student files) configures the table shown in Figure 14 and demonstrates the use of CSS to configure a table head, table body, and table footer with different styles.

The CSS styles a centered 200-pixel-wide table with a caption that is rendered in a large, bold font; a table head section with a light-gray (#eaeaea) background color; and a table body section styled with slightly smaller text (.90em) using a sans serif font; table body td element selectors set to display with some left padding and a dashed bottom border; and a table footer section that has centered, bolded text and a light gray background color (#eaeaea). The CSS code is

```
table { width: 200px;
        margin: auto; }
table, th, td { border-style: none; }
caption { font-size: 2em;
          font-weight: bold; }
thead { background-color: #eaeaea; }
tbody { font-family: Arial, sans-serif;
        font-size: .90em; }
tbody td { border-bottom: 1px #000033 dashed;
           padding-left: 25px; }
tfoot { background-color: #eaeaea;
        font-weight: bold;
        text-align: center; }
```

Table Basics

The HTML for the table is

```
<table border="1">
<caption>Time Sheet</caption>
<thead>
  <tr>
    <th id="day">Day</th>
    <th id="hours">Hours</th>
  </tr>
</thead>
<tbody>
  <tr>
    <td headers="day">Monday</td>
    <td headers="hours">4</td>
  </tr>
  <tr>
    <td headers="day">Tuesday</td>
    <td headers="hours">3</td>
  </tr>
  <tr>
    <td headers="day">Wednesday</td>
    <td headers="hours">5</td>
  </tr>
  <tr>
    <td headers="day">Thursday</td>
    <td headers="hours">3</td>
  </tr>
  <tr>
    <td headers="day">Friday</td>
    <td headers="hours">3</td>
  </tr>
</tbody>
<tfoot>
  <tr>
    <td headers="day">Total</td>
    <td headers="hours">18</td>
  </tr>
</tfoot>
</table>
```

This example demonstrates the power of CSS in styling documents. The `<td>` tags within each table row group element selector (thead, tbody, and tfoot) inherited the font styles configured for their parent group element selector. Notice how a descendant selector configures padding and border only for `<td>` tags that are contained within the `<tbody>` element. Sample code is located in the student files (chapter9/tfoot.html). Take a few moments to explore the web page code and display the page in a browser.

Table Basics

Review and Apply

Review Questions

Multiple Choice. Choose the best answer for each item.

1. Which HTML element describes the contents of a table?

   a. table

   b. summary

   c. caption

   d. thead

2. Which CSS delcaration below causes the default browser borders on a table to not display?

   a. display: none;

   b. border-style: none;

   c. border-spacing: none;

   d. border-collapse: collapse;

3. Which HTML tag pair is used to group rows in the footer of a table?

   a. <footer> </footer>

   b. <tr> </tr>

   c. <tfoot> </tfoot>

   d.

4. Which HTML element uses a border attribute to display a table with a border?

   a. <td>

   b. <tr>

   c. <table>

   d. <tableborder>

5. Which HTML tag pair is used to specify table headings?

   a. <td> </td>

   b. <th> </th>

   c. <head> </head>

   d. <tr> </tr>

6. Which CSS property replaces the use of the cellpadding attribute?

   a. cell-padding

   b. border-spacing

   c. padding

   d. border

7. Which HTML tag pair is used to begin and end a table row?

   a. <td> </td>

   b. <tr> </tr>

   c. <table> </table>

   d. <th> </th>

8. Which of the following is the recommended use of tables on web pages?

   a. configuring the layout of an entire page

   b. organizing information

   c. forming hyperlinks

   d. configuring a resume

9. Which CSS property specifies the background color of a table?

   a. background

   b. bgcolor

   c. background-color

   d. border-spacing

10. Which HTML attribute associates a table data cell with a table header cell?

   a. head

   b. headers

   c. align

   d. rowspan

Hands-On Exercises

1. Write the HTML for a two-column table that contains the names of your friends and their birthdays. The first row of the table should span two columns and contain the following heading: "Birthday List". Include at least two people in your table.

Table Basics

2. Write the HTML for a three-column table to describe the courses you are taking this semester. The columns should contain the course number, course name, and instructor name. The first row of the table should use `th` tags and contain descriptive headings for the columns. Use the table row grouping tags `<thead>` and `<tbody>` in your table.

3. Use CSS to configure a table that has a red border around both the entire table and the table cells. Write the HTML to create a table with three rows and two columns. The cell in the first column of each row will contain one of the following terms: HTML5, XML, and XHTML. The corresponding cell in the second column of each row will contain a definition of the term.

4. Create a web page about your favorite sports team with a two-column table that lists the positions and starting players. Use embedded CSS to style the table border, background color, and center the table on the web page. Place an e-mail link to yourself in the footer area. Save the file as sport9.html.

5. Create a web page about your favorite movie that uses a two-column table containing details about the movie. Use embedded CSS to style the table border and background color. Include the following in the table:

   - Title of the movie
   - Director or producer
   - Leading actor
   - Leading actress
   - Rating (R, PG-13, PG, G, NR)
   - A brief description of the movie
   - An absolute link to a review about the movie

   Place an e-mail link to yourself on the web page. Save the page as movie9.html.

Focus on Web Design

Good artists view and analyze many paintings. Good writers read and evaluate many books. Similarly, good web designers view and scrutinize many web pages. Surf the Web and find two web pages—one that is appealing to you and one that is unappealing to you. Print out each page. Create a web page that answers the following questions for each of your examples:

   a. What is the URL of the website?
   b. Does this page use tables? If so, for what purpose—page layout, organization of information, or another reason?
   c. Does this page use CSS? If so, for what purpose—page layout, text and color configuration, or another reason?
   d. Is this page appealing or unappealing? Describe three aspects of the page that you find appealing or unappealing.
   e. If this page is unappealing, what would you do to improve it?

Answers to Review Questions

1. c   **2.** b   **3.** c
4. c   **5.** b   **6.** c
7. b   **8.** b   **9.** c
10. b

Credits

Figures 1–5, 8, 9, 12–16 © Terry Ann Morris, Ed.D. | Mozilla Foundation

Form Basics

Forms are used for many purposes all over the Web. They are used by search engines to accept keywords and by online stores to process e-commerce shopping carts. Websites use forms to help with a variety of functions—accepting visitor feedback, encouraging visitors to send a news story to a friend or colleague, collecting e-mail addresses for a newsletter, and accepting order information. This chapter introduces a very powerful tool for web developers—forms that accept information from web page visitors.

You'll learn how to...

- Describe common uses of forms on web pages
- Create forms on web pages using the form, input, textarea, and select elements
- Associate form controls and groups using label, fieldset, and legend elements
- Use CSS to style a form

- Describe the features and common uses of server-side processing
- Invoke server-side processing to handle form data
- Configure new HTML5 form controls including the e-mail, URL, datalist, range, spinner, calendar, and color-well controls

From Chapter 10 of *Basics of Web Design HTML5 & CSS3*, Second Edition. Terry Ann Felke-Morris. Copyright © 2014 by Pearson Education, Inc. All rights reserved.

Every time you use a search engine, place an order, or join an online mailing list, you use a form. A **form** is an HTML element that contains and organizes objects called **form controls**—such as text boxes, check boxes, and buttons—that can accept information from website visitors.

FIGURE 1 *The search form on Google's home page.*

For example, you may have used Google's search form (Figure 1) many times but never thought about how it works. The form is quite simple; it contains just three form controls—the text box that accepts the keywords used in the search and two buttons. The "Google Search" button submits the form and invokes a process to search the Google databases and display a results page. The whimsical "I'm Feeling Lucky" button submits the form and displays the top page for your keywords.

Figure 2 shows a more detailed form, used to enter shipping information at irs.gov. This form contains text boxes to accept information such as name and address. Select lists are used to capture information with a limited number of correct values, such as state and country information. When a visitor clicks the "Continue" button, the form information is submitted and the ordering process continues.

Whether a form is used to search for web pages or to place an order, the form alone cannot do all the processing. The form needs to invoke a program or script on the server in order to search a database or record an order. There are usually two components of a form:

1. The HTML form itself, which is the web page user interface

2. The server-side processing, which works with the form data and sends e-mail, writes to a text file, updates a database, or performs some other type of processing on the server

The Form Element

Now that you have a basic understanding of what forms do, let's focus on the HTML to create a form. The **form element** contains a form on a web page. The `<form>` tag specifies the beginning of a form area. The closing `</form>` tag specifies the end of a form area. There can be multiple forms on a web page, but they cannot be nested inside each other. The form element can be

Shipping Address Entry

Name:

Company:

Address Line 1:

Address Line 2:

City:

State:

Zip Code:

Country: United States

Continue   Clear All

FIGURE 2 *This form accepts order information.*

Form Basics

configured with attributes that specify what server-side program or file will process the form, how the form information will be sent to the server, and the name of the form. These attributes are listed in Table 1.

TABLE 1 *Common Attributes of the Form Element*

Attribute	Value	Purpose
`action`	URL or file name/path of server-side processing script	Required; indicates where to send the form information when the form is submitted; `mailto:youre-mailaddress` will launch the visitor's default e-mail application to send the form information
`autocomplete`	`on`	HTML5 attribute; default value; browser will use autocompletion to fill form fields
	`off`	HTML5 attribute; browser will not use autocompletion to fill form fields
`id`	Alphanumeric, no spaces; the value must be unique and not used for other id values on the same web page document	Optional; provides a unique identifier for the form
`method`	`get`	Default value; the value of `get` causes the form data to be appended to the URL and sent to the web server
	`post`	The `post` method is more private and transmits the form data in the body of the HTTP response; this method is preferred by the W3C
`name`	Alphanumeric, no spaces, begins with a letter; choose a form name value that is descriptive but short; for example, OrderForm is better than Form1 or WidgetsRUsOrderForm	Optional; names the form so that it can be easily accessed by client-side scripting languages, such as JavaScript, to edit and verify the form information before the server-side processing is invoked

For example, to configure a form called order, using the post method, and invoking a script called demo.php on your web server, the code is

```
<form name="order" method="post" id="order" action="demo.php">
... form controls go here ...
</form>
```

Form Controls

The purpose of a form is to gather information from a web page visitor; form controls are the objects that accept the information. Types of form controls include text boxes, scrolling text boxes, select lists, radio buttons, check boxes, and buttons. HTML5 offers new form controls including those customized for e-mail addresses, URLs, dates, times, numbers, color selection. HTML elements that configure form controls will be introduced in the following sections.

Form Basics

Text Box

The **input element** is used to configure several different types of form controls. The input element is not coded as a pair of opening and closing tags. It is considered to be a stand-alone or void element. Use the `type` attribute to specify the type of form control that the browser should display. The `<input>` tag with `type="text"` configures a text box. The **text box** form control accepts text or numeric information such as names, e-mail addresses, phone numbers, and other text. A sample text box is shown in Figure 3. The code for the text box is shown below.

```
E-mail: <input type="text" name="email" id="email">
```

FIGURE 3 *The `<input>` tag with* `type="text"` *configures this form element.*

Common input element attributes for text boxes are listed in Table 2. Several attributes are new in HTML5. The new **required attribute** is exciting because it will cause supporting browsers to perform form validation. Browsers that support the HTML5 `required` attribute will automatically verify that information has been entered in the text box and display an error message when the condition is not met. A code sample is

```
E-mail: <input type="text" name="email" id="email"
                required="required">
```

FIGURE 4 *The Firefox browser displayed an error message.*

Figure 4 shows an error message automatically generated by Firefox that displayed after the user clicked the form's submit button without entering information in the required text. Browsers that do not support HTML5 or the `required` attribute will ignore the attribute.

Although web designers are enthusiastic about the `required` attribute and other new form processing functions offered by HTML5, it will be some time before all browsers support these new features. In the meantime, be aware that verification and validation of form information also must be done the old-fashioned way—with client-side or server-side scripting.

Form Basics

TABLE 2 *Common Input Element Attributes*

Attribute	Value	Usage
type	text	Configures the text box
name	Alphanumeric, no spaces, begins with a letter	Names the form element so that it can be easily accessed by client-side scripting languages (such as JavaScript) or by server-side processing; the name should be unique
id	Alphanumeric, no spaces, begins with a letter	Provides a unique identifier for the form element
size	Numeric	Configures the width of the text box as displayed by the browser; if size is omitted, the browser displays the text box with its own default size
maxlength	Numeric	Configures the maximum length of data accepted by the text box
value	Text or numeric characters	Assigns an initial value to the text box that is displayed by the browser; accepts information typed in the text box; this value can be accessed by client-side scripting languages and by server-side processing
disabled	disabled	Form control is disabled
readonly	readonly	Form control is for display; cannot be edited
autocomplete	on	HTML5 attribute; default; browser will use autocompletion to fill the form control
	off	HTML5 attribute; browser will not use autocompletion to fill the form control
autofocus	autofocus	HTML5 attribute; form control has cursor focus
list	Datalist element id value	HTML5 attribute; associates the form control with a datalist element
placeholder	Text or numeric characters	HTML5 attribute; tip or hint to aid the user
required	required	HTML5 attribute; browser verifies entry of information
accesskey	Keyboard character	Configures a hot key for the form control
tabindex	Numeric	Configures the tab order of the form control

Why use both the `name` and `id` attributes on form controls?

The `name` attribute names the form element so that it can be easily accessed by client-side scripting languages such as JavaScript or by server-side processing languages such as PHP. The value given to a `name` attribute for a form element should be unique for that form. The `id` attribute is included for use with CSS and scripting. The value of the `id` attribute should be unique to the entire web page document that contains the form. Typically, the values assigned to the `name` and `id` attribute on a particular form element are the same.

Form Basics

Submit Button and Reset Button

The Submit Button

The **submit button** form control is used to submit the form. When clicked, it triggers the action method on the `<form>` tag and causes the browser to send the form data (the name and value pairs for each form control) to the web server. The web server will invoke the server-side processing program or script listed on the form's `action` attribute.

The `<input>` tag with `type="submit"` configures a submit button. For example,

```
<input type="submit">
```

The Reset Button

The **reset button** form control is used to reset the form fields to their initial values. A reset button does not submit the form.

Sample Form

E-mail: _____

Submit Query   Reset

FIGURE 5 *The form contains a text box, a submit button, and a reset button.*

The `<input>` tag with `type="reset"` configures a reset button. For example,

```
<input type="reset">
```

Sample Form

A form with a text box, a submit button, and a reset button is shown in Figure 5. Common attributes for submit buttons and reset buttons are listed in Table 3.

TABLE 3 *Common Attributes for Submit Buttons and Reset Buttons*

Attribute	Value	Usage
`type`	`submit`	Configures a submit button
	`reset`	Configures a reset button
`name`	Alphanumeric, no spaces, begins with a letter	Names the form element so that it can be easily accessed by client-side scripting languages (such as JavaScript) or by server-side processing; the name should be unique
`id`	Alphanumeric, no spaces, begins with a letter	Provides a unique identifier for the form element
`value`	Text or numeric characters	Configures the text displayed on the button; a submit button displays text "Submit Query" by default; a reset button displays "Reset" by default
`accesskey`	Keyboard character	Configures a hot key for the form control
`tabindex`	Numeric	Configures the tab order of the form control

Form Basics

Hands-On Practice 1 ——————————————————————

You will code a form in this Hands-On Practice. To get started, launch a text editor and open the template file located at chapter1/template.html in the student files on the companion website at www.pearsonhighered.com/felke-morris. Save the file with the name form1.html. You will create a web page with a form similar to the example in Figure 6.

1. Modify the title element to display the text "Form Example".

2. Configure an h1 element with the text "Join Our Newsletter".

3. You are ready to configure the form area. A form begins with the form element. Place your cursor on a blank line under the heading you just added and type in a `<form>` tag as follows:

```
<form method="get">
```

As you read through the chapter you will find that a number of attributes can be used with the `<form>` element. In your first form, we are using the minimal HTML needed to create the form.

FIGURE 6 *The text on the submit button says, "Sign Me Up!"*

4. To create the form control for the visitor's e-mail address to be entered, type the following code on a blank line below the form element:

```
E-mail: <input type="text" name="email" id="email"><br><br>
```

This places the text "E-mail:" in front of the text box used to enter the visitor's e-mail address. The input element has a `type` attribute with the value of `text` that causes the browser to display a text box. The `name` attribute assigns the name `email` to the information entered into the text box (the `value`) and could be used by server-side processing. The `id` attribute uniquely identifies the element on the page. The `<br>` elements configure line breaks.

5. Now you are ready to add the submit button to the form on the next line. Add a `value` attribute set to "Sign Me Up!":

```
<input type="submit" value="Sign Me Up!">
```

This causes the browser to display a button with "Sign Me Up!" instead of the default value of "Submit Query".

6. Add a blank space after the submit button and code a reset button:

```
<input type="reset">
```

7. Next, code the closing form tag:

```
</form>
```

Save your form1.html file. Test your page in a browser. It should look similar to the page shown in Figure 6.

You can compare your work with the solution found in the student files (chapter10/form1.html) folder. Try entering some information into your form. Try clicking the submit button. Don't worry if the form redisplays but nothing seems to happen when you click the button—you haven't configured this form to work with any server-side processing. Connecting forms to server-side processing is demonstrated later in this chapter. The next sections will introduce you to more form controls.

Check Box and Radio Button

The Check Box

The **check box** form control allows the user to select one or more of a group of predetermined items. The `<input>` tag with `type="checkbox"` configures a check box. Figure 7 shows an example with several check boxes—note that more than one check box can be selected by the user. Common check box attributes are listed in Table 4. The HTML is

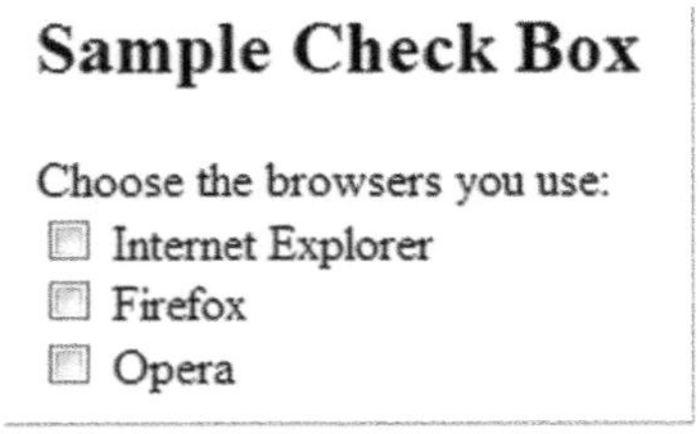

Sample Check Box

Choose the browsers you use:
- Internet Explorer
- Firefox
- Opera

FIGURE 7 *Check box.*

```
Choose the browsers you use: <br>
<input type="checkbox" name="IE" id="IE"
       value="yes"> Internet Explorer<br>
<input type="checkbox" name="Firefox" id="Firefox"
       value="yes"> Firefox<br>
<input type="checkbox" name="Opera" id="Opera"
       value="yes"> Opera<br>
```

TABLE 4 *Common Check Box Attributes*

Attribute	Value	Usage
type	checkbox	Configures the check box
name	Alphanumeric, no spaces, begins with a letter	Names the form element so that it can be easily accessed by client-side scripting languages or by server-side processing; the name of each check box should be unique
id	Alphanumeric, no spaces, begins with a letter	Provides a unique identifier for the form element
checked	checked	Configures the check box to be checked by default when displayed by the browser
value	Text or numeric characters	Assigns a value to the check box that is triggered when the check box is checked; this value can be accessed by client-side and by server-side processing
disabled	disabled	Form control is disabled and will not accept information
autofocus	autofocus	HTML5 attribute; form control has cursor focus
required	required	HTML5 attribute; browser verifies entry of information
accesskey	Keyboard character	Configures a hot key for the form control
tabindex	Numeric	Configures the tab order of the form control

Form Basics

234

The Radio Button

The **radio button** form control allows the user to select exactly one (and only one) choice from a group of predetermined items. Each radio button in a group is given the same `name` attribute and a unique `value` attribute. Because the `name` attribute is the same, the elements are identified as part of a group by the browsers and only one may be selected.

The `<input>` tag with `type="radio"` configures a radio button. Figure 8 shows an example with a radio button group—note that only one radio button can be selected at a time by the user. Common radio button attributes are listed in Table 5. The HTML is

```
Select your favorite browser:<br>
<input type="radio" name="favbrowser" id="favIE" value="IE"> Internet Explorer<br>
<input type="radio" name="favbrowser" id="favFirefox" value="Firefox"> Firefox<br>
<input type="radio" name="favbrowser" id="favOpera" value="Opera"> Opera<br>
```

Notice that all the `name` attributes have the same value: `favbrowser`. Radio buttons with the same `name` attribute are treated as a group by the browser. Each radio button in the same group can be uniquely identified by its `value` attribute.

TABLE 5 *Common Radio Button Attributes*

Attribute	Value	Usage
type	radio	Configures the radio button
name	Alphanumeric, no spaces, begins with a letter	Required; all radio buttons in a group must have the same `name`; names the form element so that it can be easily accessed by client-side scripting languages or by server-side processing
id	Alphanumeric, no spaces, begins with a letter	Provides a unique identifier for the form element
checked	checked	Configures the radio button to be selected by default when displayed by the browser
value	Text or numeric characters	Assigns a value to the radio button that is triggered when the radio button is selected; this should be a unique value for each radio button in a group; this value can be accessed by client-side and by server-side processing
disabled	disabled	Form control is disabled and will not accept information
autofocus	autofocus	HTML5 attribute; form control has cursor focus
required	required	HTML5 attribute; browser verifies entry of information
accesskey	Keyboard character	Configures a hot key for the form control
tabindex	Numeric	Configures the tab order of the form control

Form Basics

Hidden Field and Password Box

The Hidden Field

The **hidden field** form control stores text or numeric information, but it is not visible in the browser viewport. Hidden fields can be accessed by both client-side and server-side scripting.

The `<input>` tag with `type="hidden"` configures a hidden field. Common hidden field attributes are listed in Table 6.

The HTML to create a hidden form control with the `name` attribute set to "sendto" and the `value` attribute set to an e-mail address as follows:

```
<input type="hidden" name="sendto" id="sendto" value="order@site.com">
```

TABLE 6 *Common Hidden Field Attributes*

Attribute	Value	Usage
type	hidden	Configures the hidden form element
name	Alphanumeric, no spaces, begins with a letter	Names the form element so that it can be easily accessed by client-side scripting languages (such as JavaScript) or by server-side processing; the name should be unique
id	Alphanumeric, no spaces, begins with a letter	Provides a unique identifier for the form element
value	Text or numeric characters	Assigns a value to the hidden control; this value can be accessed by client-side scripting languages and by server-side processing
disabled	disabled	Form control is disabled

Form Basics

The Password Box

The **password box** form control is similar to the text box, but it is used to accept information that must be hidden as it is entered, such as a password. The `<input>` tag with `type="password"` configures a password box. Common password box attributes are listed in Table 7.

When the user types information in a password box, asterisks (or another symbol, depending on the browser) are displayed instead of the characters that have been typed, as shown in Figure 9. This hides the information from someone looking over the shoulder of the person typing. The actual characters typed are sent to the server, and the information is not really secret or hidden. The HTML is

Sample Password Box

Password: ●●●●●●●

FIGURE 9 *The characters secret9 were typed, but the browser does not display them.*

```
Password: <input type="password" name="pword" id="pword">
```

TABLE 7 *Common Password Box Attributes*

Attribute	Value	Usage
type	password	Configures the password box
name	Alphanumeric, no spaces, begins with a letter	Names the form element so that it can be easily accessed by client-side scripting languages or by server-side processing; the name should be unique
id	Alphanumeric, no spaces, begins with a letter	Provides a unique identifier for the form element
size	Numeric	Configures the width of the password box as displayed by the browser; if size is omitted, the browser displays the password box with its own default size
maxlength	Numeric	Optional; configures the maximum length of data accepted by the password box
value	Text or numeric characters	Assigns an initial value to the password box that is displayed by the browser; accepts the information typed in the password box; This value can be accessed by client-side and by server-side processing
disabled	disabled	Form control is disabled
readonly	readonly	Form control is for display; cannot be edited
autocomplete	on	HTML5 attribute; default; browser will use autocompletion to fill the form control
	off	HTML5 attribute; autocompletion is not used
autofocus	autofocus	HTML5 attribute; form control has cursor focus
placeholder	Text or numeric characters	HTML5 attribute; tip or hint to aid the user
required	required	HTML5 attribute; browser verifies entry of information
accesskey	Keyboard character	Configures a hot key for the form control
tabindex	Numeric	Configures the tab order of the form control

Form Basics

Textarea Element

Sample Scrolling Text Box

Comments:

| Enter comments | ▲ |
| | ▼ |

FIGURE 10 *Scrolling text box.*

The **scrolling text box** form control accepts free-form comments, questions, or descriptions. The **textarea element** configures a scrolling text box. The `<textarea>` tag denotes the beginning of the scrolling text box. The closing `</textarea>` tag denotes the end of the scrolling text box. Text contained between the tags will display in the scrolling text box area. A sample scrolling text box is shown in Figure 10. Common attributes are listed in Table 8. The HTML is

```
Comments:<br>
<textarea name="cm" id="cm" cols="40" rows="2">Enter comments</textarea>
```

TABLE 8 *Common Scrolling Text Box Attributes*

Attribute	Value	Usage
name	Alphanumeric, no spaces, begins with a letter	Names the form element so that it can be easily accessed by client-side scripting languages (such as JavaScript) or by server-side processing; the name should be unique
id	Alphanumeric, no spaces, begins with a letter	Provides a unique identifier for the form element
cols	Numeric	Required; configures the width in character columns of the scrolling text box; if cols is omitted, the browser displays the scrolling text box with its own default width
rows	Numeric	Required; configures the height in rows of the scrolling text box; if rows is omitted, the browser displays the scrolling text box with its own default height
maxlength	Numeric	Maximum number of characters accepted
disabled	disabled	Form control is disabled
readonly	readonly	Form control is for display; cannot be edited
autofocus	autofocus	HTML5 attribute; form control has cursor focus
placeholder	Text or numeric characters	HTML5 attribute; tip or hint to aid the user
required	required	HTML5 attribute; browser verifies entry of information
wrap	hard or soft	HTML5 attribute; configures line breaks within the information entered
accesskey	Keyboard character	Configures a hot key for the form control
tabindex	Numeric	Configures the tab order of the form control

Form Basics

In this Hands-On Practice you will create a contact form with the following form controls: a First Name text box, a Last Name text box, an E-mail text box, and a Comments scrolling text box. You'll use the form you created in Hands-On Practice 1 (see Figure 6) as a starting point. Launch a text editor and open the form1.html file located at chapter10/form1.html in the student files. Save the file with the name form2.html. The new contact form is shown in Figure 11.

1. Modify the title element to display the text "Contact Form".

2. Configure the h1 element with the text "Contact Us".

3. A form control for the e-mail address is already coded. Refer to Figure 11 and note that you'll need to add text box form controls for the first name and last name above the e-mail form control. Position your cursor after the opening form tag and press the enter key twice to create two blank lines. Add the following code to accept the name of your web page visitor:

```
First Name: <input type="text" name="fname"
               id="fname"><br><br>
Last Name: <input type="text" name="lname"
               id="lname"><br><br>
```

FIGURE 11 *A typical contact form.*

4. Now you are ready to add the scrolling text box form control to the form using a `<textarea>` tag on a new line below the e-mail form control. The code is

```
Comments:<br>
<textarea name="comments" id="comments"></textarea><br><br>
```

Save your file and display in a browser to view the default display of a scrolling text box. Note that this default display will differ by browser. At the time this was written, Internet Explorer always rendered a vertical scroll bar, but the Firefox browser only rendered scroll bars once enough text was entered to require them. The writers of browser rendering engines keep the lives of web designers interesting!

5. Let's configure the `rows` and `cols` attributes for the scrolling text box form control. Modify the `<textarea>` tag and set `rows="4"` and `cols="40"` as follows:

```
Comments:<br>
<textarea name="comments" id="comments" rows="4" cols="40"></textarea><br><br>
```

6. Next, modify the text displayed on the submit button. Set the `value` attribute to "Contact". Save your form2.html file. Test your page in a browser. It should look similar to the page shown in Figure 11.

You can compare your work with the solution found in the student files (chapter10/form2.html) folder. Try entering some information into your form. Try clicking the submit button. Don't worry if the form redisplays but nothing seems to happen when you click the button—you haven't configured this form to work with any server-side processing. Connecting forms to server-side processing is demonstrated later in this chapter.

Form Basics

Select Element and Option Element

The **select list** form control shown in Figures 12 and 13 is also known by several other names, including select box, drop-down list, drop-down box, and option box. A select list is configured with one select element and multiple option elements.

The Select Element

The **select element** contains and configures the select list form control. The `<select>` tag denotes the beginning of the select list. The closing `</select>` tag denotes the end of the select list. Attributes configure the number of options to display and whether more than one option item may be selected. Common attributes are listed in Table 9.

TABLE 9   *Common Select Element Attributes*

Attribute	Value	Usage
name	Alphanumeric, no spaces, begins with a letter	Names the form element so that it can be easily accessed by client-side scripting languages (such as JavaScript) or by server-side processing; the name should be unique
id	Alphanumeric, no spaces, begins with a letter	Provides a unique identifier for the form element
size	Numeric	Configures the number of choices the browser will display; if set to 1, element functions as a drop-down list; scroll bars are automatically added by the browser if the number of options exceeds the space allowed
multiple	multiple	Configures a select list to accept more than one choice; by default, only one choice can be made from a select list
disabled	disabled	Form control is disabled
tabindex	Numeric	Configures the tab order of the form control

Form Basics

The Option Element

The **option element** contains and configures an option item displayed in the select list form control. The `<option>` tag denotes the beginning of the option item. The closing `</option>` tag denotes the end of option item. Attributes configure the value of the option and whether they are preselected. Common attributes are listed in Table 10.

TABLE 10 *Common Option Element Attributes*

Attribute	Value	Usage
value	Text or numeric characters	Assigns a value to the option; this value can be accessed by client-side and by server-side processing
selected	selected	Configures an option to be initially selected when displayed by a browser
disabled	disabled	Form control is disabled

The HTML for the select list in Figure 12 is

```
<select size="1" name="favbrowser" id="favbrowser">
  <option>Select your favorite browser</option>
  <option value="Internet Explorer">Internet Explorer</option>
  <option value="Firefox">Firefox</option>
  <option value="Opera">Opera</option>
</select>
```

Select List: One Initial Visible Item

Select your favorite browser ▼

FIGURE 12 *A select list with size set to 1 functions as a drop-down box when the arrow is clicked.*

The HTML for the select list in Figure 13 is

```
<select size="4" name="jumpmenu" id="jumpmenu">
  <option value="index.html">Home</option>
  <option value="products.html">Products</option>
  <option value="services.html">Services</option>
  <option value="about.html">About</option>
  <option value="contact.html">Contact</option>
</select>
```

Select List: Four Items Visible

FIGURE 13 *Since there are more than four choices, the browser displays a scroll bar.*

Form Basics

Label Element

The **label element** is a container tag that associates a text description with a form control. This is helpful to visually challenged individuals using assistive technology such as a screen reader to match up the text descriptions on forms with their corresponding form controls. The label element also benefits individuals without fine motor control. Clicking anywhere on either a form control or its associated text label will set the cursor focus to the form control.

There are two different methods to associate a label with a form control.

1. The first method places the label element as a container around both the text description and the HTML form element. Notice that both the text label and the form control must be adjacent elements. The code is

   ```
   <label>E-mail: <input type="text" name="email" id="email"></label>
   ```

2. The second method uses the `for` attribute to associate the label with a particular HTML form element. This is more flexible and is does not require the text label and the form control to be adjacent. The code is

   ```
   <label for="email">E-mail: </label>
   <input type="text" name="email" id="email">
   ```

   Notice that the value of the **for attribute** on the label element is the same as the value of the `id` attribute on the input element. This creates the association between the text label and the form control. The input element uses both the `name` and `id` attributes for different purposes. The `name` attribute can be used by client-side and by server-side scripting. The `id` attribute creates an identifier that can be used by the label element, anchor element, and CSS selectors.

The label element does not display on the web page—it works behind the scenes to provide for accessibility.

Form Basics

 **Hands-On Practice 3**

In this Hands-On Practice you will add the label element to the text box and scrolling text area form controls on the form you created in Hands-On Practice 2 (see Figure 11) as a starting point. Launch a text editor and open the form2.html file located at chapter10/form2.html in the student files. Save the file with the name form3.html.

1. Locate the text box for the first name. Add a label element to wrap around the input tag as follows:

   ```
   <label>First Name: <input type="text" name="fname" id="fname">
   </label>
   ```

2. Using the method shown previously, add a label element for the last name and e-mail form controls.

3. Configure a label element to contain the text "Comments". Associate the label with the scrolling text box form control. Sample code is

   ```
   <label for="comments">Comments:</label><br>
   <textarea name="comments" id="comments" rows="4" cols="40"></textarea>
   ```

   Save your form3.html file. Test your page in a browser. It should look similar to the page shown in Figure 11—the label elements do not change the way the page displays, but a web visitor with physical challenges should find the form easier to use.

You can compare your work with the solution found in the student files (chapter10/form3.html) folder. Try entering some information into your form. Try clicking the submit button. Don't worry if the form redisplays but nothing seems to happen when you click the button—you haven't configured this form to work with any server-side processing. Connecting a form to server-side processing is demonstrated later in this chapter.

Form Basics

Fieldset Element and Legend Element

Fieldset and legend elements work together to visually group form controls together and increase the usability of the form.

The Fieldset Element

A technique that can be used to create a more visually pleasing form is to group elements of a similar purpose together using the **fieldset element**, which will cause the browser to render a visual cue, such as an outline or a border, around form elements grouped together within the fieldset. The `<fieldset>` tag denotes the beginning of the grouping. The closing `</fieldset>` tag denotes the end of the grouping.

The Legend Element

The **legend element** provides a text description for the fieldset grouping. The `<legend>` tag denotes the beginning of the text description. The closing `</legend>` tag denotes the end of the text description.

The HTML to create the grouping shown in Figure 14 is

```
<fieldset>
<legend>Billing Address</legend>
<label>Street: <input type="text" name="street" id="street"
                    size="54"></label><br><br>
<label>City: <input type="text" name="city" id="city"></label>
<label>State: <input type="text" name="state" id="state" maxlength="2"
                    size="5"></label>
<label>Zip: <input type="text" name="zip" id="zip" maxlength="5"
                    size="5"></label>
</fieldset>
```

Fieldset and Legend

Billing Address
Street:

City: State: Zip:

FIGURE 14 *Form controls that are all related to a mailing address.*

The grouping and visual effect of the fieldset element creates an organized and appealing web page containing a form. Using the fieldset and legend elements to group form controls enhances accessibility by organizing the controls both visually and semantically. The

Form Basics

244

fieldset and legend elements can be accessed by screen readers and are useful tools to configure groups of radio buttons and check boxes on web pages.

A Look Ahead—Styling a Fieldset Group with CSS

The next section focuses on styling a form with CSS. But how about a quick preview?

Figures 14 and 15 show the same form elements, but the form in Figure 15 is styled with CSS— the same functionality with increased visual appeal. Access the example page at chapter10/form4.html in the student files. The style rules are

```
fieldset { width: 500px; border: 2px ridge #ff0000;
           font-family: Arial, sans-serif; padding: 10px; }
legend { font-family: Georgia, "Times New Roman", serif;
         font-weight: bold; }
label { padding-left: 10px; }
```

Fieldset and Legend Styled with CSS

Billing Address

Street:

City: State: Zip:

FIGURE 15 *The fieldset, legend, and label elements are configured with CSS.*

Accessibility and Forms

Using the HTML elements label, fieldset, and legend will increase the accessibility of your web forms. This makes it easier for individuals with vision and mobility challenges to use your form pages. An added benefit is that the use of label, fieldset, and legend elements may increase the readability and usability of the web form for all visitors. Be sure to include contact information (e-mail address and/or phone number) just in case a visitor is unable to submit your form successfully and requires additional assistance.

Some of your website visitors may have difficulty using the mouse and will access your form with a keyboard. The Tab key can be used to move from one form control to another. The default action for the Tab key within a form is to move to the next form control in the order in which the form controls are coded in the web page document. This is usually appropriate. However, if the tab order needs to be changed for a form, use the **tabindex attribute** on each form control.

Another technique that can make your form keyboard-friendly is the use of the **accesskey attribute** on form controls. Assigning accesskey a value of one of the characters (letter or number) on the keyboard will create a hot key that your website visitor can press to move the cursor immediately to a form control. Windows users will press the Alt key and the character key. Mac users will press the Ctrl key and the character key. When choosing accesskey values, avoid combinations that are already used by the operating system (such as Alt+F to display the File menu). Testing hot keys is crucial.

Form Basics

Style a Form with CSS

FIGURE 16 *The alignment of the text and form controls needs improvement.*

The form in Figure 16 looks a little "messy" and you might be wondering how that can be improved. Back in the day, web designers typically used a table to configure the display of form elements, often placing the text labels and form field elements in separate table data cells. However, the table approach is outdated, does not provide support for accessibility, and can be difficult to maintain over time. The modern approach is to style the form with CSS. This section will demonstrate using CSS to style a form layout without using an HTML table.

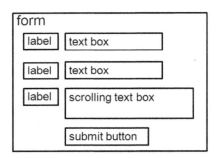

FIGURE 17 *A sketch of the box model used to configure the form.*

When styling a form with CSS, the box model is used to create a series of boxes, as shown in Figure 17. The outermost box defines the form area. Other boxes indicate label elements and form controls. CSS is used to configure these components.

FIGURE 18 *The layout and format of this form are configured with CSS.*

Figure 18 displays a web page with a form configured in this manner (see chapter10/formcss.html in the student files). As you view the following CSS and HTML, note that the label element selector is configured with block display, a 100 pixel width, and floats to the left side of the form, and clears any previous left floats. The input and textarea elements have a top margin and are also configured with block display. The submit button is assigned to an id with a left margin. The styles result in a well-aligned form.

The CSS is

```
form { background-color: #eaeaea;
       font-family: Arial, sans-serif;
       width: 350px;
       padding: 10px; }
label { float: left;
        clear: left;
        display: block;
        width: 100px;
        text-align: right;
        padding-right: 10px;
        margin-top: 10px; }
input, textarea { margin-top: 10px;
                  display: block; }
#mySubmit { margin-left: 110px; }
```

The HTML is

```
<form>
  <label for="myName">Name:</label>
  <input type="text" name="myName" id="myName">
  <label for="myEmail">E-mail:</label>
  <input type="text" name="myEmail" id="myEmail">
  <label for="myComments">Comments:</label>
  <textarea name="myComments" id="myComments"
  rows="2" cols="20"></textarea>
  <input id="mySubmit" type="submit" value="Submit">
</form>
```

This section provided you with a method to style a form with CSS. Testing the way that different browsers render the form is crucial.

As you've coded and displayed the forms in this chapter, you may have noticed that when you click the submit button, the form just redisplays—the form doesn't "do" anything. This is because there is no `action` attribute in the `<form>` tag. The next section focuses on the second component of using forms on web pages—server-side processing.

Form Basics

Server-Side Processing

VideoNote
*Connect
a form to
Server-side
Processing*

Your web browser requests web pages and their related files from a web server. The web server locates the files and sends them to your web browser. Then the web browser renders the returned files and displays the requested web pages. Figure 19 illustrates the communication between the web browser and the web server.

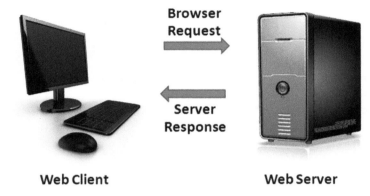

FIGURE 19 *The web browser (client) communicates with the web server.*

Sometimes a website needs more functionality than static web pages—possibly a site search, order form, e-mail list, database display, or other type of interactive, dynamic processing. This is when server-side processing is needed. Early web servers used a protocol called **Common Gateway Interface** (CGI) to provide this functionality. CGI is a protocol, or standard method, for a web server to pass a web page user's request (which is typically initiated through the use of a form) to an application program and to accept information to send to the user. The web server typically passes the form information to a small application program that is run by the operating system and processes the data, and it usually sends back a confirmation web page or message. Perl and C are popular programming languages for CGI applications.

Server-side scripting is a technology in which a server-side script is run on a web server to dynamically generate web pages. Examples of server-side scripting technologies include PHP, Ruby on Rails, Microsoft Active Server Pages, Adobe ColdFusion, Sun JavaServer Pages, and Microsoft.NET. Server-side scripting differs from CGI in that it uses **direct execution**—the script is run either by the web server itself or by an extension module to the web server.

A web page invokes server-side processing by either an attribute on a form or by a hyperlink—the URL of the script is used. Any form data that exists is passed to the script. The script completes its processing and may generate a confirmation or response web

Form Basics

page with the requested information. When invoking a server-side script, the web developer and the server-side programmer must communicate about the form `method` **attribute** (`get` or `post`), form `action` **attribute** (URL of the server-side script), and any special form element control(s) expected by the server-side script.

The `method` attribute is used on the form tag to indicate the way in which the name and value pairs should be passed to the server. The `method` attribute value of `get` causes the form data to be appended to the URL, which is easily visible and not secure. The `method` attribute value of `post` does not pass the form information in the URL; it passes it in the entity body of the HTTP request, which makes it more private. The W3C recommends the `method="post"` method.

The `action` attribute is used on the `<form>` tag to invoke a server-side script. The `name` attribute and the `value` attribute associated with each form control are passed to the server-side script. The `name` attribute may be used as a variable name in the server-side processing.

Privacy and Forms

A **privacy policy** lists the guidelines that you develop to protect the privacy of your visitors' information. Websites either indicate this policy on the form page itself or create a separate page that describes the privacy policy (and other company policies). For example, the order form page at mymoney.gov (http://mymoney.gov/mymoneyorder.shtml) indicates the following:

> "WE WILL NOT SHARE OR SELL ANY PERSONAL INFORMATION OBTAINED FROM YOU WITH ANY OTHER ORGANIZATION, UNLESS REQUIRED BY LAW TO DO SO."

If you browse popular sites such as Amazon.com or eBay.com you'll find links to their privacy policies (sometimes called a privacy notice) in the page footer area. The Better Business Bureau provides a sample privacy notice at www.bbbonline.org/privacy/sample_privacy.asp. Include a privacy notice in your site to inform your visitors how you plan to use the information they share with you.

Sources of Free Remote-Hosted Form Processing

If your web host provider does not support server-side processing, free remotely hosted scripts may be an option. Try out the free form processing offered by http://formbuddy.com, www.expressdb.com, or www.formmail.com.

Sources of Free Server-Side Scripts

To use free scripts, you need to have access to a web server that supports the language used by the script. Contact your web host provider to determine what is supported. Be aware that many free web host providers do not support server-side processing (you get what you pay for!). Visit http://scriptarchive.com and http://php.resourceindex.com for free scripts and related resources.

Form Basics

Practice with a Form

 Hands-On Practice 4

In this Hands-On Practice you will modify the form page that you created earlier in this chapter, configuring the form so that it uses the post method to invoke a server-side script. Your computer must be connected to the Internet when you test your work. The post method is more secure than the get method because the post method does not pass the form information in the URL; it passes it in the entity-body of the HTTP Request, which makes it more private.

When using a server-side script you will need to obtain some information, or documentation, from the person or organization providing the script. You will need to know the location of the script, whether it requires the get or post method, whether it requires any specific names for the form controls, and whether it requires any hidden form elements. The `action` attribute is used on the `<form>` tag to invoke a server-side script. A server-side script has been created at http://webdevbasics.net/scripts/demo.php for students to use for this exercise. The documentation for the server-side script is listed in Table 11.

TABLE 11 *Server-Side Script Documentation*

Script URL	http://webdevbasics.net/scripts/demo.php
Form method	`post`
Script purpose	This script will accept form input and display the form control names and values in a web page. This is a sample script for student assignments. It demonstrates that server-side processing has been invoked. A script used by an actual website would perform a function such as sending an e-mail message or updating a database.

Launch a text editor and open the form3.html file you created in Hands-On Practice 3, also found in the student files (chapter10/form3.html). Modify the `<form>` tag by adding a `method` attribute with a value of "post" and an `action` attribute with a value of "http://webdevbasics.net/scripts/demo.php". The HTML for the revised `<form>` tag is

```
<form method="post" action="http://webdevbasics.net/scripts/demo.php">
```

Save your page as contact.html and test it in a browser. Your screen should look similar to Figure 11. Compare your work with the solution in the student files (chapter10/contact.html).

Now you are ready to test your form. You must be connected to the Internet to test your form successfully. Enter information in the form controls and click the submit button. You should see a confirmation page similar to the one shown in Figure 20.

The demo.php script creates a web page that displays a message and the form information you entered. This confirmation page was created by the server-side script on the `action` attribute in the `<form>` tag. Writing scripts for server-side processing is beyond the scope of this chapter. However, if you are curious, visit http://webdevbasics.net/2e/chapter10.html to see the source code for the demo.php script.

FIGURE 20 *The server-side script has created this page in response to the form.*

 What should I do if nothing happened when I tested my form?
Try these troubleshooting hints:

▶ Verify that your computer is connected to the Internet.

▶ Verify the spelling of the script location in the `action` attribute.

▶ Recall that attention to detail is crucial!

Form Basics

HTML5 Text Form Controls

The E-mail Address Input Form Control

The **e-mail address** form control is similar to the text box. Its purpose is to accept information that must be in e-mail format, such as "DrMorris2010@gmail.com". The `<input>` element with `type="email"` configures an e-mail address form control. Only browsers that support the HTML5 `email` attribute value will verify the format of the information. Other browsers will treat this form control as a text box. Figure 21 (see chapter10/email.html in the student files) shows an error message displayed by Firefox when text other than an e-mail address is entered. Note that the browser does not verify that the e-mail address actually exists—just that the text entered is in the correct format. The HTML is

```
<label for="email">E-mail:</label>
<input type="email" name="myEmail" id="myEmail">
```

FIGURE 21 *The browser displays an error message.*

The URL Form Input Control

The **URL** form control is similar to the text box. It is intended to accept any type of URL or URI, such as "http://webdevbasics.net". The `<input>` element with `type="url"` configures a URL form control. Only browsers that support the HTML5 `url` attribute value will verify the format of the information. Other browsers render this form control as a text box. Figure 22 (see chapter10/url.html in the student files) shows an error message displayed by Firefox when text other than a URL is entered. Note that the browser does not verify that the URL actually exists—just that the text entered is in the correct format. The HTML is

```
<label for="myWebsite">Suggest a Website:</label>
<input type="url" name="myWebsite" id="myWebsite">
```

Form Basics

FIGURE 22 *The browser displays an error message.*

The Telephone Number Input Form Control

The **telephone number** form control is similar to the text box. Its purpose is to accept a telephone number. The `<input>` element with `type="tel"` configures a telephone number form control. An example is in the student files (chapter10/tel.html). Browsers that do not support `type="tel"` will render this form control as a text box. Some mobile devices display a numeric keypad for entry into telephone number input form controls. The HTML is

```
<label for="mobile">Mobile Number:</label>
<input type="tel" name="mobile" id="mobile">
```

The Search Input Form Control

The **search** form control is similar to the text box and is used to accept a search term. The `<input>` element with `type="search"` configures a search input form control. An example is in the student files (chapter10/search.html). Browsers that do not support `type="search"` will render this form control as a text box. The HTML is

```
<label for="keyword">Search:</label>
<input type="search" name="keyword" id="keyword">
```

Valid Attributes for HTML5 Text Form Controls

Attributes supported by the HTML5 text form controls are listed in Table 2.

 FAQ **How can I tell which browsers support the new HTML5 form elements?**

There's no substitute for testing. With that in mind, several resources are listed below that provide information about browser support for new HTML5 elements:

 ▶ http://caniuse.com (also CSS3 browser support information)
 ▶ http://findmebyip.com/litmus (also CSS3 browser support information)
 ▶ http://html5readiness.com
 ▶ http://html5test.com
 ▶ www.standardista.com/html5

HTML5 Datalist Element

Figure 23 shows the **datalist** form control in action. Notice how a selection of choices is offered to the user along with a text box for entry. The datalist is configured using three elements: an input element, the datalist element, and one or more option elements. Only browsers that support the HTML5 datalist element will display and process the datalist items. Other browsers ignore the datalist element and render the form control as a text box.

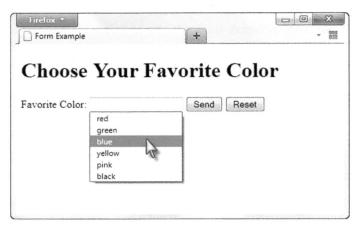

FIGURE 23 *Firefox displays the datalist form control.*

The source code for the datalist is available in the student files (chapter10/list.html). The HTML is

```
<label for="color">Favorite Color:</label>
<input type="text" name="color" id="color" list="colors">
  <datalist id="colors">
    <option value="red">
    <option value="green">
    <option value="blue">
    <option value="yellow">
    <option value="pink">
    <option value="black">
  </datalist>
```

Notice that the value of the **list attribute** on the input element is the same as the value of the id attribute on the datalist element. This creates the association between the text box and the datalist form control. One or more option elements can be used to offer predefined

Form Basics

choices to your web page visitor. The option element's `value` attribute configures the text displayed in each list entry. The web page visitor can choose an option from the list (see Figure 23) or type directly in the text box, as shown in Figure 24.

The datalist form control offers a convenient way to offer choices yet provide for flexibility on a form. At the time this was written, only the Firefox, Chrome, and Opera browsers supported this new HTML5 element. Check out http://webdevbasics.net/2e/chapter10.html for new developments on this intriguing form control.

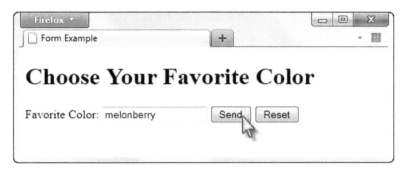

FIGURE 24 *The list disappeared when the user began typing in the text box.*

? FAQ **Why should I learn about the new HTML5 form controls if they are not yet supported by all browsers?**

The display and support of the new HTML5 form controls will vary by browser, but you really can use them right now! The new form controls offer increased usability for your web page visitors who have modern browsers. For example, some new form controls offer built-in browser edits and validation. Future web designers will probably take these features for granted some day, but you are right in the midst of this huge advance in web page coding—so now is a great time to become familiar with these new elements. Finally, browsers that do not support the new input types will display them as text boxes and ignore unsupported attributes or elements. Figure 25 depicts the display of a datalist in the Internet Explorer 9 browser. Notice that, unlike Firefox, the browser does not render the list—it only renders a text box.

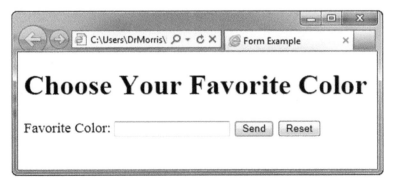

FIGURE 25 *Browsers that do not support the datalist form control display a text box.*

Form Basics

HTML5 Slider and Spinner Controls

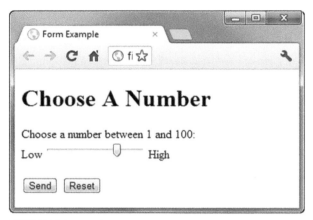

FIGURE 26 *The Google Chrome browser displays the range form control.*

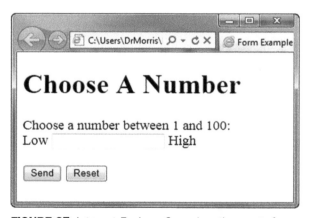

FIGURE 27 *Internet Explorer 9 renders the range form control as a text box.*

The Slider Input Form Control

The **slider** form control provides a visual, interactive user interface that accepts numerical information. The `<input>` element with `type="range"` configures a slider control in which a number within a specified range is chosen. The default range is from 0 to 100. Only browsers that support the HTML5 `range` attribute value will display the interactive slider control, shown in Figure 26 (see chapter10/range.html in the student files). Note the position of the slider in Figure 26; this resulted in the value 80 being chosen. The nondisplay of the value to the user may be a disadvantage of the slider control. Nonsupporting browsers render this form control as a text box, as shown in Figure 27.

The slider control accepts attributes listed in Tables 2 and 12. The `min`, `max`, and `step` attributes are new. Use the **min attribute** to configure the minimum range value. Use the **max attribute** to configure the maximum range value. Use the **step attribute** to configure a value for the step between values to be other than 1.

The HTML for the slider control rendered in Figures 26 and 27 is shown below.

```
<label for="myChoice">Choose a number between 1 and 100:</label><br>
Low <input type="range" min="1" and max="100" name="myChoice" id="myChoice"> High
```

The Spinner Input Form Control

The **spinner** form control displays an interface that accepts numerical information and provides feedback to the user. The `<input>` element with `type="number"` configures a spinner control in which the user can either type a number into the text box or select a number from a specified range. Only browsers that support the HTML5 `number` attribute value will display the interactive spinner control, shown in Figure 28 (see chapter10/spinner.html in the student files). Other browsers render this form control as a text box. Expect increased support in the future.

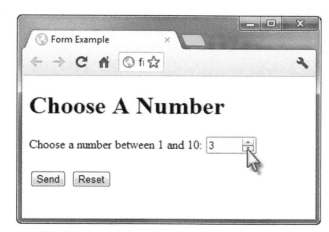

FIGURE 28 *A spinner control displayed in the Google Chrome browser.*

The spinner control accepts attributes listed in Tables 2 and 12. Use the `min` attribute to configure the minimum value. Use the `max` attribute to configure the maximum value. Use the `step` attribute to configure a value for the step between values to be other than 1. The HTML for the spinner control displayed in Figure 28 is

```
<label for="myChoice">Choose a number between 1 and 10:</label>
<input type="number" name="myChoice" id="myChoice" min="1" max="10">
```

TABLE 12 *Additional Attributes for Slider, Spinner, and Date/Time Form Controls*

Attribute	Value	Usage
max	Maximum value	HTML5 attribute for range, number, and date/time input controls; specifies a maximum value
min	Minimum value	HTML5 attribute for range, number, and date/time input controls; specifies a minimum value
step	Incremental step value	HTML5 attribute for range, number, and date/time input controls; specifies a value for incremental steps

HTML5 and Progressive Enhancement

Use HTML5 form elements with the concept of progressive enhancement in mind. Nonsupporting browsers will display text boxes in place of form elements that are not recognized. Supporting browsers will display and process the new form controls. This is progressive enhancement in action—everyone sees a usable form, and those using modern browsers benefit from enhanced features.

HTML5 Calendar and Color-Well Controls

The Calendar Input Form Control

HTML5 provides a variety of calendar form controls to accept date- and time-related information. Use the `<input>` element and configure the `type` attribute to specify a date or time control. Table 13 lists the HTML5 date and time controls.

TABLE 13 *Date and Time Controls*

Type Attribute	Value	Purpose Format
date	A date	YYYY-MM-DD Example: January 2, 2014, is represented by "20140102"
datetime	A date and time with time zone information; note that the time zone is indicated by the offset from UTC time	YYYY-MM-DDTHH:MM:SS-##:##Z Example: January 2, 2014, at exactly 9:58 AM Chicago time (CST) is represented by "2014-01-02T09:58:00-06:00Z"
datetime-local	A date and time without time zone information	YYYY-MM-DDTHH:MM:SS Example: January 2, 2014, at exactly 9:58 AM is represented by "2014-01-02T09:58:00"
time	A time without time zone information	HH:MM:SS Example: 1:34 PM is represented by "13:34"
month	A year and month	YYYY-MM Example: January, 2014, is represented by "2014-01"
week	A year and week	YYYY-W##, where ## represents the week in the year Example: The third week in 2014 is represented by "2014-W03"

The form in Figure 29 (see chapter10/date.html in the student files) uses the `<input>` element with `type="date"` to configure a calendar control with which the user can select a date.

Form Basics

The HTML for the date control displayed in Figure 29 is

```
<label for="myDate">Choose a
Date</label>
<input type="date" name="myDate"
id="myDate">
```

The date and time controls accept attributes listed in Tables 2 and 12. At the time this was written, only the Google Chrome and Opera browsers displayed a calendar interface for date and time controls. Other browsers currently render the date and time form controls as a text box, but you should expect increased support in the future.

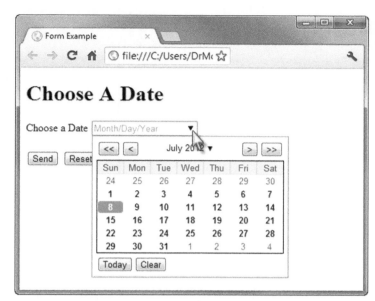

FIGURE 29 *A date form control displayed in the Google Chrome browser.*

The Color-Well Form Control

The **color-well** form control displays an interface that offers a color-picker interface to the user. The input element with `type="color"` configures a control with which the user can choose a color. At the time this was written, only the Google Chrome and Opera browsers supported the color-picker interface, shown in Figure 30 (see chapter10/color.html in the student files). Other browsers render this form control as a text box.

The HTML for the color-well form control rendered in Figure 30 is

```
<label for="myColor">Choose
a color:</label>
<input type="color"
name="myColor" id="myColor">
```

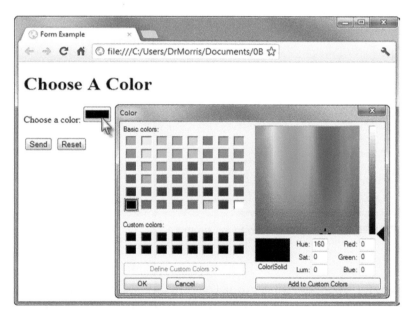

FIGURE 30 *The Google Chrome browser supports the color-well form control.*

In the next section, you'll get some experience with the new HTML5 form controls.

Form Basics

Practice with an HTML5 Form

Hands-On Practice 5

FIGURE 31 *The form displayed in Chrome.*

In this Hands-On Practice you will code HTML5 form controls as you configure a form that accepts a first name, a last name, an e-mail address, a rating value, and comments from a website visitor. Figure 31 displays the form in the Google Chrome browser, which supports the HTML5 features used in the Hands-On Practice. Figure 32 displays the form in Internet Explorer 9, which does not support the HTML5 features. Notice that the form is enhanced in Google Chrome but is still usable in both browsers—demonstrating the concept of progressive enhancement.

To get started, launch a text editor, and open the file located at chapter1/template.html in the student files. Save the file with the name form5.html. You will modify the file to create a web page similar to the examples in Figures 31 and 32.

1. Modify the title element to display the text "Comment Form". Configure the text contained within the h1 element to be "Comment Form". Add a paragraph to indicate "Required fields are marked with an asterisk *".

2. Configure the form element to submit the form information to the text's form processor at http://webdevbasics.net/scripts/demo.php.

```
<form method="post" action="http://webdevbasics.net/scripts/demo.php">
```

3. Code the form labels and controls. Configure the first name, last name, e-mail, and comment information to be required. Use an asterisk to inform your web page visitor about the required fields. Use `type="email"` instead of `type="input"` for the e-mail address. Use the `placeholder` attribute to provide hints to the user in the name and e-mail form controls. Add a slider control (use `type="range"`) to generate a value from 1 to 10 for the rating. The HTML follows:

```
<form method="post" action="http://webdevbasics.net/scripts/demo.php">
  <label for="myFirstName">* First Name</label>
  <input type="text" name="myFirstName" id="myFirstName"
         required="required" placeholder="your first name">
  <label for="myLastName">* Last Name</label>
```

Form Basics

```
<input type="text" name="myLastName"
        id="myLastName" required="required"
        placeholder="your last name">
<label for="myEmail">* E-mail</label>
<input type="email" name="myEmail" id="myEmail"
        required="required"
        placeholder="you@yourdomain.com">
<label for="myRating">Rating (1 &mdash; 10)
        </label>
<input type="range" name="myRating"
        id="myRating" min="1" max="10">
<label for="myComments">* Comments</label>
<textarea name="myComments" id="myComments"
        rows="2" cols="40"
        required="required"
        placeholder="your comments here">
</textarea>
<input type="submit" value="Submit">
</form>
```

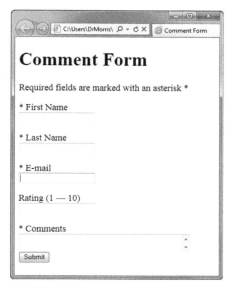

FIGURE 32 *The form displayed in Internet Explorer 9.*

4. Code embedded CSS. Configure the label element selector to use block display with a 20px top margin. Configure the input element selector to use block display with a 20 pixel bottom margin. The CSS follows:

```
label { display: block;
        margin-top: 20px; }
input { display: block;
        margin-bottom: 20px; }
```

5. Save your form5.html file. Test your page in a browser. If you use a browser that supports the HTML5 features used in the form (such as Google Chrome), your page should look similar to Figure 31. If you use a browser that does not offer support of the form's HTML5 attributes (such as Internet Explorer 9), your form should look similar to Figure 32. The display in other browsers will depend on the level of HTML5 support.

6. Try submitting the form without entering any information. Figure 33 shows the error message displayed by Google Chrome.

Compare your work with the solution in the student files (chapter10/form5.html). As this Hands-On Practice demonstrated, support of the new HTML5 form control attributes and values is not uniform. It will be some time before all browsers support these new features. Design forms with progressive enhancement in mind and be aware of both the benefits and the limitations of using new HTML5 features.

FIGURE 33 *The Chrome browser displays an error message.*

Review and Apply

Review Questions

Multiple Choice. Choose the best answer for each item.

1. Which of the following form controls would be appropriate for an area that your visitors can use to type in comments about your website?

   a. text box
   b. select list
   c. radio button
   d. scrolling text box

2. Which attribute of the `<form>` tag is used to specify the name and location of the script that will process the form field values?

   a. `action`
   b. `process`
   c. `method`
   d. `id`

3. Forms contain various types of _____, such as text boxes and buttons, that accept information from a web page visitor.

   a. hidden elements
   b. labels
   c. form controls
   d. legends

4. Choose the tag that would configure a text box with the name "city" and a width of 40 characters.

   a. `<input type="text" id="city" width="40">`
   b. `<input type="text" name="city" size="40">`
   c. `<input type="text" name="city" space="40">`
   d. `<input type="text" name="city" width="40">`

5. Which of the following form controls would be appropriate for an area that your visitors can use to type in their e-mail address?

   a. select list
   b. text box
   c. scrolling text box
   d. check box

6. You would like to conduct a survey and ask your web page visitors to vote for their favorite search engine. Which of the following form controls is best to use for this purpose?

   a. check box
   b. radio button
   c. text box
   d. scrolling text box

7. You would like to accept a number that's in a range from 1 to 50. The user needs visual verification of the number they selected. Which of the following form controls is best to use for this purpose?

   a. spinner
   b. radio button
   c. check box
   d. slider

8. What will happen when a browser encounters a new HTML5 form control that it does not support?

   a. The computer will shut down.
   b. The browser will crash.
   c. The browser will display an error message.
   d. The browser will display an input text box.

9. Which tag would configure a scrolling text box with the name comments, two rows, and thirty characters?

   a. `<textarea name="comments" width="30" rows="2"></textarea>`
   b. `<input type="textarea" name="comments" size="30" rows="2">`
   c. `<textarea name="comments" rows="2" cols="30"></textarea>`
   d. `<textarea name="comments" width="30" rows="2">`

Form Basics

10. Choose the item that would associate a label displaying the text E-mail: with the text box named email.

a. `E-mail: <input type="textbox" name="email" id="email">`

b. `<label>E-mail: <input type="text" name="email" id="email"></label>`

c. `<label for="email">E-mail:</label> <input type="text" name="email" id="email">`

d. both b and c

Hands-On Exercises

1. Write the code to create the following:

   a. A text box named username that will accept the user name of web page visitors. The text box should allow a maximum of thirty characters to be entered.

   b. A group of radio buttons that website visitors can check to vote for their favorite day of the week.

   c. A select list that asks website visitors to select their favorite social networking website.

   d. A fieldset and legend with the text "Shipping Address" around the form controls for the following fields: AddressLine1, AddressLine2, City, State, Zip Code.

   e. A hidden form control with the name of userid.

   f. A password form control with the name of password.

2. Create a web page with a form that accepts requests for a brochure to be sent in the mail. Use the HTML5 `required` attribute to configure the browser to verify that all fields have been entered by the user. Sketch out the form on paper before you begin.

3. Create a web page with a form that accepts feedback from website visitors. Use the HTML5 input `type="email"` along with the `required` attribute to configure the browser to verify the data entered. Also configure the browser to require user comments with a maximum length of 1600 characters accepted. Sketch out the form on paper before you begin.

4. Create a web page with a form that accepts a website visitor's name, e-mail, and birthdate. Use the HTML5 `type="date"` attribute to configure a calendar control on browsers that support the attribute value.

Focus on Web Design

1. Search the Web for a web page that uses an HTML form. Print the browser view of the page. Print out the source code of the web page. Using the printout, highlight or circle the tags related to forms. On a separate sheet of paper, create some notes by listing the tags and attributes related to forms found on your sample page along with a brief description of their purpose. Place your name in an e-mail link on the web page.

Form Basics

2. Choose one server-side technology mentioned in this chapter: Ruby on Rails, PHP, JSP, or ASP.NET. Use the resources listed in the chapter as a starting point, but also search the Web for additional resources on the server-side technology you have chosen. Create a web page that lists at least five useful resources along with information about each that provides the name of the site, the URL, a brief description of what is offered, and a recommended page (such as a tutorial, free script, and so on). Place your name in an e-mail link on the web page.

Answers to Review Questions

1. d	2. a	3. c
4. b	5. b	6. b
7. a	8. d	9. c
10. d		

Credits

Media and Interactivity Basics

Videos and sounds on your web pages can make them more interesting and informative. This chapter introduces you to working with multimedia and interactive elements on web pages. Methods to add audio, video, and Flash to your web pages are introduced. Sources of these media types, the HTML code needed to place the media on a web page, and suggested uses of the media are discussed. You'll also create an interactive image gallery with CSS and explore new CSS3 properties. Adding the right touch of multimedia and interactivity to a web page can make it engaging and compelling for your visitors.

You'll learn how to...

- Describe types of multimedia files used on the Web
- Configure hyperlinks to multimedia files
- Configure audio and video on a web page with HTML5 elements
- Configure a Flash animation on a web page
- Use the CSS3 transform property
- Use the CSS3 transition property
- Describe the purpose of the HTML5 canvas element

Plug-ins, Containers, and Codecs

Helper Applications and Plug-ins

Web browsers are designed to display certain file types such as .html, .htm, .gif, .jpg, and .png, among others. When the media is not one of these file types, the browser searches for a **plug-in** or **helper application** configured to display the file type. If it cannot find a plug-in or helper application (which runs in a separate window from the browser) on the visitor's computer, the web browser offers the visitor the option of saving the file to their computer. Several commonly used plug-ins are as follows:

- **Adobe Flash Player** (www.adobe.com/products/flashplayer). The Flash Player displays **.swf** format files. These can contain audio, video, and animation, along with interactivity.

- **Adobe Shockwave Player** (www.adobe.com/products/shockwaveplayer). The Shockwave Player displays high-performance multimedia created using the Adobe Director application.

- **Adobe Reader** (www.adobe.com/products/acrobat/readstep2.html). Adobe Reader is commonly used to exchange information stored in .pdf format.

- **Java Runtime Environment** (www.java.com/en/download/manual.jsp). The Java Runtime Environment (JRE) is used to run applications and applets using Java technology.

- **RealPlayer** (http://real.com). The RealPlayer plug-in plays streaming audio, video, animations, and multimedia presentations.

- **Windows Media Player** (www.microsoft.com/windows/windowsmedia/download). The Windows Media plug-in plays streaming audio, video, animations, and multimedia presentations.

- **Apple QuickTime** (www.apple.com/quicktime/download). The Apple QuickTime plug-in displays QuickTime animation, music, audio, and video directly within the web page.

The plug-ins and helper applications listed above have been used on the Web for many years. What is new about HTML5 video and audio is that it is native to the browser—with no plug-in needed. When working with native HTML5 video and audio, you need to be aware of the **container** (which is designated by the file extension) and the **codec** (which is the algorithm used to compress the media). There is no single codec that is supported by all popular browsers. For example, the H.264 codec requires licensing fees and is not supported by the Firefox and Opera web browsers, which support royalty-free Vorbis and Theora codecs. Explore Tables 1 and 2, which list common media file extensions, the container file type, and a description with codec information (if applicable for HTML5).

Media and Interactivity Basics

TABLE 1 *Common Audio File Types*

Extension	Container	Description
.wav	Wave	This format was originally created by Microsoft. It is a standard on the PC platform but is also supported by the Mac platform.
.aiff or .aif	Audio Interchange	A popular audio file format on the Mac platform. It is also supported on the PC platform.
.mid	Musical Instrument Digital Interface	Contains instructions to recreate a musical sound rather than a digital recording of the sound itself. However, a limited number of types of sounds can be reproduced.
.au	Sun UNIX Sound File	This is an older type of sound file that generally has poorer sound quality than the newer audio file formats.
.mp3	MPEG-1 Audio Layer-3	This sound file format is popular for music files due to the MP3 codec, which supports two channels and advanced compression.
.ogg	Ogg	An open-source audio file format (see www.vorbis.com) that uses the Vorbis codec.
.m4a	MPEG 4 Audio	This audio-only MPEG-4 format uses the Advanced Audio Coding (AAC) codec; supported by QuickTime, iTunes, and mobile devices such as the iPod and iPad.

TABLE 2 *Common Video File Types*

Extension	Container	Description
.mov	QuickTime	Created by Apple and initially used on the Macintosh platform; also supported by Windows.
.avi	Audio Video Interleaved	Microsoft's original standard video format for PC platforms.
.flv	Flash Video	A Flash-compatible video file container; supports H.264 codec.
.wmv	Windows Media Video	A streaming video technology developed by Microsoft. The Windows Media Player supports this file format.
.mpg	MPEG	Developed under the sponsorship of the Moving Picture Experts Group (MPEG), www.chiariglione.org/mpeg; supported on both Windows and Mac platforms.
.m4v and .mp4	MPEG-4	MPEG4 (MP4) codec; H.264 codec; played by QuickTime, iTunes, and mobile devices such as the iPod and iPad.
.3gp	3GPP Multimedia	H.264 codec; a standard for delivery of multimedia over third-generation, high-speed wireless networks.
.ogv or .ogg	Ogg	This open-source video file format uses the Theora codec (see www.theora.org).
.webm	WebM	This open media file format sponsored by Google, uses the VP8 video codec and Vorbis audio codec (see www.webmproject.org).

Media and Interactivity Basics

Configure Audio and Video

Accessing an Audio or Video File

The easiest way to give your website visitors access to an audio or a video file is to create a simple hyperlink to the file. For example, the code to hyperlink to a sound file named WDFpodcast.mp3 is

```
<a href="WDFpodcast.mp3">Podcast Episode 1</a> (MP3)
```

When your website visitor clicks the link, the plug-in for .mp3 files that is installed on the computer (such as QuickTime) will typically display embedded in a new browser window or tab. Your web page visitor can then use the plug-in to play the sound.

 Hands-On Practice 1

In this Hands-On Practice you will create a web page similar to Figure 1 that contains an h1 element and a hyperlink to an MP3 file. The web page will also provide a hyperlink to a text transcript of that file to provide for accessibility. It can also be useful to your web page visitors if you indicate the type of file (such as an MP3) and, optionally, the size of the file to be accessed.

FIGURE 1 *The default MP3 player will launch in the browser when the visitor clicks on Podcast Episode 1.*

Copy the podcast.mp3 and podcast.txt files from the chapter11/starters folder in the student files on the companion website at www.pearsonhighered.com/felke-morris and save them to a folder named podcast. Use the chapter1/template.html file as a starting point and create a web page containing a page title of "Podcast", an h1 element with the text "Web Design Podcast", a hyperlink to the MP3 file, and a hyperlink to the text transcript. Save your page as podcast2.html. Display the file in a browser. Try to test your page in different browsers and browser versions. When you click on the MP3 hyperlink, an audio player (whichever player or plug-in is configured for the browser) will launch to play the file. When you click on the hyperlink for the text transcript, the text will display in the browser. Compare your work to the sample in the student files (chapter11/podcast/podcast.html).

Multimedia and Accessibility

Provide alternate content for the media files you use on your website in transcript, caption, or printable PDF format.

▶ Provide a text transcript for audio files such as podcasts. Often you can use the podcast script as the basis of the text transcript file that you create as a PDF and upload to your website.

▶ Provide captions for video files. Apple QuickTime Pro includes a captioning function— view an example in the student files at chapter11/starters/sparkycaptioned.mov. Captions can be added to your YouTube Videos. For more information about video captioning visit www.webaim.org/techniques/captions.

Multimedia and Browser Compatibility Issues

Providing your website visitor a hyperlink to download and save a multimedia file is the most basic method to provide access to your media, although your visitor will need an application installed on their computer (such as Adobe Quicktime, Apple iTunes, or Windows Media Player) to play the file after download. You are dependent on whether your website visitors have installed the corresponding player. For this reason, many websites began to use the Adobe Flash file format to share video and audio files.

In response to these browser plug-in compatibility issues and in an effort to reduce reliance on a proprietary technology like Adobe Flash, HTML5 introduces new audio and video elements that are native to the browser and do not require browser plug-ins or players. However, because HTML5 is not yet an official standard and not supported by older browsers, web designers still need to provide for a fallback option, such as providing a hyperlink to the media file or displaying a Flash version of the multimedia. You'll work with Flash, HTML5 video, and HTML5 audio later in this chapter.

FAQ Why doesn't my audio or video file play?

Playing audio and video files on the Web depends on the plug-ins installed in your visitor's web browsers. A page that works perfectly on your home computer may not work for all visitors—depending on the configuration of their computer. Some visitors will not have the plug-ins properly installed. Some visitors may have file types associated with incorrect plug-ins or incorrectly installed plug-ins. Some visitors may be using low bandwidth and have to wait an overly long time for your media file to download. Are you detecting a pattern here? Sometimes multimedia on the Web can be problematic.

Flash and the HTML5 Embed Element

Adobe Flash is an application that can be used to add visual interest and interactivity to web pages with slideshows, animations, and other multimedia effects. Flash animation can be interactive—it can be scripted, with a language called ActionScript, to respond to mouse clicks, accept information in text boxes, and invoke server-side scripting. Flash can also be used to play audio and video files. Flash multimedia files are stored in a **.swf** file extension and require the Flash Player browser plug-in.

FIGURE 2 *The embed element was used to configure the Flash media.*

The Embed Element

The **embed element** is a self-contained, or void, element whose purpose is to provide a container for external content (such as Flash) that requires a plug-in or player. Although used for many years to display Flash on web pages, the embed element was never an official W3C element until HTML5. One of the design principles of HTML5 is to "pave the cowpaths"—to smooth the way for valid use of techniques that, although supported by browsers, were not part of the official W3C standard. Figure 2 (also in the student files at chapter11/flashembed.html) shows a web page using an embed element to display a Flash .swf file. The attributes of the embed element commonly used with Flash media are listed in Table 3.

TABLE 3 *Embed Element Attributes*

Attribute	Description and Value
`src`	File name of the Flash media (.swf file)
`height`	Specifies the height of the object area in pixels
`type`	The MIME type of the object; use `type="application/x-shockwave-flash"`
`width`	Specifies the width of the object area in pixels
`bgcolor`	Optional; background color of the Flash media, using a hexadecimal color value
`quality`	Optional; describes the quality of the media, usually set to "high"
`title`	Optional; specifies a brief text description
`wmode`	Optional; set to "transparent" to configure transparent background

In this Hands-On Practice you will launch a text editor and create a web page that displays a Flash slideshow of photographs. Your page will look like the one shown in Figure 3.

Create a folder called embed. Copy the lighthouse.swf file from the student files chapter11/starters folder and save it in your embed folder.

Use the chapter1/template.html file as a starting point, and create a web page containing a page title and an h1 element with the text "Door County Lighthouse Cruise" and an `<embed>` tag to display a Flash file named lighthouse.swf that is 320 pixels wide and 240 pixels high. A sample embed tag is

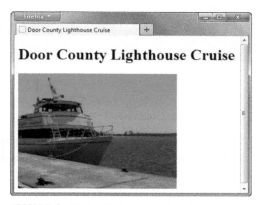

FIGURE 3 *Flash slideshow of images configured with the embed element.*

```
<embed type="application/x-shockwave-flash"
       src="lighthouse.swf" quality="high"
       width="320" height="240"
       title="Door County Lighthouse Cruise">
```

Notice the value of the `title` attribute in the code sample. The descriptive text could be accessed by assistive technologies such as a screen reader application.

Save your page as index.html in the embed folder. Test it in a browser. Compare your work to the sample in the student files (chapter11/lighthouse/embed.html).

 What will happen if my web page visitor uses a browser that does not support Flash?

If you used the code in this section to display Flash media on a web page and your visitor's browser does not support Flash, the browser will typically display a message about a missing plug-in. The code in this section passes W3C HTML5 conformance checks and is the minimum code needed to display Flash media on a web page. If you'd like more features, such as being able to offer an express install of the latest Flash player to your visitors using desktop web browsers, explore SWFObject at http://code.google.com/p/swfobject/wiki/documentation, which uses JavaScript to embed Flash content (and is W3C XHTML standards compliant).

Although the Flash player is installed on most desktop web browsers, be aware that many users of mobile devices will not be able to view your Flash multimedia. There is no Flash support in the iPhone, iTouch, or iPad. Adobe recently announced that the Flash Player will no longer be available for Android. Mobile devices and modern desktop browsers support the new HTML5 video and audio elements which are introduced next in this chapter. You'll also explore the potential of CSS3 animations with CSS transforms and transitions later in this chapter.

HTML5 Audio and Source Elements

The Audio Element

The new HTML5 **audio element** supports native play of audio files in the browser—without the need for plug-ins or players. The audio element begins with the `<audio>` tag and ends with the `</audio>` tag. Table 4 lists the attributes of the audio element.

TABLE 4 *Audio Element Attributes*

Attribute	Value	Description
src	file name	Optional; audio file name
type	MIME Type	Optional; the MIME type of the audio file, such as audio/mpeg or audio/ogg
autoplay	autoplay	Optional; indicates whether audio should start playing automatically; use with caution
controls	controls	Optional; indicates whether controls should be displayed; recommended
loop	loop	Optional; indicates whether audio should be played over and over
preload	none, auto, metadata	Optional; values: none (no preload), metadata (only download media file metadata), and auto (download the media file)
title		Optional; specifies a brief text description that may be displayed by browsers or assistive technologies

You'll need to supply multiple versions of the audio due to browser support of different codecs. Plan to supply audio files in at least two different containers, including ogg and mp3. It is typical to omit the src and type attributes from the audio tag and, instead, configure multiple versions of the audio file with the source element.

The Source Element

The **source element** is a self-contained, or void, tag that specifies a multimedia file and a MIME type. The src attribute identifies the file name of the media file. The type attribute indicates the MIME type of the file. Code `type="audio/mpeg"` for an MP3 file. Code `type="audio/ogg"` for audio files using the Vorbis codec. Configure a source element for each version of the audio file. Place the source elements before the closing audio tag.

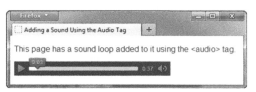

FIGURE 4 *The Firefox browser supports the HTML5 audio element.*

The following code sample configures the web page shown in Figure 4 (also in the student files chapter11/audio.html) to display a controller for an audio file:

Media and Interactivity Basics

272

```
<audio controls="controls">
  <source src="soundloop.mp3" type="audio/mpeg">
  <source src="soundloop.ogg" type="audio/ogg">
  <a href="soundloop.mp3">Download the Audio File</a> (MP3)
</audio>
```

Current versions of Safari, Chrome, Firefox, and Opera support the HTML5 audio element. The controls displayed by each browser are different. While Internet Explorer 9 supports the audio element, earlier versions of Internet Explorer offer no support. Review the code sample just given and note the hyperlink placed between the second source element and the closing audio tag. Any HTML elements or text placed in this area is rendered by browsers that do not support the HTML5 audio element. This is referred to as fallback content—if the audio element is not supported, the MP3 version of the file is made available for download. Figure 5 shows a screen shot of Internet Explorer 8 displaying "fallback content."

FIGURE 5 *Internet Explorer 8 does not recognize the audio element.*

 Hands-On Practice 3

In this Hands-On Practice you will launch a text editor and create a web page (see Figure 6) that displays an audio control to play a podcast.

Copy the podcast.mp3, podcast.ogg, and podcast.txt files from the chapter11/starters folder in the student files and save them to a folder named audio. Use the chapter1/template.html file as a starting point and create a web page containing a page title and an h1 element with the text "Web Design Podcast", an audio control (use the audio element and two source elements), and a hyperlink to the text transcript. Configure a hyperlink to the MP3 file as the fallback content. The code for the audio element is

```
<audio controls="controls">
  <source src="podcast.mp3" type="audio/mpeg">
  <source src="podcast.ogg" type="audio/ogg"><br>
  <a href="podcast.mp3">Download the Podcast</a> (MP3)
</audio>
```

Save your page as index.html in the audio folder. Display the file in a browser. Try to test your page in different browsers and browser versions. Recall that Internet Explorer versions prior to Version 9 do not support the audio element but will display the fallback content. When you click on the hyperlink for the text transcript, the text will display in the browser. Compare your work to the sample in the student files (chapter11/podcast/audio.html).

FIGURE 6 *Using the audio element to provide access to a podcast.*

How can I convert an audio file to the Ogg Vorbis codec?

The open-source Audacity application supports Ogg Vorbis. For download information see http://audacity.sourceforge.net. If you upload and share an audio file at the Internet Archive (http://archive.org), an .ogg format file will automatically be generated.

Media and Interactivity Basics

HTML5 Video and Source Elements

VideoNote
HTML5 Video

The Video Element

The new HTML5 **video element** supports native play of video files in the browser—without the need for plug-ins or players. The video element begins with the `<video>` tag and ends with the `</video>` tag. Table 5 lists the attributes of the video element.

TABLE 5   *Video Element Attributes*

Attribute	Value	Description
src	file name	Optional; video file name
type	MIME Type	Optional; the MIME type of the video file, such as video/mp4 or video/ogg
autoplay	autoplay	Optional; indicates whether video should start playing automatically; use with caution
controls	controls	Optional; indicates whether controls should be displayed
height	number	Optional; video height in pixels
loop	loop	Optional; indicates whether video plays continuously
poster	file name	Optional; specifies an image to display if the browser cannot play the video
preload	none, metadata, auto	Optional; values: none (no preload), metadata (only download media file metadata), and auto (download the media file)
title		Optional; specifies a brief text description that may be displayed by browsers or assistive technologies
width	number	Optional; video width in pixels

You'll need to supply multiple versions of the video due to browser support of different codecs. Plan to supply video files in at least two different containers, including mp4 and ogg (or ogv). See www.ibm.com/developerworks/web/library/wa-html5video/#table2 for a browser compatibility chart. It is typical to omit the `src` and `type` attributes from the video tag and, instead, configure multiple versions of the audio file with the source element.

Media and Interactivity Basics

The Source Element

The **source element** is a self-contained, or void, tag that specifies a multimedia file and a MIME type. The `src` attribute identifies the file name of the media file. The `type` attribute indicates the MIME type of the file. Code `type="video/mp4"` for video files using the MP4 codec. Code `type="video/ogg"` for video files using the Theora codec. Configure a source element for each version of the video file. Place the source elements before the closing video tag.

The following code sample configures the web page shown in Figure 7 (see the student files chapter11/sparky.html) with the native HTML5 browser controls to display and play a video.

FIGURE 7 *The Opera browser.*

```
<video controls="controls" poster="sparky.jpg"
width="160" height="150">
  <source src="sparky.m4v" type="video/mp4">
  <source src="sparky.ogv" type="video/ogg">
  <a href="sparky.mov">Sparky the Dog</a> (.mov)
</video>
```

Current versions of Safari, Chrome, Firefox, and Opera support the HTML5 video element. The controls displayed by each browser are different. Internet Explorer 9 supports the video element, but earlier versions do not. Review the code sample just given and note the anchor element placed between the second source element and the closing video tag. Any HTML elements or text placed in this area is rendered by browsers that do not support the HTML5 video element. This is referred to as fallback content. In this case, a hyperlink to a QuickTime (.mov) version of the file is supplied for the user to download. Another fallback option is to configure an embed element to play a Flash .swf version of the video. Figure 8 shows Internet Explorer 8 displaying the web page.

FIGURE 8 *Internet Explorer 8 displays the hyperlink.*

Practice with HTML5 Video

 Hands-On Practice 4

In this Hands-On Practice you will launch a text editor and create the web page in Figure 9, which displays a video control to play a movie. Copy the lighthouse.m4v, lighthouse.ogv, lighthouse.swf, and lighthouse.jpg files from the chapter11/starters folder in the student files and save them to a new folder named video.

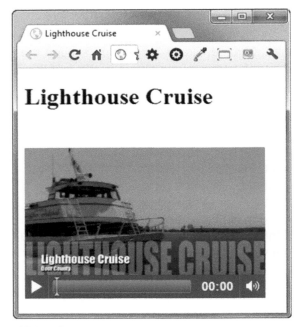

FIGURE 9 *HTML5 video element.*

Open the chapter1/template.html file in a text editor. Save the file with the name index.html in the video folder.

Edit the index.html file:

1. Modify the title element to display the text "Lighthouse Cruise".
2. Configure the h1 element with the text "Lighthouse Cruise".
3. Configure a video control (use the video element and two source elements) to display the lighthouse video.

   a. Configure an embed element to display the
      Flash content, lighthouse.swf, as fallback content.

Media and Interactivity Basics

b. Configure the lighthouse.jpg file as a poster image, which will display if the browser supports the video element but cannot play any of the video files.

The code for the video element is

```
<video controls="controls" poster="lighthouse.jpg">
  <source src="lighthouse.m4v" type="video/mp4">
  <source src="lighthouse.ogv" type="video/ogg">
  <embed type="application/x-shockwave-flash"
    src="lighthouse.swf" quality="high"
    width="320" height="240"
    title="Door County Lighthouse Cruise">
</video>
```

4. Notice that the video element does not contain height and width attributes. Using a method to configure flexible images, configure the HTML5 video to be flexible with CSS. Place your cursor in the head section and code a style element. Configure the following style rule to set 100% width, auto height, and a maximum width of 320 pixels (which is the actual width of the video).

```
video { width: 100%; height: auto; max-width: 320px; }
```

Save your page as index.html in the video folder. Display the index.html page in a browser. Try to test your page in different browsers and browser versions. Compare your work to Figure 9 and the sample in the student files (chapter11/video/video.html).

FAQ How can I convert a video file to the new codecs?

You can use Firefogg (http://firefogg.org) to convert your video file to the Ogg Theora codec. Online-Convert (http://video.online-convert.com/convert-to-webm) offers free conversion to WebM. The free, open-source MiroVideoConverter (www.mirovideoconverter.com) can convert most video files to MP4, WebM, or OGG formats.

Embed a YouTube Video

YouTube (www.youtube.com) is a popular website for sharing videos for both personal and business use. When a video is uploaded to YouTube the creator can choose to allow for video embedding by others. It's easy to display a YouTube video on your web page: On the YouTube website display the video you want to embed, select Share > Embed and then copy and paste the HTML into your web page source code. The code uses an iframe element to display a web page file within your web page. YouTube detects the browser and operating system of your web page visitor and serves the content in an appropriate format—with either Flash or HTML5 video.

The iframe Element

The **iframe element** configures an **inline frame** that displays the contents of another web page within your web page document, referred to as *nested browsing*. The iframe element begins with the `<iframe>` tag and ends with the `</iframe>` tag. Fallback content that should be displayed if the browser does not support inline frames (such as a text description or hyperlink to the actual web page) should be placed between the tags. Figure 10 shows a web page that displays a YouTube video within an iframe element. See Table 6 for a list of iframe element attributes.

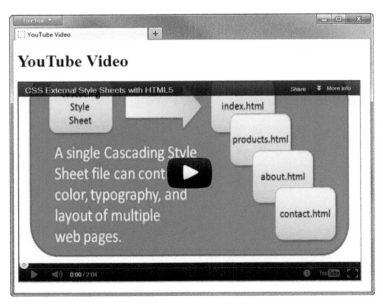

FIGURE 10 *Embedding a YouTube video.*

Media and Interactivity Basics

TABLE 6 *iframe Element Attributes*

Attribute	Description and Value
src	URL of the web page to display in the inline frame
height	Inline frame height in pixels
width	Inline frame width in pixels
id	Optional; text name, alphanumeric, beginning with a letter, no spaces—the value must be unique and not used for other id values on the same web page document
name	Optional; text name, alphanumeric, beginning with a letter, no spaces
sandbox	Optional; disallow/disable features such as plug-ins, scripts, forms (HTML5)
seamless	Optional; set seamless="seamless" to indicate streamlined browser display (HTML5)
title	Optional; specifies a brief text description

 Hands-On Practice 5

VideoNote

In this Hands-On Practice you will launch a text editor and create a web page that displays a YouTube video within an iframe element. This example embeds the video found at www.youtube.com/watch?v=1QkisJHztHI. You can choose to embed this video or select a different video. The process is to display the YouTube page for the video and copy the video identifier which is the text after the "=" in the URL. In this example, the video identifier is "1QkisJHztHI".

Use the chapter1/template.html file as a starting point and configure a web page containing a page title and an h1 element with the text "YouTube Video" and an iframe element. Code the src attribute with www.youtube.com/embed/ followed by the video identifier. In this example set the src attribute to the value www.youtube.com/embed/1QkisJHztHI. Configure a hyperlink to the YouTube video page as fallback content. The code to display the video shown in Figure 10 is

```
<iframe src="www.youtube.com/embed/1QkisJHztHI"
  width="640" height="385">
  <a href="www.youtube.com/embed/1QkisJHztHI">YouTube Video</a>
</iframe>
```

Save your page as youtubevideo.html and display it in a browser. Compare your work to Figure 10 and the sample in the student files (chapter11/iframe.html).

In addition to playing multimedia that is hosted on another server, such as the YouTube video in this example, inline frames are widely used on the Web for a variety of marketing and promotional purposes, including displaying ad banners and serving content for associate and partner sites. The advantage is separation of control. The dynamic content—such as the ad banner or multimedia clip—can be modified by the partner site at any time, just as YouTube dynamically configures the format of the video display in this section.

Media and Interactivity Basics

CSS3 Transform Property

CSS transforms allow you to change the display of an element and provides functions to rotate, scale, skew, and reposition an element. Both two-dimensional (2D) and three-dimensional (3D) transforms are possible.

FIGURE 11 *The transform property in action.*

Developers of browser-rendering engines, such as WebKit (used by Safari and Google Chrome) and Gecko (used by Firefox and other Mozilla-based browsers), have created their own proprietary properties to implement the `transform` property. So, you need to code multiple style declarations to configure a transform:

- `-webkit-transform` (for Webkit browsers)
- `-moz-transform` (for Gecko browsers)
- `-o-transform` (for the Opera browser)
- `-ms-transform` (for Internet Explorer 9)
- `transform` (W3C draft syntax)

Eventually, all browsers will support CSS3 and the `transform` property, so code this property last in the list. Table 7 lists commonly used 2D transform property function values and their purpose. See www.w3.org/TR/css3-transforms/#transform-property for a complete list. We'll focus on the rotate transform in this section.

TABLE 7 *Values of the Transform Property*

Value	Purpose
rotate(*degree*)	Rotates the element by the angle
scale(*number, number*)	Scales or resizes the element along the X and Y axis (X,Y)
scaleX(*number*)	Scales or resizes the element along the X axis
scaleY(*number*)	Scales or resizes the element along the Y axis
skewX(*number*)	Distorts the display of the element along the X axis
skewY(*number*)	Distorts the display of the element along the Y axis
translate(*number, number*)	Repositions the element along the X and Y axis (X,Y)
translateX(*number*)	Repositions the element along the X axis
translateY(*number*)	Repositions the element along the Y axis

Media and Interactivity Basics

CSS3 Rotate Transform

The `rotate()` transform function takes a value in degrees (like an angle in geometry). Rotate to the right with a positive value. Rotate to the left with a negative value. The rotation is around the origin, which, by default, is the middle of the element. The web page in Figure 11 demonstrates the use of the CSS3 transform property to slightly rotate the figure.

 Hands-On Practice 6

In this Hands-On Practice you will configure the rotation transform shown in Figure 11. Create a new folder named transform. Copy the lighthouseisland.jpg and lighthouselogo.jpg images from the chapter11/starters folder in the student files to your transform folder. Launch a text editor and open the starter.html file in the chapter11 folder. Save the file as index.html in your transform folder. Launch the file in a browser and it will look similar to Figure 12.

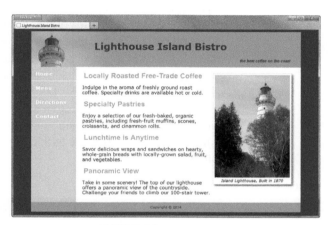

FIGURE 12 *Before the transform property.*

Open index.html in a text editor and view the embedded CSS. Locate the figure element selector. You will add new style declarations to the figure element selector that will configure a three-degree rotation transform. The new CSS is shown in blue.

```
figure { float: right; margin: 10px; background-color: #FFF;
        padding: 5px; border: 1px solid #CCC;
        box-shadow: 5px 5px 5px #828282;
        -webkit-transform: rotate(3deg);
        -moz-transform: rotate(3deg);
        -o-transform: rotate(3deg);
        -ms-transform: rotate(3deg);
        transform: rotate(3deg); }
```

Save the file and display it in a browser. You should see the figure displayed on a slight angle. Compare your work to Figure 11 and the sample in the student files (chapter11/transform/index.html).

 This section provided an overview of one type of transform: the rotation of an element. Visit www.westciv.com/tools/transforms/index.html to generate the CSS for rotate, scale, translate, and skew transforms. Find out more about transforms at www.css3files.com/transform and http://developer.mozilla.org/en/CSS/Using_CSS_transforms.

CSS Transition Property

CSS3 **transitions** provide for changes in property values to display in a smoother manner over a specified time. Transitions are supported by current versions of most modern browsers, including Internet Explorer (version 10 and later). However, for optimal browser support, code browser vendor prefixes. You can apply a transition to a variety of CSS properties including `color`, `background-color`, `border`, `font-size`, `font-weight`, `margin`, `padding`, `opacity`, and `text-shadow`. A full list of applicable properties is available at www.w3.org/TR/css3-transitions. When you configure a transition for a property, you need to configure values for the `transition-property`, `transition-duration`, `transition-timing-function`, and `transition-delay` properties. These can be combined in a single transition shorthand property. Table 8 lists the transition properties and their purpose. Table 9 lists commonly used `transition-timing-function` values and their purpose.

TABLE 8 *CSS Transition Properties*

Property	Description
transition-property	Indicates the CSS property to which the transition applies
transition-duration	Indicates the length of time to apply the transition; default value 0 configures an immediate transition; a numeric value specifies time (usually in seconds)
transition-timing-function	Configures changes in the speed of the transition by describing how intermediate property values are calculated; common values include `ease` (default), `linear`, `ease-in`, `ease-out`, `ease-in-out`
transition-delay	Indicates the beginning of the transition; default value 0 configures no delay; a numeric value specifies time (usually in seconds)
transition	Shorthand property; list the value for `transition-property`, `transition-duration`, `transition-timing-function`, and `transition-delay` separated by spaces; default values can be omitted, but the first time unit applies to `transition-duration`

TABLE 9 *Commonly used* `transition-timing-function` *values.*

Value	Purpose
ease	Default; transition effect begins slowly, speeds up, and ends slowly
linear	Transition effect has a constant speed
ease-in	Transition effect begins slowly and speeds up to a constant speed
ease-out	Transition effect begins at a constant speed and slows down
ease-in-out	Transition effect is slightly slower; Begins slowly, speeds up, and slows down

Media and Interactivity Basics

Recall that the CSS `:hover` pseudoclass provides a way to configure styles to display when the web page visitor moves the mouse over an element. The change in display happens somewhat abruptly. Web designers can use a CSS transition to create a more gradual change to the hover state. You'll try this out in this Hands-On Practice when you configure a transition for the navigation hyperlinks on a web page.

Create a new folder named transition. Copy the lighthouseisland.jpg and lighthouselogo.jpg images from the chapter11/starters folder in the student files to your transition folder. Copy the chapter11/transform/index.html file into your transition folder. Open index.html in a browser and

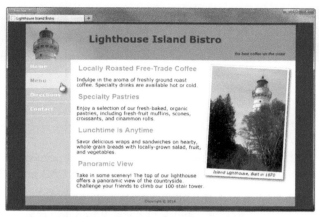

FIGURE 13 *The transition causes the hyperlinks' background color to change in a more gradual manner.*

it will look similar to Figure 11. Place your mouse over one of the navigation hyperlinks and notice that the background color and text color change immediately.

Open index.html in a text editor and view the embedded CSS. Locate the `nav a:hover` selector and notice that the color and background-color properties are configured. You will add new style declarations to the nav a selector to cause a more gradual change in the background color when the user places the mouse over the hyperlink. The new CSS is shown in blue.

```
nav a { text-decoration: none; display: block; padding: 15px;
        -webkit-transition: background-color 2s linear;
        -moz-transition: background-color 2s linear;
        -o-transition: background-color 2s linear;
        transition: background-color 2s linear; }
```

Save the file and display it in a browser. Place your mouse over one of the navigation hyperlinks and notice that while the text color changes immediately, the background color changes in a more gradual manner—the transition is working! Compare your work to Figure 13 and the student files (chapter11/transition/index.html).

 If you'd like more control over the transition than what is provided by the values listed in Table 9, explore using the cubic-bezier value for the transition-timing-function. A Bezier curve is a mathematically defined curve often used in graphic applications to describe motion. Explore the following resources:

▶ www.the-art-of-web.com/css/timing-function

▶ http://roblaplaca.com/blog/2011/03/11/understanding-css-cubic-bezier

▶ http://cubic-bezier.com

Practice with Transitions

Hands-On Practice 8

In this Hands-On Practice you will use CSS `positioning`, `opacity`, and `transition` properties to configure an interactive image gallery with CSS and HTML.

Figure 14 shows the initial display of the gallery (see the student files chapter11/gallery/gallery.html) with a semi-opaque placeholder image. When you place the mouse over a thumbnail image, the larger version of that image is gradually displayed along with a caption (see Figure 15). If you click the thumbnail, the image will display in its own browser window.

FIGURE 14 *Initial display of the gallery.*

Create a new folder called g11. Copy all the images from the chapter11/starters/gallery folder in the student files to the new g11 folder.

Launch a text editor and modify the chapter1/template.html file to configure a web page as indicated:

1. Configure the text, "Image Gallery", within an h1 element and within the title element.

2. Code a div element assigned to the id named `gallery`. This div will contain a placeholder figure element and an unordered list that contains the thumbnail images.

3. Configure a figure element within the div. The figure element will contain a placeholder img element that displays photo1.jpg.

4. Configure an unordered list within the div. Code six li elements, one for each thumbnail image. The thumbnail images will function as image links with a :hover pseudo-class that causes the larger image to display on the page. We'll make this all happen by configuring an anchor element

FIGURE 15 *The new photo gradually displays.*

Media and Interactivity Basics

containing both the thumbnail image and a span element that comprises the larger image along with descriptive text. An example of the first li element is

```
<li><a href="photo1.jpg"><img src="photo1thumb.jpg" width="100" height="75"
    alt="Golden Gate Bridge">
    <span><img src="photo1.jpg" width="400" height="300"
    alt="Golden Gate Bridge"><br>Golden Gate Bridge</span></a>
</li>
```

5. Configure all six li elements in a similar manner. Substitute the actual name of each image file for the href and src values in the code. Write your own descriptive text for each image. Use photo2.jpg and photo2thumb.jpg in the second li element. Use photo3.jpg and photo3thumb.jpg in the third li element, and so on for all six images. Save the file as index.html in the g11 folder. Display your page in a browser. You'll see the placeholder image followed by an unordered list with the thumbnail images, the larger images, and the descriptive text.

6. Now, let's add CSS. Open your file in a text editor and code a style element in the head section. Configure embedded CSS as follows:

   a. Configure the body element selector with a dark background color (#333333) and a light gray text color (#eaeaea).

   b. Configure the gallery id selector. Set position to relative. This does not change the location of the gallery but sets the stage to use absolute positioning on the span element relative to its container (#gallery) instead of relative to the entire web page document.

   c. Configure the figure element selector. Set position to absolute, left to 280px, text-align to center and opacity to .25. This will cause the figure to initially be semi-opaque.

   d. Configure the unordered list within the #gallery with a width of 300 pixels and no list marker.

   e. Configure the list item elements within the #gallery with inline display, left float, and 10 pixels of padding.

   f. Configure the img elements within the #gallery to not display a border.

   g. Configure anchor elements within the #gallery with no underline, #eaeaea text color, and italic text.

   h. Configure span elements within the #gallery. Set position to absolute, left to -1000px (which causes them not to display initially in the browser viewport), and opacity to 0. Also configure a three second ease-in-out transition.

   ```
   #gallery span { position: absolute; left: -1000px; opacity: 0;
                   -webkit-transition: opacity 3s ease-in-out;
                   -moz-transition: opacity 3s ease-in-out;
                   -o-transition: opacity 3s ease-in-out;
                   transition: opacity 3s ease-in-out; }
   ```

   i. Configure the span elements within the #gallery to display when the web visitor hovers the mouse over the thumbnail image link. Set position to absolute, top to 15px, left to 320px, centered text, and opacity to 1.

   ```
   #gallery a:hover span { position: absolute; top: 16px; left: 320px;
                           text-align: center; opacity: 1; }
   ```

Save your file in the g11 folder and display it in a browser. Compare your work to Figure 14, Figure 15, and the student files (chapter11/gallery/gallery.html).

HTML5 Canvas Element

The HTML5 **canvas element** is a container for dynamic graphics. It provides a way to dynamically draw and transform lines, shapes, images, and text on web pages. If that wasn't enough, the canvas element also provides methods to interact with actions taken by the user, like moving the mouse. The promise of the canvas element is that it can be used to create interactions as sophisticated as those developed with Adobe Flash. Recent versions of all modern browsers support the canvas element. See virtuoso examples of the canvas element in action at the following websites:

- www.chromeexperiments.com (look for experiments with "canvas" in the title)
- www.canvasdemos.com/type/applications
- www.canvasdemos.com/type/games

The canvas element begins with the `<canvas>` tag and ends with the `</canvas>` tag. However, the canvas element is configured through an **application programming interface (API)**, which means that a programming or scripting language, such as JavaScript, is

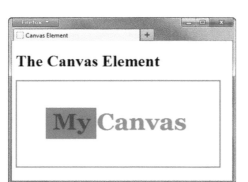

FIGURE 16 *The canvas element.*

needed to implement it. **JavaScript** is an object-based scripting language interpreted by a web browser. It's used to work with the objects associated with a web page document—the browser window, the document itself, and the elements—including form, img, and canvas. These elements are all part of the **document object model (DOM)**. JavaScript is associated with a web page using the **script element**.

The canvas API provides methods for two-dimensional (2D) bitmap drawing, including lines, strokes, arcs, fills, gradients, images, and text. However, instead of drawing visually using a graphics application, you draw programmatically by writing JavaScript statements. A very basic example of using JavaScript to draw within the canvas element is provided in this section.

Although you need to understand JavaScript to use the canvas element, learning to code JavaScript is outside of the scope of this chapter. We'll explore the very basic example of configuring the canvas element shown in Figure 16 (see the student files chapter11/canvas.html). The code is

```
<!DOCTYPE html>
<html lang="en">
<head>
<title>Canvas Element</title>
<meta charset="utf-8">
```

Media and Interactivity Basics

```
<style>
canvas { border: 2px solid red; }
</style>
<script>
function drawMe() {
  var canvas = document.getElementById("myCanvas");
  if (canvas.getContext) {
    var ctx = canvas.getContext("2d");
    ctx.fillStyle = "rgb(255, 0, 0)";
    ctx.font = "bold 3em Georgia";
    ctx.fillText("My Canvas", 70, 100);
    ctx.fillStyle = "rgba(0, 0, 200, 0.50)";
    ctx.fillRect(57, 54, 100, 65);
  }
}
</script>
</head>
<body onload="drawMe()">
<h1>The Canvas Element</h1>
<canvas id="myCanvas" width="400" height="175"></canvas>
</body>
</html>
```

If some of the code looks like a foreign language to you, don't worry—JavaScript IS a different language than CSS and HTML, with its own syntax and rules. Here's a quick overview of the code sample:

The red outline was created by applying CSS to the canvas selector.

The JavaScript function `drawMe()` is invoked when the browser loads the page.

JavaScript looks for a canvas element assigned to the `myCanvas` id.

Test for browser support of canvas and, if true, perform the actions listed below:

- Set the canvas context to 2d.
- Draw the "My Canvas" text.
  - Use the `fillStyle` attribute to set the drawing color to red.
  - Use the `font` attribute to configure the font weight, size, and family.
  - Use the `fillText` method to specify the text to display, followed by the x-value (pixels in from the left) and y-value (pixels down from the top).
- Draw the rectangle.
  - Use the `fillStyle` attribute to set the drawing color to blue with 50% opacity.
  - Use the `fillRect` method to set the x-value (pixels in from the left), y-value (pixels down from the top), width, and height of the rectangle.

This section provided a very quick overview of the canvas element. Visit www.html5canvastutorials.com, https://developer.mozilla.org/en/Canvas_tutorial, and http://dev.opera.com/articles/view/html-5-canvas-the-basics if you'd like additional examples and practice with this intriguing new element.

Media and Interactivity Basics

Review and Apply

Review Questions

Multiple Choice. Choose the best answer for each item.

1. Which property provides a way for you to rotate, scale, skew, or move an element?
   a. `display`
   b. `transition`
   c. `transform`
   d. `list-style-type`

2. Which of the following is the file extension for a Flash animation?
   a. `.swf`
   b. `.ogg`
   c. .flash
   d. .mov

3. What happens when a browser does not support the `<video>` or `<audio>` element?
   a. The computer crashes.
   b. The web page does not display.
   c. The fallback content, if it exists, will display.
   d. none of the above

4. Which property enables changes in property values to display in gradual manner over a specified time?
   a. `transition`
   b. `transform`
   c. `display`
   d. `opacity`

5. Which of the following is an open-source video codec?
   a. Theora
   b. MP3
   c. Vorbis
   d. Flash

6. Which of the following is a void element that specifies a media file name and MIME type?
   a. iframe
   b. anchor
   c. param
   d. source

7. Which of the following configures an area on a web page to not display?
   a. `hide: yes;`
   b. `display: no;`
   c. `display: none;`
   d. `display: block;`

8. What type of files are .webm, .ogv, and .m4v?
   a. audio files
   b. video files
   c. Flash files
   d. none of the above

9. Which of the following should you do to provide for usability and accessibility?
   a. Use video and sound whenever possible.
   b. Supply text descriptions of audio files and caption video files that appear in your web pages.
   c. Never use audio and video files.
   d. none of the above

10. Which of the following elements displays the contents of another web page document?
    a. `iframe`
    b. `div`
    c. `document`
    d. `object`

Hands-On Exercises

1. Write the HTML for a hyperlink to a video called lighthouse.mov on a web page.

2. Write the HTML to embed an audio file called soundloop.mp3 on a web page that can be controlled by the visitor.

Media and Interactivity Basics

3. Write the HTML to display a video on a web page. The video files are named movie.m4v and movie.ogv. The width is 480 pixels. The height is 360 pixels. The poster image is movie.jpg.

4. Write the HTML to display a Flash file named flashbutton.swf on a web page.

5. Write the HTML to configure an inline frame to display the home page of http://webdevbasics.net in your web page.

 Although you can configure an inline frame to display another website, it is an ethical practice to only do so when you have obtained permission or have an arrangement with the other website.

6. Create a web page about your favorite movie that contains an audio file with your review of the movie. Use an application of your choice to record your review (visit http://audacity.sourceforge.net/download for a free download of Audacity). Place an e-mail hyperlink to yourself on the web page. Save the page as review.html.

7. Create a web page about your favorite music group that contains either a brief audio file with your review or an audio clip of the group. Use an application of your choice to record your review (visit http://audacity.sourceforge.net/download for a free download of Audacity). Place an e-mail hyperlink to yourself on the web page. Save the page as music.html.

8. Visit the companion website at http://webdevbasics.net/flashcs5 and follow the instructions to create a Flash logo banner.

9. Add new transitions to the Lighthouse Bistro home page (found in the student files at chapter11/transition/index.html). Configure the opacity property to display the light-house figure initially at 50% opacity and slowly change the opacity to 100% when the visitor places their mouse over the figure area.

Focus on Web Design

This chapter mentioned, "pave the cowpaths" as one of the design principles of HTML5. You may be wondering about the others. The W3C has a list of the HTML5 Design Principles at www.w3.org/TR/html-design-principles. Review the page and write a one-page summary and reaction to these principles and what they mean to you as a web designer.

Answers to Review Questions

1. c   **2.** a   **3.** c
4. a   **5.** a   **6.** d
7. c   **8.** b   **9.** b
10. a

Credits

Web Publishing
Basics

Well, you've designed and built a website, but there is still much more to do. You need to obtain a domain name, select a web host, publish your files to the Web, and submit your site to search engines. In addition to discussing these tasks, this chapter introduces you to evaluating the accessibility and usability of your website.

You'll learn how to...

▷ Describe criteria to consider when you're selecting a web host

▷ Obtain a domain name for your website

▷ Publish a website using FTP

▷ Design web pages that are friendly to search engines

▷ Submit a website for inclusion in a search engine

▷ Determine whether a website meets accessibility requirements

▷ Evaluate the usability of a website

From Chapter 12 of *Basics of Web Design HTML5 & CSS3*, Second Edition. Terry Ann Felke-Morris. Copyright © 2014 by Pearson Education, Inc. All rights reserved.

Register a Domain Name

VideoNote
Choosing a Domain Name

A crucial part of establishing an effective web presence is choosing a **domain name**; it serves to locate your website on the Internet (Figure 1). If your business or organization is brand new, then it's often convenient to select a domain name while you are deciding on a company name. If your organization is well established, you should choose a domain name that relates to your existing business presence. Although many domain names have already been purchased, there are still many options available.

FIGURE 1 *Your domain name establishes your presence on the Web.*

Describe Your Business. Although there is a long-standing trend to use "fun" words as domain names (for example, yahoo.com, google.com, bing.com, woofoo.com, and so on), think carefully before doing so. Domain names for traditional businesses and organizations are the foundation of the organization's web presence and should include the business name or purpose.

Be Brief, If Possible. Although most people find new websites with search engines, some of your visitors will type your domain name in a browser. A shorter domain name is preferable to a longer one—it's easier for your web visitors to remember.

Avoid Hyphens ("-"). Using the hyphen character (commonly called a dash) in a domain name makes it difficult to pronounce the name. Also, someone typing your domain name may forget the dash and end up at a competitor's site! If you can, avoid the use of dashes in a domain name.

There's More Than .com. While the .com top-level domain name (TLD) is still the most popular for commercial and personal websites, consider also registering your domain name with other TLDs, such as .biz, .net, .us, .mobi, and so on. Commercial businesses should avoid the .org TLD, which is the first choice for nonprofit organizations. You don't have to create a website for each domain name that you register. You can arrange with your domain name

Web Publishing Basics

registrar (for example, http://register.com) for the "extra" domain names to point visitors to the domain name where your website is located. This is called **domain name redirection**.

Brainstorm Potential Keywords. Think about words that a potential visitor might type into a search engine when looking for your type of business or organization. This is the starting point for your list of **keywords**. If possible, work one or more keywords into your domain name (but still keep it as short as possible).

Avoid Trademarked Words or Phrases. The U.S. Patent and Trademark Office (USPTO) defines a **trademark** as a word, phrase, symbol, or design, or a combination of words, phrases, symbols, or designs, that identifies and distinguishes the source of the goods of one party from those of others. A starting point in researching trademarks is the USPTO Trademark Electronic Search System (TESS) at http://tess2.uspto.gov.

Know the Territory. Explore the way your potential domain name and keywords are already used on the Web. It's a good idea to type your potential domain names (and related words) into a search engine to see what may already exist.

Verify Availability. Check with one of the many **domain name registrars** to determine whether your domain name choices are available. A few of the many sites that offer domain name registration services are as follows:

- http://register.com
- http://networksolutions.com
- http://godaddy.com

Each of these sites offers a WHOIS search feature that provides a way to determine whether a potential domain name is available and, if it is owned, who owns it. Often the domain name is already taken. If that's the case, the sites listed here will provide alternate suggestions that may be appropriate. Don't give up; a domain name is out there waiting for your business.

Registering a Domain Name

Once you've found your perfect domain name, don't waste any time in registering it. The cost to register a domain name varies but is quite reasonable. The top rate for a .com one-year registration is currently $35 (and there are numerous opportunities for discounts with multiyear packages or bundled web hosting services). It's perfectly OK to register a domain name even if you are not ready to publish your website immediately. There are many companies that provide domain registration services, as listed earlier. When you register a domain name, your contact information (such as name, phone number, mailing address, and e-mail address) will be entered into the WHOIS database and available to anyone unless you choose the option for private registration. While there is usually a small annual fee for **private registration**, it shields your personal information from unwanted spam and curiosity seekers.

Obtaining a domain name is just one part of establishing a web presence—you also need to host your website somewhere. The next section introduces you to factors involved in choosing a web host.

Choose a Web Host

A **web host provider** is an organization that offers storage for your website files along with the service of making them available on the Internet. Your domain name, such as webdevbasics.net, is associated with an IP address that points to your website on the web server at the web host provider.

It is common for web host providers to charge a setup fee in addition to the monthly hosting fee. Hosting fees vary widely. The cheapest hosting company is not necessarily the one to use. Never consider using a "free" web host provider for a business website. These free sites are great for kids, college students, and hobbyists, but they are unprofessional. The last thing you or your client wants is to be perceived as unprofessional or not serious about the business at hand. As you consider different web host providers, try contacting their support phone numbers and e-mail addresses to determine just how responsive they really are. Word of mouth, web searches, and online directories such as www.hosting-review.com are all resources in your quest for the perfect web host provider.

Types of Web Hosting

▶ **Virtual Hosting**, or shared hosting, is a popular choice for small websites (Figure 2). The web host provider's physical web server is divided into a number of virtual domains, and multiple websites are set up on the same computer. You have the authority to update files in your own website space, while the web host provider maintains the web server computer and Internet connectivity.

FIGURE 2 *Virtual web hosting.*

▶ **Dedicated Hosting** is the rental and exclusive use of a computer and connection to the Internet that is housed on the web hosting company's premises. A dedicated server is usually needed for a website that could have a considerable amount of traffic, such as tens of millions of hits a day. The server can usually be configured and operated remotely from the client company, or you can pay the web host provider to administer it for you.

▶ **Co-Located Hosting** uses a computer that your organization has purchased and configured. Your web server is housed and connected to the Internet at the web host's physical location, but your organization administers this computer.

Choosing a Virtual Host

There are a number of factors to consider when choosing a web host. Table 1 provides a checklist.

TABLE 1 *Web Host Checklist*

Operating system	☐ UNIX ☐ Linux ☐ Windows	Some web hosts offer a choice of these platforms. If you need to integrate your web host with your business systems, choose the same operating system for both.
Web server	☐ Apache ☐ IIS	These two web server applications are the most popular. Apache usually runs on a UNIX or Linux operating system. Internet Information Services (IIS) is bundled with selected versions of Microsoft Windows.
Bandwidth	☐ ___ GB per month ☐ ___ Charge for overage	Some web hosts carefully monitor your data transfer bandwidth and charge you for overages. While unlimited bandwidth is great, it is not always available. A typical low-traffic website varies between 100GB and 200GB per month. A medium-traffic site should be OK with about 500GB of data transfer bandwidth per month.
Technical support	☐ E-mail ☐ Chat ☐ Forum ☐ Phone	Review the description of technical support on the web host's site. Is it available 24 hours a day, 7 days a week? E-mail or phone a question to test it. If the organization is not responsive to you as a prospective customer, be leery about the availability of its technical support later.
Service agreement	☐ Uptime guarantee ☐ Automatic monitoring	A web host that offers a Service Level Agreement (SLA) with an uptime guarantee shows that they value service and reliability. The use of automatic monitoring will inform the web host technical support staff when a server is not functioning.
Disk space	☐ ___ GB	Many virtual hosts routinely offer 100GB+ disk storage space. If you have a small site that is not graphic intensive, you may never even use more than 50MB of disk storage space.
E-mail	☐ ___ Mailboxes	Most virtual hosts offer multiple e-mail mailboxes per site. These can be used to filter messages—customer service, technical support, general inquiries, and so on.
Uploading files	☐ FTP access ☐ Web-based file manager	A web host that offers FTP access will allow the most flexibility. Others only allow updates through a web-based file manager application. Some web hosts offer both options.
Canned scripts	☐ Form processing	Many web hosts supply canned, prewritten scripts to process form information.
Scripting support	☐ PHP ☐ .NET ☐ ASP	If you plan to use server-side scripting on your site, determine which, if any, scripting is supported by your web host.
Database support	☐ MySQL ☐ MS Access ☐ MS SQL	If you plan to access a database with your scripting, determine which, if any, database is supported by your web host.
E-commerce packages	☐ _____	If you plan to enter into e-commerce, it may be easier if your web host offers a shopping cart package. Check to see if one is available.
Scalability	☐ Scripting ☐ Database ☐ E-commerce	You probably will choose a basic (low-end) plan for your first website. Note the scalability of your web host—are there other plans with scripting, database, e-commerce packages, and additional bandwidth or disk space available as your site grows?
Backups	☐ Daily ☐ Periodic ☐ No backups	Most web hosts will back up your files regularly. Check to see how often the backups are made and if they are accessible to you. Be sure to make your own site backups as well.
Site statistics	☐ Raw log file ☐ Log reports ☐ No log	The website log contains useful information about your visitors, how they find your site, and what pages they visit. Check to see if the log is available to you. Some web hosts provide reports about the log.
Domain name	☐ Included ☐ On your own	Some web hosts offer a package that includes registering your domain name. You may prefer to register your domain name yourself (see http://register.com or http://networksolutions.com) and retain control of your domain name account.
Price	☐ $___ setup fee ☐ $___ per month	Price is last in this list for a reason. Do not choose a web host based on price alone—the old adage "you get what you pay for" is definitely true here. It is not unusual to pay a one-time setup fee and then a periodic fee—monthly, quarterly, or annually.

Web Publishing Basics

Publish with File Transfer Protocol

Once you obtain your web hosting, you'll need to upload your files. While your web host may offer a web-based file manager application for client use, a common method of transferring files is to use **File Transfer Protocol** (FTP). A **protocol** is a convention or standard that enables computers to speak to one another. **FTP** is used to copy and manage files and folders over the Internet. FTP uses two ports to communicate over a network—one for the data (typically port 20) and one for control commands (typically port 21). See www.iana.org/assignments/port-numbers for a list of port numbers used on the Internet.

FTP Applications

There are many FTP applications available for download or purchase on the Web; several are listed in Table 2.

TABLE 2 *FTP Applications*

Application	Platform	URL	Cost
FileZilla	Windows, Mac, Linux	http://filezilla-project.org	Free download
SmartFTP	Windows	www.smartftp.com	Free download
CuteFTP	Windows, Mac	www.cuteftp.com	Free trial download, academic pricing available
WS_FTP	Windows	www.ipswitchft.com	Free trial download

Connecting with FTP

Your web host will provide you with the following information for connecting to your FTP server, along with any other specifications, such as whether the FTP server requires the use of active mode or passive mode:

> FTP Host: ftp://*yourhostaddress*
> Username: *your_account_username*
> Password: *your_account_password*

Web Publishing Basics

Overview of Using an FTP Application

This section focuses on FileZilla, a free FTP application with versions for the Windows, Mac, and Linux platforms. A free download of FileZilla is available at http://filezilla-project.org. After you download an FTP application of your choice, install the program on your computer using the instructions provided.

Launch and Login. Launch Filezilla or another FTP application. Enter the information required by your web host (such as FTP host, username, and password) and initiate the connection. An example screenshot of FileZilla after a connection is shown in Figure 3.

As you examine Figure 3, notice the text boxes near the top of the application for the Host, Username, and Password information. Under this area is a display of messages from the FTP server. Review this area to confirm a successful connection and the results of file transfers. Next, notice that the applica-

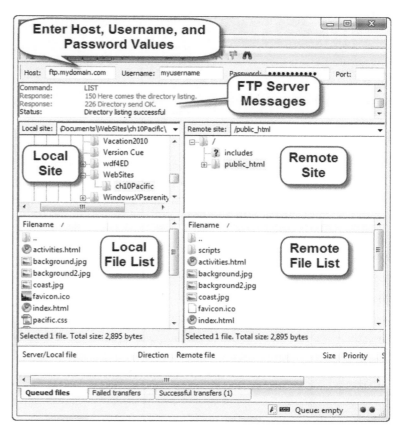

FIGURE 3 *The FileZilla FTP application.*

tion is divided into a left panel and a right panel. The left panel is the local site—it displays information about your local computer and allows you to navigate to your drives, folders, and files. The right panel is the remote site—it displays information about your website and provides a way to navigate to its folders and files.

Uploading a File. It's really easy to transfer a file from your local computer to your remote website—just select the file with your mouse in the left panel (local site list) and drag it to the right panel (remote site list).

Downloading a File. If you need to download a file from your website to your local computer, just drag the file from the right panel (remote site list) to the left panel (local site list).

Deleting a File. To delete a file on your website, right-click (Ctrl-click if using a Mac) on the file name (in the right panel) and select Delete from the context-sensitive menu.

And There's More! Explore other functions offered by FileZilla (and most FTP applications)—right-click (Ctrl-click if using a Mac) on a file in the remote site list to display a context-sensitive menu with several options, including renaming a file, creating a new directory (also known as a folder), and viewing a file.

Search Engine Submission

Using a search engine is a popular way to navigate the Web and find websites. The PEW Internet Project reports that almost 60% of online adults use search engines on a typical day and that "91% of online adults use search engines to find information on the web" (www.pewinternet.org/Press-Releases/2012/Search-Engine-Use-2012.aspx). Search engine listings can be an excellent marketing tool for your business. To harness the power of search engines and search indexes (sometimes called search directories), it helps to know how they work.

According to a survey by NetMarketShare (http://marketshare.hitslink.com/search-engine-market-share.aspx), Google (http://google.com) was the most popular site used to search the Web during a recent month. Other major search engines include Yahoo!, Bing, Baidu, and Ask. Figure 4 is a chart of the top five search sites reported in this survey. Check http://marketshare.hitslink.com for the most recent survey results.

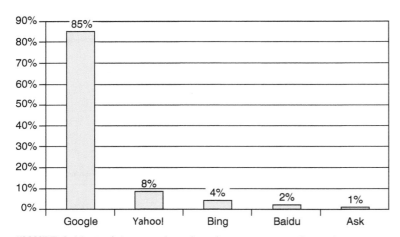

FIGURE 4 *Most of the searches done in a recent month used Google.*

Components of a Search Engine

The components of a search engine (robot, database, and search form) work together to obtain information about web pages, store information about web pages, and provide a graphical user interface to facilitate searching for and displaying a list of web pages relevant to given keywords.

Robot. A **robot** (sometimes called a spider or bot) is a program that automatically traverses the hypertext structure of the Web by retrieving a web page document and following the hyperlinks on the page. It moves like a robot spider on the Web, accessing and storing information about the web pages in a database. Visit The Web Robots Pages at www.robotstxt.org if you'd like more details about web robots.

Database. A **database** is a collection of information organized so that its contents can easily be accessed, managed, and updated. Database management systems (DBMSs) such as Oracle, Microsoft SQL Server, or IBM DB2 are used to configure and manage the database. The web page that displays the results of your search, called the Search Engine Results Page (SERP), lists information from the database accessed by the search engine.

Web Publishing Basics

Search Form. The search form is the graphical user interface that allows a user to type in the word or phrase he or she is searching for. It is typically a text box and a submit button. The visitor to the search engine types words (called keywords) related to his or her search into the text box. When the form is submitted, the keywords are sent to a server-side script that searches the database for matches. The results are displayed on a SERP and formatted with a hyperlink to each page along with additional information that might include the page title, a brief description, the first few lines of text, or the size of the page. The order in which the results are displayed may depend on paid advertisements, alphabetical order, and link popularity. The link popularity of a website is a rating determined by a search engine based on the quantity and quality of incoming hyperlinks. Each search engine has its own policy for ordering the search results. Be aware that these policies can change over time.

Listing Your Site in a Search Engine

According to a study by The Direct Marketing Association (www.the-dma.org), 66 percent of web marketers surveyed rated search engines as the top method used to drive traffic to their sites. Follow these steps to get your web site listed with a search engine:

Step 1: Visit the search engine site (such as http://google.com or http://yahoo.com) and look for an "Add site" or "List URL" link. This is typically on the home page (or About Us page) of the search engine. Be patient—these links are sometimes not obvious and you may need to click through a number of pages before you find the form to submit your website. Visit https://www.google.com/webmasters/tools/submit-url to immediately submit your website for inclusion in Google.

Step 2: Follow the directions listed on the page and submit the form to request that your site be added to the search engine. At other search engines there may be a fee for an automatic listing, called paid inclusion—more on this later. Currently, there is no fee to submit a site to Google.

Step 3: The spider from the search engine will index your site. This may take several weeks.

Step 4: Several weeks after you submit your website, check the search engine or search directory to see if your site is listed. If it is not listed, review your pages and check whether they are optimized for search engines (see the next section) and display in common browsers.

? FAQ **Is advertising on a search engine worth the cost?**

It depends. How much is it worth to your client to appear on the first page of the search engine results? You select the keywords that will trigger the display of your ad. You also set your monthly budget and the maximum amount to pay for each click. While costs and charges vary by search engine, at this time Google charges are based on cost per click—you'll be charged each time a visitor to Google clicks on your advertisement. Visit http://google.com/adwords for more information about their program.

Web Publishing Basics

Search Engine Optimization

If you have followed recommended web design practices, you've already designed your website so that the pages are appealing and compelling to your target audience. How can you also make your site work well with search engines? Here are some suggestions and hints on designing your pages for optimal ranking by search engines—a process called **Search Engine Optimization (SEO)**.

Keywords

Spend some time brainstorming about terms and phrases that people may use when searching for your site. These terms or phrases that describe your website or business are your **keywords**.

Page Titles

A descriptive page title (the text between the `<title>` tags) that includes your company and/or website name will help your site market itself. It's common for search engines to display the text in the page title in the SERP. The page title is also saved by default when a visitor bookmarks your site and is often included when a visitor prints a page of your site. Avoid using the exact same title for every page; include keywords in the page title that are appropriate for the page.

Heading Tags

Use structural tags such as `<h1>`, `<h2>`, and so on to organize your page content. If it is appropriate for the web page content, also include some keywords in the text contained within heading tags. Some search engines will give a higher list position if keywords are included in a page title or headings. Also include keywords as appropriate within the page text content. However, avoid spamming keywords—that is, do not list them over and over again. The programs behind search engines become more sophisticated all the time, and you can actually be prevented from being listed if it is perceived that you are not being honest or are trying to cheat the system.

Description

What is special about your website that would make someone want to visit? With this in mind, write a few sentences about your website or business. This description should be inviting and interesting so that a person searching the Web will choose your site from the list provided by a search engine or search directory. Some search engines will display your description on the SERP. You can configure a description for your web page by coding a meta tag in the page header area.

The Meta Tag

A **meta tag** is a self-contained tag that is placed in the header section of a web page. You've been using a meta tag to indicate character encoding. There are a number of other uses for a meta tag. We'll focus here on providing a description of a website for use by search engines. The description meta tag content is displayed on the SERP by some search engines, such as Google. The **name** attribute indicates the purpose of the meta tag. The **content** attribute provides the value needed for the specific purpose. For example, the description meta tag for a website about a web development consulting firm called Acme Design could be configured as follows:

```
<meta name="description" content="Acme Design, a web consulting group that
specializes in e-commerce, website design, development, and redesign.">
```

 What if I don't want a search engine to index a page?

Sometimes there will be pages that you don't want indexed, perhaps test pages or pages only meant for a small group of individuals (such as family or coworkers). Meta tags can be used for this purpose also. To indicate to a search engine robot that a page should not be indexed and the links should not be followed, do not place keywords and description meta tags in the page. Instead, add a "robots" meta tag to the page as follows:

```
<meta name="robots" content="noindex,nofollow">
```

Linking

Verify that all hyperlinks are working and not broken. Each page on your website should be reachable by a text hyperlink. The text should be descriptive—avoid phrases like "more info" and "click here"—and should include keywords as appropriate. Inbound links (sometimes called incoming links) are also a factor in SEO. All these linking issues can affect your website's link popularity, and its link popularity can determine its order in the search engine results page.

Images and Multimedia

Be mindful that search engine robots do not "see" the text embedded within your images and multimedia. Configure meaningful alternate text for images. Include relevant keywords in the alternate text. Although some search engine robots, such as Google's Googlebot, have recently added functionality to index text and hyperlinks contained within Flash media, be aware that a website that contains hyperlinks within Flash and Silverlight media will be less visible to search engines and may rank lower as a result.

Valid Code

Search engines do not require that your HTML and CSS code pass validation tests. However, code that is valid and well structured is likely to be more easily processed by search engine robots. This may help with your placement in the search engine results.

Content of Value

Probably the most basic, but often overlooked, component of SEO is providing content of value that follows web design best practices. Your website should contain high-quality, well-organized content that is of value to your visitors.

Web Publishing Basics

Accessibility Testing

Universal Design and Accessibility

The Center for Universal Design defines universal design as "the design of products and environments to be usable by all people, to the greatest extent possible, without the need for adaptation or specialized design." Web pages that follow the principle of universal design are **accessible** to all individuals, including those with visual, hearing, mobility, and cognitive challenges. As you've worked this book, accessibility has been an integral part of your web page design and coding rather than an afterthought. You've configured headings and subheadings, navigation within unordered lists, images with alternate text, alternate text for multimedia, and associations between text and form controls. These techniques all increase the accessibility of a web page.

Web Accessibility Standards

The accessibility recommendations presented in this text are intended to satisfy Section 508 of the Rehabilitation Act and the W3C's Web Content Accessibility Guidelines.

Section 508 of the Rehabilitation Act. Section 508 (www.access-board.gov) requires electronic and information technology, including web pages, that are used by federal agencies to be accessible to people with disabilities. At the time this was written the Section 508 standards were undergoing revision.

Web Content Accessibility Guidelines (WCAG 2.0). WCAG 2.0 (www.w3.org/TR/WCAG20) considers an accessible web page to be perceivable, operable, and understandable for people with a wide range of abilities. The page should be robust to work with a variety of browsers and other user agents, such as assistive technologies (for example, screen readers) and mobile devices. The guiding principles of WCAG 2.0 are as follows:

1. Content must be **P**erceivable.
2. Interface components in the content must be **O**perable.
3. Content and controls must be **U**nderstandable.
4. Content should be **R**obust enough to work with current and future user agents, including assistive technologies.

? FAQ What is assistive technology and what is a screen reader?

Assistive technology is a term that describes any tool that a person can use to help him or her to overcome a disability and use a computer. Examples of assistive technologies include screen readers, head- and mouth-wands, and specialized keyboards, such as a single-hand keyboard. A screen reader is a software application that can be controlled by the user to read aloud what is displayed on the computer screen. JAWS is a popular screen reader application. A free time-restricted download of JAWS is available at http://freedomscientific.com/downloads/jaws/jaws-downloads.asp. A free download of the open-source NVDA screen reader is available at www.nvda-project.org. Visit www.doit.wisc.edu/accessibility/video/intro.asp for a video introduction to the screen reader.

Testing for Accessibility Compliance

No single testing tool can automatically test for all web standards. The first step in testing the accessibility of a web page is to verify that it is coded according to W3C standards with the (X)HTML syntax validator (http://validator.w3.org) and the CSS syntax validator (http://jigsaw.w3.org/css-validator).

Automated Accessibility Testing. An automated accessibility evaluation tool is no substitute for your own manual evaluation but can be useful to quickly identify potential issues with a web page. WebAim Wave (http://wave.webaim.org) and ATRC AChecker (www.achecker.ca/checker) are two popular free online accessibility evaluation tools. The online applications typically require the URL of a web page and reply with an accessibility report. Browser toolbars can be used to assess accessibility, including the Web Developer Extension (http://chrispederick.com/work/web-developer), WAT Toolbar (www.wat-c.org/tools), and the AIS Web Accessibility Toolbar (www.visionaustralia.org.au/ais/toolbar). The browser toolbars are all multifunctional, with options to validate HTML, validate CSS, disable images, view alt text, outline block level elements, resize the browser viewport, disable styles, and more. Figure 5 shows the Web Developer Extension toolbar in action.

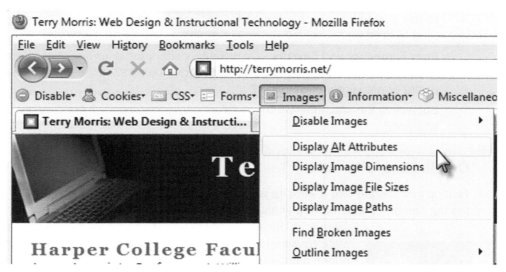

FIGURE 5 *Selecting the Images > Display Alt Attributes feature.*

Manual Accessibility Testing. It's important not to rely completely on automated tests—you'll want to review the pages yourself. For example, while an automated test can check for the presence of an `alt` attribute, it takes a human to critically think and decide whether the text of the `alt` attribute is an appropriate description for a person who cannot view the image. WebAIM provides a detailed checklist at www.webaim.org/standards/wcag/checklist that prompts you with items to review in order to verify compliance with WCAG 2.0 requirements.

Usability Testing

An addition to accessibility, another aspect of universal design is the usability of the website. **Usability** is the measure of the quality of a user's experience when interacting with a website. It's about making a website that is easy, efficient, and pleasant for your visitors. Usability.gov describes five factors that affect the user's experience: ease of learning, efficiency of use, memorability, error frequency and severity, and subjective satisfaction.

▶ **Ease of Learning**—How easy is it to learn to use the website? Is the navigation intuitive? Does a new visitor consider it easy to learn to perform basic tasks on the website or is he or she frustrated?

▶ **Efficiency of Use**—How do experienced users perceive the website—once they are comfortable, are they able to complete tasks efficiently and quickly or are they frustrated?

▶ **Memorability**—When a visitor returns to a website, does he or she remember enough to use it productively or is the visitor back at the beginning of the learning curve (and frustrated)?

▶ **Error Frequency and Severity**—Do website visitors make errors when navigating or filling in forms on the website? Are they serious errors? Is it easy to recover from errors or are visitors frustrated?

▶ **Subjective Satisfaction**—Do users "like" using the website? Are they satisfied? Why or why not?

Conducting a Usability Test

Testing how people use a website is called **usability testing**, shown in Figure 6. Usability testing can be conducted at any phase of a website's development and is often performed more than once. A usability test is conducted by asking users to complete tasks on a website, such as placing an order, looking up the phone number of a company, or finding a product. The exact tasks will vary depending on the website being evaluated. The users are monitored while they try to perform these tasks. They are asked to think out loud about their doubts and hesitations. The results are recorded (often on video) and discussed with the web design team. Often changes are made to the navigation and page layouts based on these tests.

FIGURE 6 *Observing a user perform a task on a website.*

If usability testing is done early in the development phase of a website, it may use the printed page layouts and site map. If the web development team is struggling with a design issue, sometimes a usability test can help to determine which design idea is the better choice. When usability is done during a later phase after the pages have been built, the actual website is tested. This can lead to confirmation that the site is easy to use and well designed, to last-minute changes in the website, or to a plan for website enhancements in the near future.

Hands-On Practice 1

Perform a small-scale usability test with a group of other students. Decide who will be the "typical users," the tester, and the observer. You will perform a usability test on your school's website.

 ▶ The "typical users" are the test subjects.
 ▶ The tester oversees the usability test and emphasizes that the users are not being tested—the website is being tested.
 ▶ The observer takes notes on the user's reactions and comments.

Step 1: The tester welcomes the users and introduces them to the website they will be testing.

Step 2: For each of the following scenarios, the tester introduces the scenario and questions the users as they work through the task. The tester should ask the users to indicate when they are in doubt, confused, or frustrated. The observer takes notes.

 ▶ Scenario 1: Find the phone number of the contact person for the Web Development program at your school.
 ▶ Scenario 2: Determine when to register for the next semester.
 ▶ Scenario 3: Find the requirements to earn a degree or certificate in Web Development or a related area.

Step 3: The tester and observer organize the results and write a brief report. If this were a usability test for an actual website, the development team would meet to review the results and discuss necessary improvements to the site.

Step 4: Hand in a report with your group's usability test results. Complete the report using a word processor. Write no more than one page about each scenario. Write one page of recommendations for improving your school's website.

 Continue to explore the topic of usability testing at the following resources:

 ▶ Keith Instone's Classic Presentation on How to Test Usability:
    http://instone.org/files/KEI-Howtotest-19990721.pdf
 ▶ Advanced Common Sense—the website of usability expert Steve Krug www.sensible.com
 ▶ Interview with Steve Krug: www.marketingsherpa.com/sample.cfm?contentID=3165
 ▶ Usability Basics: http://usability.gov/basics/index.html
 ▶ Usability Resources: www.infodesign.com.au/usabilityresources
 ▶ Usability Testing Materials: www.infodesign.com.au/usabilityresources/usabilitytestingmaterials

Review and Apply

Review Questions

Multiple Choice. Choose the best answer for each item.

1. Which of the following is the design of products and environments to be usable by all people, to the greatest extent possible, without the need for adaptation or specialized design?

   a. accessibility   **b.** usability

   c. universal design   **d.** assistive technology

2. In which of the following sections of a web page should meta tags be placed?

   a. head

   b. body

   c. comment

   d. none of the above

3. Which of the following statements is true?

   a. No single testing tool can automatically test for all web standards.

   b. Include as many people as possible when you conduct usability tests.

   c. Search engine listings are effective immediately after submission.

   d. None of the above statements is true.

4. Which are the four principles of the Web Content Accessibility Guidelines?

   a. contrast, repetition, alignment, proximity

   b. perceivable, operable, understandable, robust

   c. accessible, readable, maintainable, reliable

   d. hierarchical, linear, random, sequential

5. Which of the following is a protocol commonly used to transfer files over the Internet?

   a. port   **b.** http

   c. FTP   **d.** SMTP

6. Which of the following is a rating determined by a search engine based on the number and quality of hyperlinks to a website?

   a. link checking   **b.** link rating

   c. link popularity   **d.** search engine optimization

7. What is the purpose of private registration for a domain name?

   a. It protects the privacy of your web host.

   b. It is the cheapest form of domain name registration.

   c. It protects the privacy of your contact information.

   d. none of the above

8. Which of the following is true about domain names?

   a. It is recommended to register multiple domain names that are redirected to your website.

   b. It is recommended to use long, descriptive domain names.

   c. It is recommended to use hyphens in domain names.

   d. There is no reason to check for trademarks when you are choosing a domain name.

9. Which web hosting option is appropriate for the initial web presence of an organization?

   a. dedicated hosting   **b.** free web hosting

   c. virtual hosting   **d.** co-located hosting

10. What is the measure of the quality of a user's experience when interacting with a website?

   a. accessibility   **b.** usability

   c. validity   **d.** functionality

Web Publishing Basics

Hands-On Exercises

1. Run an automated accessibility test on the home page of your school website. Use both the WebAim Wave (http://wave.webaim.org) and ATRC AChecker (www.achecker.ca/checker) automated tests. Describe the differences in the way these tools report the results of the test. Did both tests find similar errors? Write a one-page report that describes the results of the tests. Include your recommendations for improving the website.

2. Search for web host providers and report on three that meet the following criteria:
   - Support PHP and MySQL
   - Offer e-commerce capabilities
   - Provide at least 1GB hard disk space

   Use your favorite search engine to find web host providers or visit web host directories such as www.hosting-review.com and www.hostindex.com. The web host survey results provided by http://uptime.netcraft.com/perf/reports/Hosters may also be useful. Create a web page that presents your findings. Include links to the three web host providers you selected. Your web page should include a table of information such as setup fees, monthly fees, domain name registration costs, amount of hard disk space, type of e-commerce package, and cost of e-commerce package. Use color and graphics appropriately on your web page. Place your name and e-mail address at the bottom of your web page.

Focus on Web Design

1. Explore how to design your website so that it is optimized for search engines (Search Engine Optimization, or SEO). Visit the following resources as a starting point as you search for three SEO tips or hints:
   - www.sitepoint.com/article/skool-search-engine-success
   - www.digital-web.com/articles/designing_for_search_engines_and_stars
   - www.seomoz.org/beginners-guide-to-seo
   - www.bruceclay.com/seo/search-engine-optimization.htm

   Write a one-page report that describes three tips that you found interesting or potentially useful. Cite the URLs of the resources you used.

2. Explore how to reach out to your current and potential website visitors with **Social Media Optimization** (SMO), which is described by Rohit Bhargava as optimizing a website so that it is "more easily linked to, more highly visible in social media searches on custom search engines (such as Technorati), and more frequently included in relevant posts on blogs, podcasts and vlogs." Benefits of SMO include increased awareness of your brand and/or site along with an increase in the number of inbound links (which can help with SEO). Visit the following resources as a starting point as you search for three SMO tips or hints:
   - http://social-media-optimization.com
   - http://rohitbhargava.typepad.com/weblog/2006/08/5_rules_of_soci.html
   - www.toprankblog.com/2009/03/sxswi-interview-rohit-bhargava

Web Publishing Basics

Write a one-page report that describes three tips that you found interesting or potentially useful. Cite the URLs of the resources you used.

Answers to Review Questions

1. c	**2.** a	**3.** a
4. b	**5.** c	**6.** c
7. c	**8.** a	**9.** c
10. b		

Credits

Figure 2 © Shutterstock | CLIPAREA | Custom Media

Figure 1 © Terry Ann Morris, Ed.D. | Microsoft Corporation

Figure 6 © Monkey Business Images | Shutterstock

Figure 5 © Terry Ann Morris, Ed.D. | Mozilla Foundation

Figure 2 © Viktor Gmyria | Shutterstock

Figure 3 © FileZilla. Reprinted with permission

HTML5 Cheat Sheet

HTML5 Cheat Sheet

Commonly Used HTML5 Tags

Tag	Purpose	Commonly Used Attributes
`<!-- -->`	Comment	
`<a>`	Anchor tag: configures hyperlinks	accesskey, class, href, id, name, rel, style, tabindex, target, title
`<abbr>`	Configures an abbreviation	class, id, style
`<address>`	Configures contact information	class, id, style
`<area>`	Configures an area in an image map	accesskey, alt, class, href, hreflang, id, media, rel, shape, style, tabindex, target, type
`<article>`	Configures an independent section of a document as an article	class, id, style
`<aside>`	Configures tangential content	class, id, style
`<audio>`	Configures an audio control native to the browser	autoplay, class, controls, id, loop, preload, src, style, title
`<b>`	Configures bold text with no implied importance	class, id, style
`<bdi>`	Configure text used in bidirectional text formatting (BliDi Isolate)	class, id, style
`<bdo>`	Specifies a BiDi override	class, id, style
`<blockquote>`	Configures a long quotation	class, id, style
`<body>`	Configures the body section	class, id, style
` `	Configures a line break	class, id, style
`<button>`	Configures a button	accesskey, autofocus, class, disabled, format, formaction, formenctype, mormmethod, formtarget, formnovalidate id, name, type, style, value
`<canvas>`	Configures dynamic graphics	class, height, id, style, title, width
`<caption>`	Configures a caption for a table	class, id, style
`<cite>`	Configures the title of a cited work	class, height, id, style, title

Tag	Purpose	Commonly Used Attributes
`<code>`	Configures a fragment of computer code	`class, id, style`
`<col>`	Configures a table column	`class, id, span, style`
`<colgroup>`	Configures a group of one or more columns in a table	`class, id, span, style`
`<command>`	Configures an area to represent commands	`class, id, style, type`
`<datalist>`	Configures a control that contains one or more option elements	`class, id, style`
`<dd>`	Configures a description area in a description list	`class, id, style`
`<del>`	Configures deleted text (with strikethrough)	`cite, class, datetime, id, style`
`<details>`	Configures a control to provide additional information to the user on demand	`class, id, open, style`
`<dfn>`	Configures the definition of a term	`class, id, style`
`<div>`	Configures a generic section or division in a document	`class, id, style`
`<dl>`	Configures a description list (formerly called a definition list)	`class, id, style`
`<dt>`	Configures a term in a description list	`class, id, style`
`<em>`	Configures emphasized text (usually displays in italics)	`class, id, style`
`<embed>`	Plug-in integration (such as Adobe Flash Player)	`class, id, height, src, style, type, width`
`<fieldset>`	Configures a grouping of form elements with a border	`class, id, style`
`<figcaption>`	Configures a caption for a figure	`class, id, style`
`<figure>`	Configures a figure	`class, id, style`
`<footer>`	Configures a footer area	`class, id, style`
`<form>`	Configures a form	`accept-charset, action, autocomplete class, enctype, id, method, name, novalidate, style, target`
`<h1>...<h6>`	Configures headings	`class, id, style`
`<head>`	Configures the head section	
`<header>`	Configures a header area	`class, id, style`
`<hgroup>`	Configures a heading group	`class, id, style`

(Continued)

HTML5 Cheat Sheet

Tag	Purpose	Commonly Used Attributes
`<hr>`	Configures a horizontal line; indicates a thematic break in HTML5	`class, id, style`
`<html>`	Configures the root element of a web page document	`lang, manifest`
`<i>`	Configures italic text	`class, id, style`
`<iframe>`	Configures an inline frame	`class, height, id, name, sandbox, seamless, src, style, width`
`<img>`	Configures an image	`alt, class, height, id, ismap, name, src, style, usemap, width`
`<input>`	Configures an input control; text box, email text box, URL text box, search text box, telephone number text box, scrolling text box, submit button, reset button, password box, calendar control, slider control, spinner control, color picker control, or hidden field form control	`accesskey, autocomplete, autofocus, class, checked, disabled, form, id, list, max, maxlength, min, name, pattern, placeholder, readonly, required, size, step, style, tabindex, type, value`
`<ins>`	Configures text that has been inserted with an underline	`cite, class, datetime, id, style`
`<kbd>`	Configures a representation of user input	`class, id, style`
`<keygen>`	Configures a control that generates a public-private key pair or submits the public key	`autofocus, challenge, class, disabled, form, id, keytype, style`
`<label>`	Configures a label for a form control	`class, for, form, id, style`
`<legend>`	Configures a caption for a fieldset element	`class, id, style`
`<li>`	Configures a list item in an unordered or ordered list	`class, id, style, value`
`<link>`	Associates a web page document with an external resource	`class, href, hreflang, id, rel, media, sizes, style, type`
`<map>`	Configures an image map	`class, id, name, style`
`<mark>`	Configures text as marked (or highlighted) for easy reference	`class, id, style`
`<menu>`	Configures a list of commands	`class, id, label, style, type`
`<meta>`	Configures meta data	`charset, content, http-equiv, name`
`<meter>`	Configures visual gauge of a value	`class, id, high, low, max, min, optimum, style, value`
`<nav>`	Configures an area with navigation hyperlinks	`class, id, style`
`<noscript>`	Configures content for browsers that do not support client-side scripting	

HTML5 Cheat Sheet

Tag	Purpose	Commonly Used Attributes
`<object>`	Configures a generic embedded object	`classid, codebase, data, form, height, name, id, style, title, tabindex, type, width`
`<ol>`	Configures an ordered list	`class, id, reversed, start, style, type`
`<optgroup>`	Configures a group of related options in a select list	`class, disabled, id, label, style`
`<option>`	Configures an option in a select list	`class, disabled, id, selected, style, value`
`<output>`	Configures result of processing in a form	`class, for, form, id, style`
`<p>`	Configures a paragraph	`class, id, style`
`<param>`	Configures a parameter for plug-ins	`name, value`
`<pre>`	Configures preformatted text	`class, id, style`
`<progress>`	Configures a visual progress indicator	`class, id, max, style, value`
`<q>`	Configures quoted text	`cite, class, id, style`
`<rp>`	Configures a ruby parentheses	`class, id, style`
`<rt>`	Configures ruby text component of a ruby annotation	`class, id, style`
`<ruby>`	Configures a ruby annotation	`class, id, style`
`<samp>`	Configures sample output from a computer program or system	`class, id, style`
`<script>`	Configures a client-side script (typically JavaScript)	`async, charset, defer, src, type`
`<section>`	Configures a section of a document	`class, id, style`
`<select>`	Configures a select list form control	`class, disabled, form, id, multiple, name, size, style, tabindex`
`<small>`	Configures a disclaimer in small text size	`class, id, style`
`<source>`	Configures a media file and MIME type	`class, id, media, src, style, type`
`<span>`	Configures a generic section of a document with inline display	`class, id, style`
`<strong>`	Configures text with strong importance (typically displayed as bold)	`class, id, style`
`<style>`	Configures embedded styles in a web page document	`media, scoped, type`
`<sub>`	Configures subscript text	`class, id, style`
`<summary>`	Configures text as a summary, caption, or legend for a details control	`class, id, style`

(Continued)

HTML5 Cheat Sheet

Tag	Purpose	Commonly Used Attributes
`<sup>`	Configures superscript text	`class, id, style`
`<table>`	Configures a table	`class, id, style, border`
`<tbody>`	Configures the body section of a table	`class, id, style`
`<td>`	Configures a table data cell in a table	`class, colspan, id, headers, rowspan`
`<textarea>`	Configures a scrolling text box form control	`accesskey, autofocus, class, cols, disabled, id, maxlength, name, placeholder, readonly, required, rows, style, tabindex, wrap`
`<tfoot>`	Configures the footer section of a table	`class, id, style`
`<th>`	Configures a table header cell in a table	`class, colspan, id, headers, rowspan, scope, style`
`<thead>`	Configures the head section of a table	`class, id, style`
`<time>`	Configures a date and/or time	`class, datetime, id, pubdate, style`
`<title>`	Configures the title of a web page document	
`<tr>`	Configures a row in a table	`class, id, style`
`<track>`	Configures a subtitle or caption track for media	`class, default, id, kind, label, src, srclang, style`
`<u>`	Configures text displayed with an underline	`class, id, style`
`<ul>`	Configures an unordered list	`class, id, style`
`<var>`	Configures text as a variable or place-holder text	`class, id, style`
`<video>`	Configures a video control native to the browser	`autoplay, class, controls, height, id, loop, poster, preload, src, style, width`
`<wbr>`	Configures a line-break opportunity	`class, id, style`

HTML5 Cheat Sheet

CSS Cheat Sheet

Commonly Used CSS Properties

Property	Description
background	Shorthand to configure all the background properties of an element Value: `background-color`, `background-image`, `background-repeat`, `background-position`
background-attachment	Configures a background image as fixed-in-place or scrolling Value: `scroll` (default) or `fixed`
background-clip	CSS3; configures the area to display the background Value: `border-box`, `padding-box`, or `content-box`
background-color	Configures the background color of an element Value: Valid color value
background-image	Configures a background image for an element Value: `url` (*file name or path to the image*), none (default) Optional new CSS3 functions: `linear-gradient()` and `radial-gradient()`
background-origin	CSS3; configures the background positioning area Value: `padding-box`, `border-box`, or `content-box`
background-position	Configures the position of a background image Value: Two percentages, pixel values, or position values (`left`, `top`, `center`, `bottom`, `right`)
background-repeat	Configures how the background image will be repeated Value: `repeat` (default), `repeat-y`, `repeat-x`, or `no-repeat`
background-size	CSS3; configures the size of the background images Value: Numeric value (px or em), percentage, `contain`, `cover`
border	Shorthand to configure the border of an element Value: `border-width`, `border-style`, `border-color`
border-bottom	Configures the bottom border of an element Value: `border-width`, `border-style`, `border-color`
border-collapse	Configures the display of borders in a table Value: `separate` (default) or `collapse`
border-color	Configures the border color of an element Value: Valid color value
border-image	CSS3; configures an image in the border of an element See http://www.w3.org/TR/css3-background/#the-border-image

(Continued)

Property	Description
border-left	Configures the left border of an element Value: border-width, border-style, border-color
border-radius	CSS3; configures rounded corners Value: One or two numeric values (px or em) or percentages that configure horizontal and vertical radius of the corner. If one value is provided, it applies to both horizontal and vertical radius. Related properties: border-top-left-radius, border-top-right-radius, border-bottom-left-radius, and border-bottom-right-radius
border-right	Configures the right border of an element Value: border-width, border-style, border-color
border-spacing	Configures the space between table cells in a table. Value: Numeric value (px or em)
border-style	Configures the style of the borders around an element Value: none (default), inset, outset, double, groove, ridge, solid, dashed, or dotted
border-top	Configures the top border of an element Value: border-width, border-style, border-color
border-width	Configures the width of an element's border Value: Numeric pixel value (such as 1 px), thin, medium, or thick
bottom	Configures the offset position from the bottom of a containing element Value: Numeric value (px or em), percentage, or auto (default)
box-shadow	CSS3; configures a drop shadow on an element Values: Three or four numerical values (px or em) to indicate horizontal offset, vertical offset, blur radius, (optional) spread distance, and a valid color value. Use the inset keyword to configure an inner shadow.
caption-side	Configures the placement of a table caption Value: top (default), or bottom
clear	Configures the display of an element in relation to floating elements Value: none (default), left, right, or both
color	Configures the color of text within an element Value: Valid color value
display	Configures how and if an element will display Value: inline, none, block, list-item, table, table-row, or table-cell
float	Configures the horizontal placement (left or right) of an element Value: none (default), left, or right
font	Shorthand to configure the font properties of an element Value: font-style, font-variant, font-weight, font-size/line-height, font-family

CSS Cheat Sheet

Property	Description
font-family	Configures the font typeface of text Value: List of valid font names or generic font family names
font-size	Configures the font size of text Value: Numeric value (px, pt, em), percentage value, xx-small, x-small, small, medium (default), large, x-large, xx-large, smaller, or larger
font-stretch	CSS3; configures a normal, condensed, or expanded face from a font family Values include: normal, wider, narrower, condensed, semi-condensed, expanded, ultra-expanded
font-style	Configures the font style of text Value: normal (default), italic, or oblique
font-variant	Configures whether text is displayed in small-caps font Value: normal (default) or small-caps
font-weight	Configures the weight (boldness) of text Value: normal (default), bold, bolder, lighter, 100, 200, 300, 400, 500, 600, 700, 800, or 900
height	Configures the height of an element Value: Numeric value (px or em), percentage, or auto (default)
left	Configures the offset position from the left of a containing element Value: Numeric value (px or em), percentage, or auto (default)
letter-spacing	Configures the space between text characters Value: Numeric value (px or em) or normal (default)
line-height	Configures the line height of text Value: Numeric value (px or em), percentage, multiplier numeric value, or normal (default)
list-style	Shorthand to configure the properties of a list list-style-type, list-style-position, list-style-image
list-style-image	Configures an image as a list marker Value: url (*file name or path to the image*) or none (default)
list-style-position	Configures the position of the list markers Value: inside, or outside (default)
list-style-type	Configures the type of list marker displayed Value: none, circle, disc (default), square, decimal, decimal-leading-zero, Georgian, lower-alpha, lower-roman, upper-alpha, or upper-roman
margin	Shorthand to configure the margin of an element Value: One to four numeric values (px or em), percentages, auto or 0

(Continued)

CSS Cheat Sheet

Property	Description
margin-bottom	Configures the bottom margin of an element Value: Numeric value (px or em), percentage, `auto` or 0
margin-left	Configures the left margin of an element Value: Numeric value (px or em), percentage, `auto` or 0
margin-right	Configures the right margin of an element Value: Numeric value (px or em), percentage, `auto` or 0
margin-top	Configures the top margin of an element Value: Numeric value (px or em), percentage, `auto` or 0
max-height	Configures the maximum height of an element Value: Numeric value (px or em), percentage, or `none` (default)
max-width	Configures the maximum width of an element Value: Numeric value (px or em), percentage, or `none` (default)
min-height	Configures the minimum height of an element Value: Numeric value (px or em), or percentage
min-width	Configures the minimum width of an element Value: Numeric value (px or em), or percentage
opacity	CSS3; configures the transparency of an element Values: Numeric value between 1 (fully opaque) and 0 (completely transparent)
outline	Shorthand to configure an outline of an element Value: `outline-width`, `outline-style`, `outline-color`
outline-color	Configures the outline color of an element Value: Valid color value
outline-style	Configures the style of the outline around an element Value: `none` (default), `inset`, `outset`, `double`, `groove`, `ridge`, `solid`, `dashed`, or `dotted`
outline-width	Description: Configures the width of an element's outline Value: Numeric pixel value (such as 1 px), `thin`, `medium`, or `thick`
overflow	Configures how content should display if it is too large for the area allocated Value: `visible` (default), `hidden`, `auto`, or `scroll`
padding	Shorthand to configure the padding of an element Value: One to four numeric values (px or em), percentages, or 0
padding-bottom	Configures the bottom padding of an element Value: Numeric value (px or em), percentage, or 0
padding-left	Configures the left padding of an element Value: Numeric value (px or em), percentage, or 0
padding-right	Configures the right padding of an element Value: Numeric value (px or em), percentage, or 0

CSS Cheat Sheet

Property	Description
padding-top	Configures the top padding of an element Value: Numeric value (px or em), percentage, or 0
page-break-after	Configures the page break after an element Value: auto (default), always, avoid, left, or right
page-break-before	Configures the page break before an element Value: auto (default), always, avoid, left, or right
page-break-inside	Configures the page break inside an element Value: auto (default) or avoid
position	Configures the type of positioning used to display an element Value: static (default), absolute, fixed, or relative
right	Configures the offset position from the right of a containing element Value: Numeric value (px or em), percentage, or auto (default)
text-align	Configures the horizontal alignment of text Value: left, right, center, justify
text-decoration	Configures the decoration added to text Value: none (default), underline, overline, line-through, or blink
text-indent	Configures the indentation of the first line of text Value: Numeric value (px or em), or percentage
text-outline	CSS3; configures an outline around text displayed within an element Values: One or two numerical values (px or em) to indicate thickness and (optionally) blur radius, and a valid color value
text-overflow	CSS3; Configures how the browser indicates content that has overflowed the container and is not visible Values: clip (default), ellipsis, string value
text-shadow	CSS3; configures a drop shadow on the text displayed within an element Values: Three or four numerical values (px or em) to indicate horizontal offset, vertical offset, blur radius, (optional) spread distance, and a valid color value
text-transform	Configures the capitalization of text Value: none (default), capitalize, uppercase, or lowercase
top	Configures the offset position from the top of a containing element Value: Numeric value (px or em), percentage, or auto (default)
transform	CSS3; configures change or transformation in the display of an element Values: A transform function such as scale(), translate(), matrix(), rotate(), skew(), or perspective()

(Continued)

CSS Cheat Sheet

Property	Description
transition	CSS3; Shorthand property to configure the presentational transition of a CSS property value Value: list the value for `transition-property`, `transition duration`, `transition-timing-function`, and `transition-delay` separated by spaces; default values can be omitted, but the first time unit applies to `transition-duration`
transition-delay	CSS3; Indicates the beginning of the transition; default value 0 configures no delay, otherwise use a numeric value to specify time (usually in seconds)
transition-duration	CSS3; Indicates the length of time to apply the transition; default value 0 configures an immediate transition, otherwise use a numeric value to specify time (usually in seconds)
transition-property	CSS3; Indicates the CSS property that the transition applies to; a list of applicable properties is available at http://www.w3.org/TR/css3-transitions
transition-timing-function	CSS3; Configures changes in the speed of the transition by describing how intermediate property values are calculated; common values include `ease` (default), `linear`, `ease-in`, `ease-out`, `ease-in-out`
vertical-align	Configures the vertical alignment of an element Value: Numeric value (px or em), percentage, baseline (default), `sub`, `super`, `top`, `text-top`, `middle`, `bottom`, or `text-bottom`
visibility	Configures the visibility of an element Value: `visible` (default), `hidden`, or `collapse`
white-space	Configures white space inside an element Value: `normal` (default), `nowrap`, `pre`, `pre-line`, or `pre-wrap`
width	Configures the width of an element Value: Numeric value (px or em), percentage, or `auto` (default)
word-spacing	Configures the space between words within text Value: Numeric value (px or em) or `auto` (default)
z-index	Configures the stacking order of an element Value: A numeric value or `auto` (default)

CSS Cheat Sheet

Commonly Used CSS Pseudo-Classes and Pseudo-Elements

Name	Purpose
`:active`	Configures an element that is being clicked
`:after`	Inserts and configures content after an element
`:before`	Inserts and configures content before an element
`:first-child`	Configures an element that is the first child of another element
`:first-letter`	Configures the first character of text
`:first-line`	Configures the first line of text
`:first-of-type`	CSS3; Configures the first element of the specified type
`:focus`	Configures an element that has keyboard focus
`:hover`	Configures an element that has a mouse placed over it
`:last-child`	CSS3; configures the last child of an element
`:last-of-type`	CSS3; configures the last element of the specified type
`:link`	Configures a hyperlink that has not been visited
`:nth-of-type(n)`	CSS3; configures the "nth" element of the specified type. Values: a number, odd, or even
`:visited`	Configures a hyperlink that has been visited

CSS Cheat Sheet

Comparison of XHTML and HTML5

Comparison of XHTML and HTML5

As you traverse the Web and view the source code of pages created by others, you may notice that the style and syntax of the coding sometimes uses XHTML syntax.

XHTML, eXtensible HyperText Markup Language, utilizes the tags and attributes of HTML along with the syntax of XML (eXtensible Markup Language). For the most part, you will use the same tags and attributes in HTML and XHTML; the major change is the syntax and additional restrictions in XHTML. The W3C has created a draft recommendation for HTML5, which is intended to be the successor to HTML4 and to replace XHTML. HTML5 incorporates features of both HTML and XHTML, adds new elements and attributes, provides new features, such as form edits and native video, and is intended to be backward compatible.

In this section we'll concentrate on the differences between XHTML and HTML5—introducing you to some specific examples of syntax differences.

XML Declaration

Since XHTML follows XML syntax, each document should begin with an XML declaration. HTML5 has no such requirement.

XHTML

```
<?xml version="1.0" encoding="UTF-8"?>
```

HTML5

Not required

Document Type Definition

XHTML 1.0, the first version of XHTML (and the version that has been most widely used on the Web), has three distinct document type definitions: strict, transitional, and frameset. HTML5 has one document type definition. The Document Type Definitions (DTDs) follow:

XHTML 1.0 Strict DTD

```
<!DOCTYPE html PUBLIC "-//W3C//DTD XHTML 1.0 Strict//EN"
"http://www.w3.org/TR/xhtml1/DTD/xhtml1-strict.dtd">
```

XHTML 1.0 Transitional DTD

```
<!DOCTYPE html PUBLIC "-//W3C//DTD XHMTL 1.0 Transitional//EN"
"http://www.w3.org/TR/xhtml1/DTD/xhmtl1-transitional.dtd">
```

XHTML 1.0 Frameset DTD

```
<!DOCTYPE html PUBLIC "-//W3C//DTD XHMTL 1.0 Frameset//EN"
"http://www.w3.org/TR/xhtml1/DTD/xhmtl1-frameset.dtd">
```

HTML5

```
<!doctype html>
```

The `<html>` Tag

XHTML requires that the root element (immediately after the DTD) is an `<html>` tag which refers to the XML namespace. HTML5 has no such namespace requirement. To assist the interpreting of page content by search engines and screen readers, use the `lang` attribute to indicate the spoken language of the web page content. See http://www.w3.org/TR/REC-html40/struct/dirlang.html\#adef-lang.

XHTML

```
<html xmlns="http://www.w3.org/1999/xhtml" lang="en" xml:lang="en">
```

HTML5

```
<html lang="en">
```

Uppercase Versus Lowercase

The XHTML standard follows XML syntax, which requires lowercase. HTML5 allows both upper and lowercase letters; lowercase is preferred.

XHTML

```
<table>
```

HTML5

Either `<TABLE>` or `<table>`

Note: lowercase is preferred.

Quotation Marks with Attributes

The XHTML standard requires that the values for all attributes be enclosed in quotation marks. This is recommended (but not required) when coding HTML5.

XHTML

```
<p id="article">
```

HTML5

Either `<p id=article>` or `<p id="article">`

Start and End Tags

The XHTML standard requires both opening (start) and closing (end) tags for all elements except self-closing (void) elements (such as br, hr, img, input, link, and meta). HTML5

Comparison of XHTML and HTML5

requires both start and end tags for all non-void elements except body, dd, dt, head, html, li, option, p, tbody, td, tfoot, th, thead, and tr. However, it is good coding practice to always code both start and end tags for non-void elements.

XHTML

```
<p>This is the first paragraph.</p>
<p>This is the second paragraph.</p>
```

HTML5

```
<p>This is the first paragraph.</p>
<p>This is the second paragraph.</p>
```

Self-Closing Elements

The XHTML standard requires that all self-closing elements are properly closed using " />". HTML5 does not require this and refers to self-closing elements as void elements.

XHTML

```
This is the first line.<br />
This is the second line.
```

HTML5

```
This is the first line.<br>
This is the second line.
```

Attribute Values

The XHTML standard requires that all attributes be assigned values. HTML5 allows some attributes, such as checked, to be minimized. Since these attributes only have a single value, HTML5 does not require that the value be provided.

XHTML 1.0

```
<input type="radio" checked="checked" name="gender" id="gender"
value="male" />
```

HTML5

Either
```
<input type="radio" checked id="gender" name="gender" value="male">
```
or
```
<input type="radio" checked="checked" id="gender" name="gender"
value="male">
```

Elements New to HTML5

The following elements are new in HTML5: article, aside, audio, bdi, canvas, command, datalist, details, embed, figcaption, figure, footer, header, hgroup, keygen, mark, meter, nav, output, progress, ruby, rt, rp, section, source, time, track, video, and wbr. See the HTML5 Cheat Sheet appendix and http://www.w3.org/TR/html5-diff/#new-elements for information about these new elements.

Comparison of XHTML and HTML5

Attributes New to HTML5

HTML5 includes a variety of new attributes and new attribute values. The `autocomplete`, `autofocus`, `min`, `max`, `multiple`, `pattern`, `placeholder`, `required`, and `step` attributes are new for the input element. The textarea element now supports the following new attributes: `autofocus`, `maxlength`, `placeholder`, `required`, and `wrap`. The `autofocus` and `required` attributes are new for the select element. The input element supports the following new values for the type attribute: `color`, `date`, `datetime`, `datetime-local`, `email`, `month`, `number`, `range`, `search`, `tel`, `time`, `url`, and `week`. See http://www.w3.org/TR/html5-diff/#new-elements and http://www.w3.org/TR/htmlmarkup/elements.html#elements for more information about these new attributes and attribute values.

Elements Considered Obsolete in HTML5

The following elements are obsolete in HTML5: acronym, applet, basefont, big, center, dir, font, frame, frameset, isindex, noframes, strike, and tt. An obsolete element may be displayed by a browser. However, the code will not pass syntax validation and browsers may drop support of obsolete elements/attributes at any time. See http://www.whatwg.org/specs/webapps/current-work/multipage/obsolete.html#non-conforming-features for suggestions on replacing these elements.

Attributes Considered Obsolete in HTML5

A number of attributes present in XHTML and HTML4 are obsolete in HTML5, including align, alink, background, bgcolor, border, cellpadding, cellspacing, clear, frameborder, hspace, link, marginheight, marginwidth, noshade, nowrap, summary, text, valign, and vspace. See http://www.w3.org/TR/html5-diff/#obsolete-attributes for a complete list.

Elements Changed in HTML5

The purpose of the address, b, cite, dl, hr, I, label, menu, noscript, s, script, small, strong, and u elements was changed in HTML5. Visit http://www.w3.org/TR/html5-diff/#changed-elements for detailed information.

Attributes Changed in HTML5

The use of over 20 attributes was changed in HTML5. Of note is that the id value can now begin with any non-space character. Visit http://www.w3.org/TR/html5-diff/#changedattributes for detailed information.

Video and Audio Support

XHTML required the use of the object element to provide a video or audio player on a web page and was dependent on the visitor's browser having the corresponding plug-in or helper application installed. HTML5 supports video and audio native to the browser using the video, audio, and source elements. Because all browsers do not support the same media encoding formats, multiple versions of the media file should be provided when using HTML5 video and audio elements. The following code samples configure an audio file player on a web page.

Comparison of XHTML and HTML5

XHTML

```
<object data="soundloop.mp3" height="50" width="100" type="audio/mpeg"
title="Music Sound Loop">
  <param name="src" value="soundloop.mp3" />
  <param name="controller" value="true" />
  <param name="autoplay" value="false" />
</object>
```

HTML5

```
<audio controls="controls">
  <source src="soundloop.mp3" type="audio/mpeg">
  <source src="soundloop.ogg" type="audio/ogg">
  <a href="soundloop.mp3">Download the Soundloop</a> (MP3)
</audio>
```

Adobe Flash Support

XHTML required the use of the object element to play a Flash .swf file on a web page, although the embed element had been used and supported by browsers for many years. HTML5 still supports the use of the object element. However, the embed element is now officially supported in HTML5.

XHTML

```
<object type="application/x-shockwave-flash" data="lighthouse.swf"
width="320" height="240" title="Door County Lighthouse Cruise">
  <param name="movie" value="lighthouse.swf">
  <param name="bgcolor" value="#ffffff">
  <param name="quality" value="high">
</object>
```

HTML5

```
<embed type="application/x-shockwave-flash" src="lighthouse.swf"
quality="high" width="320" height="240"
title="Door County Lighthouse Cruise">
```

Document Outline

The document outline is the structure of a document indicated by the heading-level elements, such as h1, h2, and so on. XHTML coding practice is to use only one h1 element on a web page and to configure the heading-level elements in outline format. Outlining is different in HTML5. Instead of a solely heading-level outline, the HTML5 outline is also configured using sectioning elements (such as section, article, nav, and aside), each of which may contain headings. Try out an HTML5 outliner at http://gsnedders.html5.org/outliner.

JavaScript and the `<script>` Tag

XHTML considers JavaScript statements to be arbitrary character data (CDATA). The XML parser should not process them. The CDATA statement tells the XML parser to ignore the JavaScript. This is not part of HTML and not supported by many current browsers.

Comparison of XHTML and HTML5

XHTML

```
<script type="text/javascript">
<![CDATA[
```

...JavaScript statements go here

```
]]>
</script>
```

HTML5

```
<script>
```

...JavaScript statements go here

```
</script>
```

An alternative method for using JavaScript on a web page that is supported by XHTML standards is to place JavaScript statements in a separate (.js) file. This file can be configured by the `<script>` tag. HTML5 also supports this syntax.

XHTML

```
<script src="myscript.js" type="text/javascript"></script>
```

HTML5

```
<script src="myscript.js">
```

Wrap-Up

Visit the W3C's website for the most up-to-date information about XHTML (http://www.w3.org/TR/xhtml1) and HTML5 (http://www.w3.org/TR/html5).

JavaJam
Coffee House
Case Study

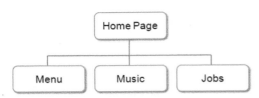

FIGURE 1 *JavaJam site map.*

header
nav
content div
footer

FIGURE 2 *JavaJam wireframe.*

Julio Perez is the owner of the JavaJam Coffee House, a gourmet coffee shop that serves snacks, coffee, tea, and soft drinks. Local folk music performances and poetry readings are held a few nights during the week. The customers of JavaJam are mainly college students and young professionals. Julio would like a web presence for his shop that will display his services and provide information about performances. He would like a home page, menu page, music performance schedule page, and job opportunities page. A site map for the JavaJam Coffee House website is shown in Figure 1. The site map describes the architecture of the website, which consists of a Home page with three main content pages: Menu, Music, and Jobs.

Figure 2 displays a wireframe sketch of the page layout for the website. It contains a site logo, a navigation area, a content area, and a footer area for copyright information. You have three tasks in this case study:

1. Create a folder for the JavaJam website.

2. Create the Home page: index.html.

3. Create the Menu page: menu.html.

Hands-On Practice Case Study

Task 1: Create a folder on your hard drive or portable storage device (thumb drive or SD card) called javajam to contain your JavaJam website files.

Task 2: The Home Page. You will use a text editor to create the Home page for the JavaJam Coffee House website. The Home page is shown in Figure 3.

JavaJam Coffee House

Home Menu Music Jobs

- Specialty Coffee and Tea
- Bagels, Muffins, and Organic Snacks
- Music and Poetry Readings
- Open Mic Night Every Friday

54321 Route 42
Ellison Bay, WI 54210
888-555-5555

Copyright © 2014 JavaJam Coffeee House
yourfirstname@yourlastname.com

FIGURE 3 *JavaJam index.html.*

All student files can be found on the companion website at www.pearsonhighered.com/felke-morris.

JavaJam Coffee House Case Study

Launch a text editor, and create a web page with the following specifications:

1. **Web Page Title:** Use a descriptive page title. The company name is a good choice for a business website.

2. **Wireframe Header Area:** Code the header element with the text, "JavaJam Coffee House" contained within a heading 1 element.

3. **Wireframe Navigation Area:** Place the following text within a nav element with bold text (use the <b> element):

   Home   Menu   Music   Jobs

   Code anchor tags so that "Home" links to index.html, "Menu" links to menu.html, "Music" links to music.html, and "Jobs" links to jobs.html. Add extra blank spaces between the hyperlinks with the   special character as needed.

4. **Wireframe Content Area:** Code the main page content within a div element. Use Hands-On Practice 2.11 as a guide.
   a. Configure the following content in an unordered list:

      Specialty Coffee and Tea
      Bagels, Muffins, and Organic Snacks
      Music and Poetry Readings
      Open Mic Night Every Friday Night

   b. Code the following address and phone number contact information within a div element. Use line break tags to help you configure this area and add extra space between the phone number and the footer area.

      54321 Route 42
      Ellison Bay, WI 54210
      1-888-555-5555

5. **Wireframe Footer Area:** Configure the following copyright and e-mail link information within a footer element. Format it with small text size (use the <small> tag) and italics font style (use the <i> tag).
   Copyright © 2014 JavaJam Coffee House
   Place your name in an e-mail link on the line under the copyright.

   The page in Figure 3 may seem a little sparse, but don't worry; as you gain experience and learn to use more advanced techniques, your pages will look more professional. White space (blank space) on the page can be added with <br> tags where needed. Your page does not need to look exactly the same as the sample. Your goal at this point should be to practice and get comfortable using HTML. Save your page in the javajam folder, and name it index.html.

Task 3: The Menu Page. Create the Menu page shown in Figure 4. A technique that improves productivity is to create new pages based on existing pages so that you can benefit from your previous work. Your new Menu page will use the index.html page as a starting point.

Open the index.html page for the JavaJam website in a text editor. Select File > Save As, and save the file with the new name of menu.html in the javajam folder. Now you are ready to edit the page.

FIGURE 4 *JavaJam menu.html.*

1. **Web Page Title:** Modify the page title. Change the text contained between the `<title>` and `</title>` tags to the following:

JavaJam Coffee House Menu

2. **Wireframe Content Area:**
   a. Delete the Home page content unordered list and contact information.
   b. Use a description list to add the menu content to the page. Use the `<dt>` tag to contain each menu item name. Configure the menu item name to have strong importance and display in bold font weight with the `<strong>` tag. Use the `<dd>` tag to contain the menu item description. The menu item names and descriptions are as follows:

   Just Java
   Regular house blend, decaffeinated coffee, or flavor of the day.
   Endless Cup $2.00

   Cafe au Lait
   House blended coffee infused into a smooth, steamed milk.
   Single $2.00 Double $3.00

   Iced Cappuccino
   Sweetened espresso blended with icy-cold milk and served in a chilled glass.
   Single $4.75 Double $5.75

Save your page, and test it in a browser. Test the hyperlink from the menu.html page to index.html. Test the hyperlink from the index.html page to menu.html. If your links do not work, review your work, paying close attention to these details:

- Verify that you have saved the pages with the correct names in the correct folder.
- Verify your spelling of the page names in the anchor tags.

Test again after you make changes.

JavaJam Coffee House Case Study

Part 1

Now you will use the existing JavaJam website as a starting point while you create a new version of the website that uses an external style sheet to configure color (see Figure 5).

#000000

#2E0000

#D2B48C

#F5F5DC

FIGURE 5 *New JavaJam Coffee House home page with color swatches.*

You have four tasks:

1. Create a new folder for the JavaJam Coffee House website.

2. Create an external style sheet named javajam.css.

3. Update the Home page: index.html.

4. Update the Menu page: menu.html.

Task 1: Create a folder called ch4javajam to contain your JavaJam Coffee House website files. Copy the index.html and menu.html files from the Chapter 2 Case Study javajam folder.

Task 2: The External Style Sheet. Launch a text editor. You will create an external style sheet named javajam.css. A sample wireframe is shown in Figure 6.

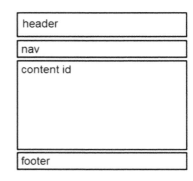

FIGURE 6 *The wireframe for the JavaJam Coffee House home page.*

Code CSS to configure the following:

- Global styles for the document (use the body element selector) with a beige background color (#F5F5DC) and dark brown text color (#2E0000).

- Styles for the header element selector that configure a tan background color (#D2B48C).

- Styles for the footer element selector that configure background color (#D2B48C) and text color (#000000).

Save the file as javajam.css in the ch4javajam folder. Check your syntax with the CSS validator at http://jigsaw.w3.org/css-validator. Correct and retest if necessary.

Task 3: **The Home Page.** Launch a text editor and open the home page, index.html.

 a. Associate the javajam.css external style sheet. Add a `<link>` element in the head section to associate the web page with the javajam.css external style sheet file.

 b. Assign the div that contains the main page content to an id named `content`. Change the first `<div>` tag to `<div id="content">`. We'll configure CSS for this id in a future case study.

FIGURE 7 *The new index.html page.*

Save and test your index.html page in a browser. It should be similar to the page shown in Figure 7, and you'll notice that the styles you configured in the external CSS file are applied!

Task 4: **The Menu Page.** Launch a text editor, and open the menu.html file. An example of the new version of the web page is shown in Figure 8.

 a. Code a `<link>` element in the head section to associate the web page with the javajam.css external style sheet file.

 b. Refer to Task 3 and configure the `content` div.

Save and test your new menu.html page. It should look similar to Figure 8.

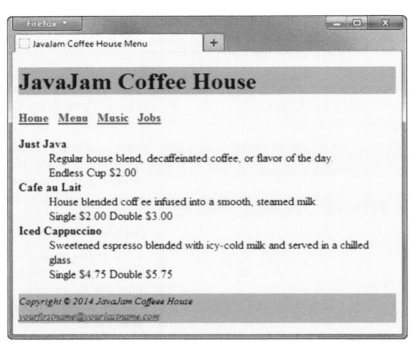

FIGURE 8 *The new menu.html page.*

This demonstrates the power of CSS. Just a few lines of code have transformed the display of the web pages in the browser.

Part 2

Now you will use the existing JavaJam website as a starting point while you create a new version of the website that incorporates images.

You have five tasks:

1. Create a new folder for the JavaJam Coffee House website.
2. Update the javajam.css external style sheet.
3. Update the Home page: index.html.
4. Update the Menu page: menu.html.
5. Create a new Music page: music.html.

Task 1: Create a folder called ch5javajam to contain your JavaJam Coffee House website files. Copy the files from the Chapter 4 Case Study ch4javajam folder and place them in your ch5javajam folder. Copy the following files from the chapter5/casestudystarters/javajam folder in the student files and place them in your ch5javajam folder: windingroad.jpg, marker.gif, favicon.ico, greg.jpg, gregthumb.jpg, melanie.jpg, and melaniethumb.jpg.

FIGURE 9 *JavaJam Coffee House home page.*

Task 2: **The External Style Sheet.** Launch a text editor and open the javajam.css external style sheet file.

1. Configure an img element selector not to display a border.
2. Configure an h3 element selector to display with a light tan #E6D6A9 background color.
3. Configure a ul element selector to display the marker.gif file as the list marker ("bullet").

Save your file. Use the CSS Validator (http://jigsaw.w3.org/css-validator) to check your syntax. Correct and retest if necessary.

Task 3: **The Home Page.** Launch a text editor and open the home page, index.html. Locate the div assigned to the id named con-tent. Configure an h2 element with the text, "Follow the Winding Road to JavaJam," on a new line below the opening div tag. Add an <img> tag on a new line below the h2 element. Configure the <img> tag to display the windingroad.jpg image. Configure the alt, height, and width attributes for the image. Save and test your page in a browser. It should look similar to Figure 9.

Task 4: **The Menu Page.** Launch a text editor and open the menu page, menu.html. Locate the div assigned to the id named `content`. Configure an h2 element with the text, "Coffee at JavaJam," on a new line below the opening div tag. Save and test your page in a browser. It should look similar to Figure 10.

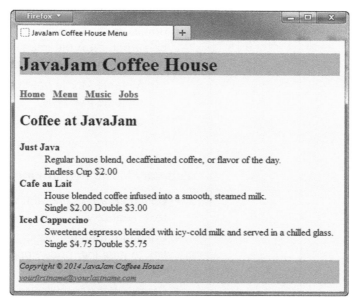

FIGURE 10 *JavaJam Coffee House menu page.*

Task 5: **The Music Page.** Use the Menu page as the starting point for the Music page. Launch a text editor and open the menu.html file in the ch5javajam folder. Save the file as music.html.

Modify the music.html file to look similar to the Music page, as shown in Figure 11:

1. Change the page title to an appropriate phrase.

2. Replace the text contained within the h2 element with the following: Music at JavaJam

3. Delete the description list from the page.

4. Configure a paragraph below the h2 element. The text of the paragraph follows:

   The first Friday night each month at JavaJam is a special night. Join us from 8pm to 11pm for some music you won't want to miss!

   Hint: Use the special character `&rsquo;` for the apostrophe character.

5. The remaining content on the page consists of two announcements: January and February. Each announcement is configured within a div element and contains an h3 element, an image link, and a paragraph.

FIGURE 11 *JavaJam Coffee House music page.*

January Music Performance:

- Configure an h3 element with the following text: January
- Configure the melaniethumb.jpg as an image link to melanie.jpg. Code appropriate attributes on the `<img>` tag.
- Configure the following text within the paragraph after the image. Code a line break tag after each sentence.

  > Melanie Morris entertains with her melodic folk style.

  > Check out the podcast!

  > CDs are now available.

February Music Performance:

- Configure an h3 element with the following text: February
- Configure the gregthumb.jpg as an image link to greg.jpg. Code appropriate attributes on the `<img>` tag.
- Configure the following text within the paragraph after the image. Code a line break tag after each sentence.

  > Tahoe Greg is back from his tour.

  > New songs.

  > New stories.

  > CDs are now available.

Save the music.html file. When you test your page in a browser, it should look similar to Figure 11.

Part 3

Now you will use the existing JavaJam website as a starting point to create a new version of the website. The new design is a centered page layout that takes up 80% of the browser viewport. You'll use CSS to configure the new page layout, a background image, and other styles, including font and padding. Figure 12 displays a wireframe with the wrapper div, which contains the other web page elements.

You have six tasks:

1. Create a new folder for the JavaJam Coffee House website.
2. Update the javajam.css external style sheet.
3. Update the Home page: index.html.
4. Update the Menu page: menu.html.
5. Update the Music page: music.html.
6. Configure shadow with CSS3.

FIGURE 12 *The* wrapper *div contains the other page elements.*

Task 1: Create a folder called ch6javajam to contain your JavaJam Coffee House website files. Copy the files from the Chapter 5 Case Study ch5javajam folder. Copy the javabackground.gif and javalogo.gif files from the chapter6/starters folder in the student files into your ch6javajam folder.

Task 2: The External Style Sheet. Launch a text editor and open the javajam.css external style sheet file.

- **The body element selector.** Add style declarations to display a background image named javabackground.gif and to configure Verdana, Arial, or any sans-serif font typeface.

- **The wrapper id selector.** Code a selector for an id named `wrapper`. Configure the `wrapper` id to be centered (see Hands-On Practice 6.7) with a width of 80%, background color #F5F5DC, and a minimum width of 960 pixels.

- **The h1 element selector.** Code an h1 element selector with a height of 100 pixels that displays a background image of javalogo.gif. The background image should be centered and should not repeat. Recall that the h1 element contains the text "JavaJam Coffee House." Configure text-indent: -9999px; so that the text will not overlay the image and will not display unless images are turned off or CSS is not supported.

- **The h3 element selector.** Add a style declaration to display in uppercase text (use the `text-transform` property).

- **The nav element selector.** Code a nav element selector that configures bold text that is centered (use the `text-align` property).

- **The content id selector.** Code a selector for an id named `content` and configure this with 1 pixel of padding on the top and 20 pixels of padding the right, bottom, and left sides.

- **The dt element selector.** Code a dt element selector that configures bold text.

- **The footer element selector.** Add style declarations to configure 20 pixels of padding, small font size (.60em), italics, and centered text.

JavaJam Coffee House Case Study

Save your javajam.css file. Use the CSS validator (http://jigsaw.w3.org/css-validator) to check your syntax. Correct and retest if necessary.

Task 3: The Home Page. Launch a text editor and open the home page, index.html. Code div tags to add a `wrapper` div that contains the content of the web page. Use Hands-On Practice 6.7 as a guide. Remove the tags for the b element, the i element, and the small element—they are no longer needed since CSS is now used to configure the text. Save the file.

Task 4: The Menu Page. Launch a text editor and open the menu.html file. Code div tags to add a `wrapper` div that contains the content of the web page. Use Hands-On Practice 6.7 as a guide. Remove the tags for the strong element, the b element, the i element, and the small element—they are no longer needed since CSS is now used to configure the text. Save the file.

Task 5: The Music Page. Launch a text editor and open the music.html file. Code div tags to add a `wrapper` div that contains the content of the web page. Use Hands-On Practice 6.7 as a guide. Remove the tags for the b element, the i element, and the small element— they are no longer needed since CSS is now used to configure the text. Save the file.

Test your web pages in a browser. Your home page should be similar to the example in Figure 13.

FIGURE 13 *The new JavaJam home page with centered layout.*

Task 6: Configure Shadow with CSS3. Launch a text editor and open the javajam.css file. Apply a shadow effect the to the `wrapper` id. Add the following style to the `#wrapper` selector:

```
box-shadow: 5px 5px 5px #2E0000;
```

Save the file. Launch a modern browser such as Safari, Google Chrome, or Firefox and test the home page (index.html) shown in Figure 14.

JavaJam Coffee House Case Study

FIGURE 14 *The JavaJam home page with a shadow effect.*

Part 4

Now you will use the existing JavaJam website as a starting point to create a new version of the website that uses a two-column layout. Figure 15 displays a wireframe with the new layout.

You have three tasks:

1. Create a new folder for the JavaJam Coffee House website.

2. Edit the javajam.css external style sheet.

3. Edit the Home page (index.html), Menu page (menu.html), and Music page (music.html) to configure the navigation hyperlinks within an unordered list.

Task 1: Create a folder called ch7javajam to contain your JavaJam Coffee House website files. Copy the files from the Chapter 6 Case Study ch6javajam folder.

Task 2: Configure the CSS. Launch a text editor and open the javajam.css external style sheet file.

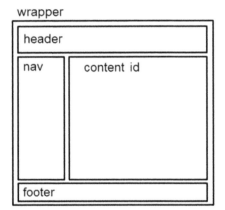

wrapper

FIGURE 15 *JavaJam two-column page layout.*

- **The wrapper id selector.** Change the background color from off-white (#F5F5DC) to light tan (#E2D2B0).

- **The h1 element selector.** Add a new style declaration to set the bottom margin to 0.

- **The h3 element selector.** Add a new style declaration to set the background color to light tan (#E2D2B0).

- **The nav element selector.** This is the area that will float on the page. Configure left float and a width of 160 pixels.

- **The content id selector.** Add new style declarations to configure an off-white (#F5F5DC) background color and a 175 pixel left margin.

- **Configure the content area.**

- **Content images.** Create a new style rule using a descendant selector that causes the images in the content id (`#content img`) to float to the left, with 40 pixels of right padding and 40 pixels of left padding.

- **Content ul elements.** The marker.gif image should only be used in the content id area. Replace the ul element selector with a descendant selector that specifies only ul elements within the content id (`#content ul`). Also configure the `list-style-position: inside;` style declaration for this selector.

- **Content div elements.** Create a new style rule using a descendant selector (`#content div`) that configures div elements within the `content` id (such as the announcements on the music page) to display with overflow set to auto, with 40 pixels of left padding, and 40 pixels of right padding.

- **Configure the navigation area.** Use descendant selectors to configure the unordered list and anchor elements *within the nav element*.

  - **Style the unordered list.** Configure the ul element selector with no list markers, zero left padding, and 1.2em font size.

  - **Remove the underline from navigation anchor tags.** Configure the a element selector to display text without an underline.

JavaJam Coffee House Case Study

- **Style unvisited navigation hyperlinks.** Configure the `:link` pseudo-class with medium tan text color (#795240).

- **Style visited navigation hyperlinks.** Configure the `:visited` pseudo-class with medium brown text color (#A58366).

- **Style interactive hyperlinks.** Configure the `:hover` pseudo-class with offwhite text color (#F5F5DC).

- **Configure the footer area.** Use a descendant selector to configure the anchor tags within the footer element to display with dark brown text color (#2E0000) for unvisited hyperlinks, black text color (#000000) for visited hyperlinks, and off-white text color (#F5F5DC) when the `:hover` pseudo-class is active.

Save your javajam.css file. Use the CSS validator (http://jigsaw.w3.org/css-validator) to check your syntax. Correct and retest if necessary.

Task 3: **Edit the Web Pages.** Launch a text editor and open the index.html file. Configure the navigation hyperlinks using an unordered list. Remove the ` ` special characters.

Save the file. Test your web page in a browser. Your home page should be similar to the example in Figure 16 with a two-column page layout. Modify the music.html and menu.html files in a similar manner. Test your web page in a browser. The Music page is shown in Figure 17.

FIGURE 16 *The new Javajam Home page with a two-column layout.*

FIGURE 17 *The new JavaJam Music page with a two-column layout.*

JavaJam Coffee House Case Study

Part 5

Now you will use the existing JavaJam website as a starting point to create a new version of the website that utilizes media queries to configure display for mobile devices. Figure 18 displays wireframes for desktop browser, typical tablet screen, and typical smartphone screen display. When you have finished, the website will look the same in desktop browsers (see Figures 16 and 19). The mobile displays should be similar to the screen captures in Figure 19.

Desktop Browser   Tablet Display   Smartphone Display

FIGURE 18 *JavaJam wireframes.*

You have five tasks:

1. Create a new folder for the JavaJam Coffee House website.

2. Edit the javajam.css external style sheet to include media queries and styles needed for appropriate desktop, tablet, and smartphone display.

3. Edit the Home page (index.html).

4. Edit the Menu page (menu.html).

5. Edit the Music page (music.html).

FIGURE 19 *Resize the browser window to approximate the new tablet and smartphone display.*

Task 1: Create a folder called ch8javajam to contain your JavaJam Coffee House website files. Copy the files from the Chapter 7 Case Study ch7javajam folder. Copy the file javalogomobile.gif from the student files chapter8/starters folder into the ch8javajam folder.

Task 2: Configure the CSS. Launch a text editor and open the javajam.css external style sheet file.

a. Configure Support of HTML5. Add the following style rule to configure most older browsers to render HTML5 block display elements as expected.

```
header, hgroup, nav, footer, figure, figcaption, aside, section,
article { display: block; }
```

JavaJam Coffee House Case Study

b. **Configure Tablet Display.**

1. Code a media query to select for typical tablet device viewport size.

   ```
   @media only screen and (max-width: 768px) {
   }
   ```

2. Configure the following new styles within the media query:

   a. **The body element selector.** Set margin to 0.

   b. **The wrapper id selector.** Set minimum width to 0 and width to auto.

   c. **The h1 element selector.** Set margin to 0 and configure javalogomobile.gif as the background image.

   d. **The content id selector.** Set left margin to 0.

   e. **The nav element selector.** Eliminate float (*Hint*: Use `float: none;`), set the width to auto, and configure 0 padding.

   f. **Navigation unordered list.** Use a descendant selector to configure ul elements within the navigation area to display centered text.

   g. **Navigation list items.** Use a descendant selector to configure li elements within the navigation area with inline display, 0 top and bottom padding, and 0.75em left and right padding.

   h. **The section element selector.** Configure section elements to have 0 padding.

   i. **Content unordered list.** Use a descendant selector to configure ul elements within the `content` id to clear float and have 1em of top padding.

c. **Configure Smartphone Display.**

1. Code a media query to select for typical smartphone device viewport size.

   ```
   @media only screen and (max-width: 480px) {
   }
   ```

2. Configure the following new styles within the media query:

   a. **The body element selector.** Set margin to 0.

   b. **The wrapper id selector.** Set the width to auto, minimum width to 0, and margin to 0.

   c. **The h1 element selector.** Set margin to 0 and configure javalogomobile.gif as the background image.

   d. **The content id selector.** Set top and bottom padding to 0.1em, left and right padding to 1em, margin to 0, and font size to 90%.

   e. **Navigation unordered list.** Use a descendant selector to configure ul elements within the navigation area with 0 padding.

   f. **Navigation list items.** Use a descendant selector to configure li elements within the navigation area with `inline-block` display, 5em width, 120% font size, centered text, a 2px box shadow (use #330000), #F5F5DC background color, 1% margin, and 2.5% padding.

   g. **Navigation hyperlinks.** Use a descendant selector to configure anchor elements within the navigation area with block display. This will provide the user a larger area to tap when selecting a hyperlink.

JavaJam Coffee House Case Study

h. **Content images.** Use a descendant selector to configure img elements within the `content` id to not float, set padding to 0, and set margin to 0.1em.

i. **The section element selector.** Configure section elements to have 0 padding.

j. **Section Images.** Use a descendant selector to configure img elements within a section element to not display.

k. **The mobile id.** Set display to inline. You'll apply this id when you edit the home page (index.html).

l. **The desktop id.** Set display to none. You'll apply this id later when you edit the home page (index.html).

d. **Configure Desktop Display.** Code the following new styles *above* the media queries.

1. **The mobile id.** Set display to none. You'll apply this id when you edit the home page (index.html).

2. **The desktop id.** Set display to inline. You'll apply this id later when you edit the home page (index.html).

e. **Configure Flexible Images.** Configure a new style for the img element selector *above* the media queries. Set maximum width to 100% and height to auto.

f. **Configure Sections.** Later in the case study you will rework the music.html page to show each announcement in a section element instead of within a div element. Let's get the CSS configured now. Review the CSS and locate the #`content div` selector. Replace #`content div` with `section`. Change the left and right padding to 20%.

Save your javajam.css file. Use the CSS validator (http://jigsaw.w3.org/css-validator) to check your syntax. Correct and retest if necessary.

Task 3: **Edit the Home Page.** Launch a text editor and open the index.html file. Edit the code as follows:

a. Configure a viewport meta tag in the head section that configures the `width` to the `device-width` and sets the `initial-scale` to 1.0.

b. Add statements needed to the head section to apply the HTML5 shim so that older browsers will successfully display the HTML5 elements.

c. The home page displays a phone number in the contact information area. Wouldn't it be handy if a person using a smartphone could click on the phone number to call the coffee house? You can make that happen by using `tel:` in a hyperlink. Configure a hyperlink assigned to an id named `mobile` that contains the phone number as shown below:

```
<a id="mobile" href="tel:888-555-5555">888-555-5555</a>
```

But wait a minute, a telephone link could confuse those visiting the site with a desktop browser. Code another phone number directly after the hyperlink. Code a span element assigned to an id named `desktop` around the phone number as shown here:

```
<span id="desktop">888-555-5555</span>
```

d. Remove the `height` and `width` attributes from the img tag.

Save the index.html file. Remember that validating your HTML can help you find syntax errors. Validate and correct this page before you continue. Display your page in a browser. While your home page will look unchanged in maximized desktop browsers (see Figure 16), as you resize and reduce the browser viewport dimensions, the displays should be similar to the screen captures in Figure 19.

Task 4: **Edit the Menu Page.** Launch a text editor and open the menu.html file. Edit the code as follows:

a. Configure a viewport meta tag in the head section that configures the width to the device-width and sets the initial-scale to 1.0.

b. Add statements needed to the head section to apply the HTML5 shim so that older browsers will successfully display the HTML5 elements.

Save the menu.html file. Remember that validating your HTML can help you find syntax errors. Validate and correct this page before you continue. Display your page in a browser. Resize the browser window to test the media queries. Compare your work with Figure 20, which shows screen captures of the menu page.

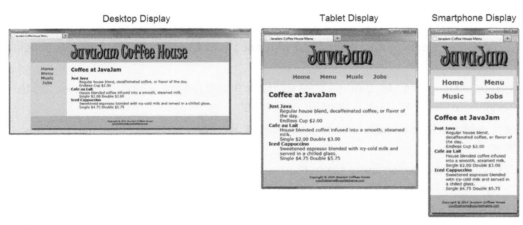

FIGURE 13 *Browser approximation of the menu.html page display*

Task 5: **Edit the Music Page.** Launch a text editor and open the music.html file. Edit the code as follows:

a. Configure a viewport meta tag in the head section that configures the width to the device-width and sets the initial-scale to 1.0.

b. Add statements needed to the head section to apply the HTML5 Shim so that older browsers will successfully display the HTML5 elements.

c. Remove the height and width attributes from the img tags.

d. Each performance announcement is contained within a div element. A section element is more descriptive of this type of content than the generic div element. Replace the div tags that surround each performance announcement with section tags.

Save the music.html file. Remember that validating your HTML can help you find syntax errors. Validate and correct this page before you continue. Display your page in a browser. Resize the browser window to test the media queries. Compare your work with Figure 21, which shows screen captures of the music page. JavaJam Coffee House is mobile!

FIGURE 21 *Browser approximation of the music.html page display.*

Part 6

Now you will use the JavaJam Coffee House existing website as a starting point and modify the Menu page to display information in a table. Your new page will be similar to Figure 22 when you have completed this case study. You have three tasks:

1. Create a new folder for this JavaJam case study.
2. Modify the style sheet (javajam.css) to configure style rules for the new table.
3. Modify the Menu page to use a table to display information as shown in Figure 22.

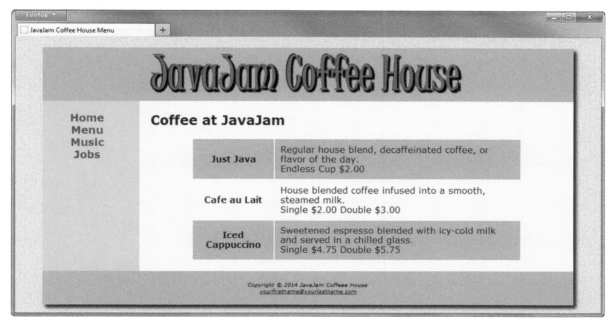

FIGURE 22 *Menu page with a table.*

Task 1: Create a folder called ch9javajam to contain your JavaJam Coffee House website files. Copy the files from the Chapter 8 Case Study ch8javajam folder into the new ch9javajam folder.

Task 2: **Configure the CSS.** You will add styles to configure the table on the Menu page. Launch a text editor and open the javajam.css external style sheet file. You will add the new style rules above the media queries.

> **Configure the table.** Code a new style rule for the table element selector that configures a centered table (use `margin: auto;`) with an 80% width.

> **Configure the table cells.** Code a new style rule for the td and th element selectors that configures 10 pixels of padding.

> **Configure alternate-row background color.** The table looks more appealing if the rows have alternate background colors but is still readable without them. Apply the `:nth-of-type` CSS3 pseudo-class to configure the odd table rows with a medium brown background color (#D2B48C).

Save the javajam.css file.

Task 3: **Update the Menu Page.** Open the menu.html page for the JavaJam Coffee House website in a text editor. The menu descriptions are configured with a description list. Replace the description list with a table that has three rows and two columns. Use th and td elements where appropriate. Save your page and test it in a browser. If the page does not display as you intended, review your work, validate the CSS, validate the HTML, modify as needed, and test again.

JavaJam Coffee House Case Study

Part 7

Now you will use the existing JavaJam website as a starting point. You will add a new page to the JavaJam website—the Jobs page. Refer back to the site map for the JavaJam website in Figure 1. The Jobs page will use the same page layout as the other JavaJam web pages. You'll apply your new skills and code a form in the content area of the Jobs page.

You have four tasks:

1. Create a new folder for this JavaJam case study.
2. Modify the style sheet (javajam.css) to configure style rules for the new Jobs page.

FIGURE 23 *The new JavaJam Jobs page.*

3. Create the Jobs page: jobs.html. Your new page will be similar to Figure 23 when you have completed this step.
4. Configure HTML5 form control features on the Jobs page.

Task 1: Create a folder called ch10javajam to contain your JavaJam Coffee House website files. Copy the files from the Chapter 9 Case Study ch9javajam folder to your new ch10javajam folder.

Task 2: Configure the CSS. Review Figure 23 and the wireframe in Figure 24. Notice how the text labels for the form controls are on the left side of the content area but contain right-aligned text. Notice the empty vertical space between each form control. Open javajam.css in a text editor. Place your cursor on a new blank line above the media queries.

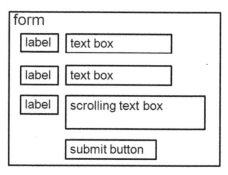

FIGURE 24 *The sketch of the form.*

1. Configure a label element selector. Set left float, block display, right alignment for text, and assign a width of 120 pixels, and an appropriate amount of right padding.

2. Configure the input element and textarea element selectors. Set block display and 20 pixels of bottom margin.

3. Configure style rules to optimize the display on smartphone-sized mobile devices by rendering the label text above each form control. Add the following style rule to the media query that targets a maximum width of 480 pixels:

   ```
   label { float: none; text-align: left; }
   ```

   Save the javajam.css file.

Task 3: Create the Jobs Page. Use the Menu page as the starting point for the Jobs page. Launch a text editor and open menu.html. Save the file as jobs.html. Modify your jobs.html file to look similar to the Jobs page (shown in Figure 23) as follows:

1. Change the page title to an appropriate phrase.

2. Replace the text contained within the `<h2>` tags with "Jobs at JavaJam".

3. The Jobs page will contain a paragraph and a form in the `content` div. Delete the table in the `content` div. Add a paragraph that contains the following text: "Want to work at JavaJam? Fill out the form below to start your application."

4. Prepare to code the HTML for the form area. Begin with a form element that uses the post method and the `action` attribute to invoke server-side processing. Unless directed otherwise by your instructor, configure the `action` attribute to send the form data to http://webdevbasics.net/scripts/javajam.php.

5. Configure the form control for the Name information. Create a label element that contains the text "Name:". Create a text box configured with "myName" as the value of the `id` and `name` attributes. Use the `for` attribute to associate the label element with the form control.

6. Configure the form control for the E-mail information. Create a label element that contains the text "E-mail:". Create a text box configured with "myEmail" as the value of the `id` and `name` attributes. Use the `for` attribute to associate the label element with the form control.

7. Configure the Experience area on the form. Create a label element that contains the text "Experience:". Create a textarea element configured with "myExperience" as the value of the `id` and `name` attributes, `rows` set to 2, and `cols` set to 20. Use the `for` attribute to associate the label element with the form control.

8. Configure the submit button. Code an input element with `type="submit"` and `value="Apply Now"`.

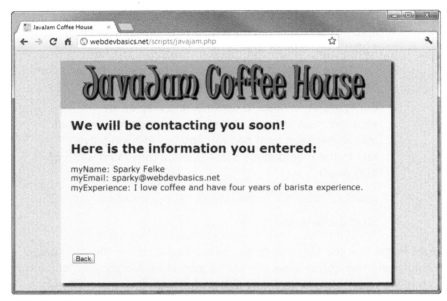

FIGURE 25 *The form confirmation page.*

9. Code an ending `</form>` tag on a blank line after the submit button.

Save your file and test your web page in a browser. It should look similar to the page shown in Figure 23. If you are connected to the Internet, submit the form. This will send your form information to the server-side script configured in the form tag. A confirmation page similar to Figure 25 will be displayed that lists the form control names and the values you entered.

Task 4: Configure the Form with HTML5 Attributes and Values. Get more practice with the new HTML5 elements by modifying the form on the Jobs page to use HTML5 attributes and values. Modify the jobs.html file in a text editor.

1. Add the following sentence to the paragraph above the form: "Required fields are marked with an asterisk *".

2. Use the `required` attribute to require the name, e-mail, and experience form controls to be entered. Add an asterisk at the beginning of each label text.

3. Configure the input element for the e-mail address with `type="email"`.

4. Code a label element containing the text "Start Date" that is associated with a calendar form control to accept the date that the applicant is available to start the job (use `type="date"`).

Save your file and display your web page in a browser. Submit the form with missing information or only a partial e-mail address. Depending on the browser's level of HTML5 support, the browser may perform form validation and display an error message. Figure 26 shows the Jobs page rendered in the Firefox browser with an incorrectly formatted e-mail address.

JavaJam Coffee House Case Study

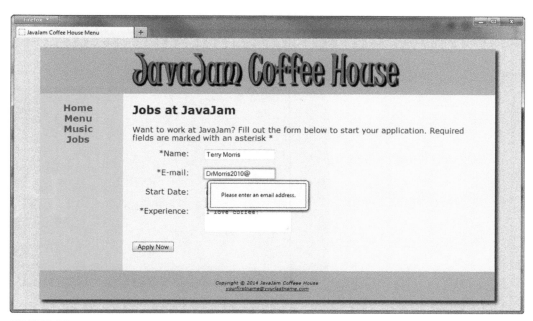

FIGURE 26 *The Jobs page with HTML5 form controls.*

Task 4 provided you with additional practice using the new HTML5 attributes and values. The display and functioning of browsers will depend on the level of HTML5 support. See http://www.standardista.com/html5/html5-web-forms for an HTML5 browser support list.

JavaJam Coffee House Case Study

Part 8

Now you will use the existing JavaJam website as a starting point to create a new version of the website that incorporates multimedia and interactivity. You have three tasks:

1. Create a new folder for this JavaJam case study.
2. Modify the style sheet (javajam.css) to configure a transition for the navigation hyperlink color.
3. Edit the text and configure two audio elements on the music page (music.html), and update the external CSS file as needed.

Task 1: Create a folder called ch11javajam to contain your JavaJam Coffee House website files. Copy the files from the Chapter 10 Case Study ch10javajam folder to your new ch11javajam folder. Copy the following files from the chapter11/casestudystarters folder in the student files and save them in your ch11javajam folder: melanie.mp3, melanie.ogg, greg.mp3, greg.ogg.

Task 2: **Configure a Navigation Transition with CSS.** Open javajam.css in a text editor. Locate the nav a selector. Code additional style declarations to configure a three-second ease-out transition in the color property. Save the file. Display any of the web pages in a browser that supports transitions and place your mouse over a navigation link. You should see a gradual change in the color of the text in the navigation link.

Task 3: **Configure the Audio.** Launch a text editor and open the music page (music.html). Look for the paragraph about Melanie. Remove the text, "Check out the podcast!". Code an audio element before the closing paragraph tag. Configure the audio element to play the melanie.mp3 and melanie.ogg files. Provide a hyperlink to the melanie.mp3 file as fallback content. Configure a second audio element within the paragraph about Tahoe Greg. Configure the audio element to play the greg.mp3 and greg.ogg files. Provide a hyperlink to the greg.mp3 file as fallback content. Save the file. Check your HTML syntax using the W3C validator (http://validator.w3.org). Correct and retest if necessary.

Next, configure the CSS. Launch a text editor. Open javajam.css. Configure a style above the media queries for the audio element selector that clears float and sets the top padding to 20 pixels.

Save the javajam.css file. Launch a browser and test your new music.html page. It should look similar to Figure 27.

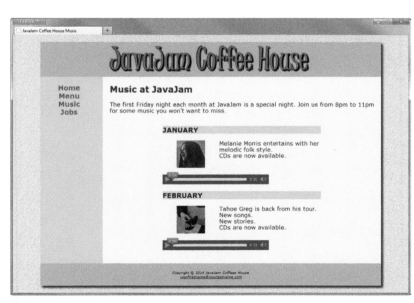

FIGURE 27 *New JavaJam music page.*

JavaScript is often used to respond to events such as moving the mouse, clicking a button, and loading a web page. As you continue your web design studies, a good next step would be to explore client-side scripting with JavaScript. Visit the following resources to get started:

- www.echoecho.com/javascript.htm
- www.w3schools.com/js
- www.tizag.com/javascriptT

Just as JavaScript was needed to configure the HTML5 canvas element in this section, other more advanced features of HTML5 also provide APIs that work with JavaScript. These include web storage, web databases, offline application caching, drag and drop, geolocation, and web messaging.

JavaScript is also the "J" in **AJAX**, which stands for Asynchronous JavaScript and XML, a technology that powers interactive web applications including Gmail (http://gmail.google.com), Flickr (http://flickr.com, and Delicious (http://del.icio.us). Recall the client/server model discussed in Chapters 1 and 10. The browser makes a request to the server (often triggered by clicking a hyperlink or a submit button), and the server returns an entire new web page for the browser to display. AJAX pushes more of the processing on the client (browser) with JavaScript and XML and often uses "behind the scenes" asynchronous requests to the server to refresh a portion of the browser display instead of the entire web page. The key is that when using AJAX technology, JavaScript code (which runs on the client computer within the confines of the browser) can communicate directly with the server—exchanging data and modifying parts of the web page display without reloading of the entire web page.

For example, as soon as a website visitor types a Zip Code into a form, the value could be looked up on a Zip Code database and the city/state automatically populated using AJAX—and all this takes place while the visitor is entering the form information before he or she clicks the submit button. The result is that the visitor perceives the web page as being more responsive and has a more interactive experience. Visit the following websites to explore this topic further:

- www.w3schools.com/ajax/ajax_intro.asp
- www.alistapart.com/articles/gettingstartedwithajax
- www.tizag.com/ajaxTutorial

JavaJam Coffee House Case Study

Part 9

Now you will use the existing JavaJam website as a starting point to create a new version of the website that implements the description meta tag on each page. You have three tasks:

1. Create a new folder for this JavaJam case study.
2. Write a description of the JavaJam Coffee House business.
3. Code a description meta tag on each page in the website.

Task 1: Create a folder called ch12javajam to contain your JavaJam Coffee House website files. Copy the files from the Chapter 11 Case Study ch11javajam folder.

Task 2: **Write a Description.** Review the JavaJam Coffee House pages that you created earlier. Write a brief paragraph that describes the JavaJam Coffee House site. Edit the paragraph down to a description that is only a few sentences and less than 25 words in length.

Task 3: **Update Each Page.** Open each page in a text editor and add a description meta tag to the head section. Save the files and test them in a browser. They will not look different, but they are much friendlier to search engines!

Web Project
Case Study

The purpose of this Web Project Case Study is to design a website using recommended design practices. Your website might be about a favorite hobby or subject, your family, a church or club you belong to, a company that a friend owns, the company you work for, and so on. Your website will contain a home page and at least six (but no more than ten) content pages. The Web Project Case Study provides an outline for a semester-long project in which you design, create, and publish an original website.

Project Milestones

- Web Project Topic Approval (must be approved before moving on to other milestones)
- Web Project Planning Analysis Sheet
- Web Project Site Map
- Web Project Page Layout Design
- Web Project Update 1
- Web Project Update 2
- Publish and Present Project

1. **Web Project Topic Approval.** The topic of your website must be approved by your instructor. Write a one-page paper with a discussion of the following items:
   - What is the name and purpose of the site?

     List the website name and the reasons you are creating the site.
   - What do you want the site to accomplish?

     Explain the goal you have for the site. Describe what needs to happen for you to consider your site a success.
   - Who is your target audience?

     Describe your target audience by age, gender, socioeconomic characteristics, and so on.
   - What opportunity or issue is your site addressing?

     Note: Your site might be addressing the opportunity of providing information about a topic to others, creating an initial web presence for a company, and so on.
   - What type of content might be included in your site?

     Describe the type of text, graphics, and media you will need for the site.
   - List at least two related or similar sites found on the Web.

2. **Web Project Planning Analysis Sheet**. Write a one-page paper with a discussion of the following items. Include the following headings:

Website Goal

List the website name and describe the goal of your site in one or two sentences.

What results do I want to see?

List the working title of each page on your site. A suggested project scope is seven to eleven pages.

What information do I need?

List the sources of the content (facts, text, graphics, sounds, video) for the web pages you listed. While you should write the text content yourself, you may use outside sources for royalty-free images and multimedia. Review copyright considerations.

3. **Web Project Site Map**. Use the drawing features of a word processing program, a graphic application, or paper and pencil to create a site map of your website that shows the hierarchy of pages and relationships between pages.

4. **Web Project Page Layout Design**. Use the drawing features of a word processing program, a graphic application, or paper and pencil to create wireframe page layouts for the home page and content pages of your site. Indicate where the logo, navigation, text, and images will be located. Do not worry about exact wording or exact images.

5. **Project Update Meeting 1**. You should have at least three pages of your website completed by this time. If you have not done so already, your instructor will help you to publish your pages to the Web. Unless prior arrangements to meet are made, the Project Update Meeting will be held during class lab time. Bring the following items to discuss with your instructor:

   - The URL of your website
   - Source files of your web pages and images
   - Site map (revise as needed)

6. **Project Update Meeting 2**. You should have at least six pages of your website completed by this time. They should be published to the Web. Unless prior arrangements to meet are made, the Project Update Meeting will be held during class lab time. Prepare the following items to discuss with your instructor:

   - The URL of your website
   - Source files of your web pages and images
   - Site map (revise as needed)

7. **Publish and Present Project**. Finish publishing your project to your website. Be prepared to show your website to the class, explaining project goal, target audience, use of color, and any challenges you faced (and how you overcame them) while you completed the project.

Index